YOUNG PEOPLE IN EUROPE

Labour markets and citizenship

Edited by Harriet Bradley and Jacques van Hoof

First published in Great Britain in April 2005 by

The Policy Press
University of Bristol
Fourth Floor
Beacon House
Queen's Road
Bristol BS8 1QU
UK

Tel +44 (0)117 331 4054
Fax +44 (0)117 331 4093
e-mail tpp-info@bristol.ac.uk
www.policypress.org.uk

British Library Cataloguing in Publication Data
A catalogue record for this book is available from the British Library.

Library of Congress Cataloging-in-Publication Data
A catalog record for this book has been requested.

ISBN 1 86134 588 7 hardback

A paperback version of this book is also available

Harriet Bradley is Dean of the Faculty of Social Sciences and Law, and Professor of Sociology at the University of Bristol, UK. **Jacques van Hoof** is Professor of Labour Management, Radboud University Nijmegen, the Netherlands.

Cover design by Qube Design Associates, Bristol.
Front cover: photograph supplied by kind permission of www.JohnBirdsall.co.uk
Printed and bound in Great Britain by MPG Books, Bodmin

Contents

Part Three: Policy options

List of tables and figures

Tables

Figures

Acknowledgements

The editors and authors wish to thank DG4 of the European Commission for its funding for the COST Action 14 initiative, which facilitated the collaboration upon which this book is based. Thanks are also due to Francis Bailleau and Torild Hammer for their work in organising and coordinating Working Group 4 of COST Action 14.

COST is an intergovernmental organisation for coordination of scientific and technical research, aiming at coordination and formation of networks on a European level between nationally funded research projects.

Special thanks to Karen Paton of the University of Bristol for her help in preparing the final version of the text.

Notes on contributors

José Luis Álvaro is Professor of Social Psychology at the Faculty of Social and Political Sciences, Complutense University, Madrid. His research interests include: social theory, psychological effects of unemployment, social and psychological influences on mental health. E-mail: jlalvaro@cps.ucm.es

Francesca Bianchi teaches Sociology of Education, Training and Human Resources Management at the University of Florence in the Faculty of Political Sciences Cesare Alfieri. She is a member of the HRM Masters degree Organising Committee at the University of Florence. Her last publications were 'La riforma dell'apprendistato in Italia: alcune valutazioni preliminari' (with M.Trentini), *Diritto delle relazioni industriali*, no 1, 2004; 'L'analisi delle azioni di sistema Avviso No.2/98. I formulari, le schede di rilevazione e il ruolo degli incontri tematici' in F.Frigo and M.Benincampi (eds) *Formazione aziendale e azioni di sistema nell'esperienza della Legge 236/93*, 2003; *Il lavoro nei paesi d'Europa* (with P. Giovannini), 2000. E-mail: bianchi@unifi.it

Harriet Bradley is Dean of the Faculty of Social Sciences and Law and Professor of Sociology at the University of Bristol. Her books include *Men's work, women's work, fractured identities* and *Gender and power in the workplace*. Her current research deals with the Connexions youth programme in the UK and with the labour market position of young minority ethnic workers. E-mail: harriet.bradley@bris.ac.uk

Jan Carle is Assistant Professor and Director of Studies in Sociology at Gothenberg University, Sweden. He is currently working within two different research projects on youth, family and generations: Youth Unemployment and Social Exclusion in Europe, a joint research project between nine European countries funded by TSER (Targeted Social and Economic Research) and national funding, and, together with Ulla Björnberg and Ann Britt Sand, a project with three-year funding from Swedish Council for Working Life and Social Research, *Family solidarity between generations: Economic and social transfers between individuals in various family forms*. E-mail jan.carle@sociology.gu.se

Gary Craig is Professor of Social Justice at the University of Hull, President of the International Association for Community Development and an Academician of the Academy of Learned Societies in the Social Sciences. His research interests include 'race' and ethnicity, poverty and inequality, young people, community development and local governance. E-mail: g.craig@hull.ac.uk

Hans Dietrich is Head of Research in the Department of Education, Training and Employment, and Life Courses at the Institut für Arbeitsmarkt- und Berufsforschung in Nürnberg, Germany. His research work and publications are focused on qualification and labour market, school-to work transition and the life course. E-mail: hans.dietrich@iab.de

Manuela du Bois-Reymond is Professor for Youth Studies and Youth Policy at the Department of Education, Leiden University, the Netherlands. She is member of the European network EGRIS (European Group for Integrated Research) and has conducted research in the field of youth transition, the relationship between young people and parents and research on intercultural childhood. She has published widely in these areas. She has also worked for the Council of Europe, especially in the field of non-formal education. She is board member of several international journals. E-mail: dubois@fsw.leidenuniv.nl

Klára Fóti is Senior Research Fellow at the Institute for World Economics of the Hungarian Academy of Sciences, in Budapest, Hungary. She has been Visiting Fellow in the Institute of Development Studies at the University of Sussex, and has a special interest in labour market issues. As Honorary Research Fellow in the Department of Sociology, University of Liverpool, she conducted comparative research on youth transitions. Over the past couple of years she has participated in various international projects comparing employment situation in some East European countries and has published extensively on these issues. Since 1998 she has been editing the Human Development Reports for Hungary, commissioned by the United Nations Development Programme (UNDP). The last report, entitled *Alleviating poverty: Analysis and recommendations*, was published in 2003. E-mail: kfoti@vki3.vki.hu

Alicia Garrido Luque is Associate Professor in Social Psychology at the Faculty of Social and Political Sciences, Complutense University, Madrid, Spain. Her research fields include: social theory, youth transitions to the labour market, psychological effects of unemployment and research methods in social sciences. E-mail: agarrido@cps.ucm.es

Jerome Gautié is Professor of Economics at the University of Reims (France), and Senior Researcher at the Centre d' Etudes de l' Emploi. His research fields include: the labour market positions of young people and older workers, labour market policies, and low-wage workers. E-mail: jerome.gautie@ens.fr

Torild Hammer is Senior Research Fellow at NOVA, Norwegian Social Research. Her main research interests are youth unemployment, employment and European social policy. E-mail: torild.hammer@nova.no

Miroljub Ignjatović was born in Belgrade. He is a researcher at the Organisations and Human Resource Research Centre, Faculty of Social Sciences, University of Ljubljana, Slovenia. His main research interests are labour market, unemployment and employment issues, labour market flexibilisation, social policy, post-modern society and issues of vocational education and training. E-mail: miroljub.ignjatovic@guest.arnes.si

Gill Jones is Emeritus Professor of Sociology, Keele University, and an Honorary Fellow of the School of Social and Political Sciences, University of Edinburgh. She has been conducting research on young people, their families and youth policies over many years. Publications include *Youth, family and citizenship* (with C. Wallace, 1992), *Leaving home* (1995), *Balancing acts: Youth parenting and public policy* (with R. Bell, 2000), *The youth divide: Diverging paths to adulthood* (2002), and a review for the Social Exclusion Unit of the impact of government policy on social exclusion among young people (with J. Bynner and M. Londra, 2004). E-mail: gill.jones@blueyonder.co.uk

Ilse Julkunen is Professor in Social Work at Helsinki University, Department of Social Policy and Social Work. She is also the Research Director for the Evaluation of Social Services at the National Research and Development Centre for Welfare and Health in Helsinki, Finland. E-mail: julkunen@helsinki.fi

Ira Malmberg-Heimonen is a doctoral student and an Assistant Lecturer in Social Policy and Social Work at the Swedish School of Social Sciences, Helsinki University, Finland. Her main research interests are related to welfare and labour market policies, and labour market integration. E-mail: ira.malmberg-heimonen@helsinki.fi

Wim Plug has worked as a sociological researcher at the University of Leiden, the Netherlands. His scientific interests lie in the fields of young people's life courses, their transition from education to work, their labour market attitudes and their transition to adulthood, in both national and international perspectives. E-mail: wa.plug@hccnet.nl

Herwig Reiter is Researcher at the Department of Political and Social Sciences of the European University Institute in Florence, Italy. His main fields of interest are youth research and youth policy, both within a European perspective. His focus is on issues of work and unemployment as well as the combination of qualitative and quantitative research methods. E-mail: herwig.reiter@iue.it

Martina Trbanc is Researcher at the Organisations and Human Resource Research Centre, Faculty of Social Sciences, University of Ljubljana, Slovenia. She is involved in teaching and research on the labour market, unemployment, marginalisation and social exclusion, employment policy and social policy and links between education and employment. E-mail: martina.trbanc@guest.arnes.si

Jacques van Hoof is Professor of Labour Management at the Radboud University, Nijmegen, the Netherlands. He has researched extensively into vocational education and training, work orientations and problems of work–life balance. He is co-editor and co-author of the books *Comparative industrial and employment relations* and *Women and the European labour markets*. E-mail: jacvhoof@wxs.nl

Introduction

Jacques van Hoof and Harriet Bradley

The starting point of the policy debate in Europe on youth, labour markets and citizenship is usually the existence of youth unemployment and the attendant risks of marginalisation for a sizable group of young people. That unemployment may endanger the integration of young people into the labour market and, by consequence, their transition to independent adulthood and full citizenship, is a disturbing thought for politicians and scientists alike. It is a reason for several policy initiatives addressed specifically at the reduction of youth unemployment in both the 'old' and the 'new' Europe. It lies behind the recent efforts of the European Union (EU) to achieve some coordination of youth policies in the member states. It is also the motive for many research projects within single countries, and studies of a more comparative nature.

Youth unemployment is unevenly distributed among European countries. These differences are portrayed in Table 0.1, which presents the youth unemployment figures for 2003 and compares them with

Table 0.1: Youth unemployment (ages 15-24) in Europe at the end of 2003, compared with 1997

	2003	1997
Italy	27.0	33.1
Greece	26.3	30.8
Spain	22.7	39.1
Belgium	21.5	23.0
Finland	21.8	25.2
France	20.9	29.1
Slovenia	15.9	17.2
Portugal	14.4	15.1
Sweden	13.4	20.6
Hungary	13.2	13.2
UK	12.3	14.2
Norway	11.6	10.6
Germany	11.1	10.8
Luxembourg	10.4	8.1
Denmark	10.3	8.4
Ireland	8.3	15.3
Austria	8.1	6.7
Netherlands	6.7	9.6

Source: Eurostat

the situation in 1997. The table includes the 15 countries that constituted the EU up until 2004 and adds in Norway, Hungary and Slovenia (three countries that will be discussed in later chapters of this book).

Overall, youth unemployment declined during the period 1997-2003, in particular in those countries that had extremely high unemployment (>25%) in 1997. As a result, the differences between countries in 1997 and 2003 became smaller. However, there are still six countries in which 20-27% of the youth labour force are currently unemployed. Nine countries have a youth unemployment rate of 10-16%. Only in three countries is youth unemployment at present less than 10%. Still more significant is the proportion of unemployed youth whose unemployment is long term. According to OECD data for 2002, in the 15 EU countries 26.6% of all young unemployed people were out of work for more than a year. Exclusion is therefore looming large for more than a quarter of unemployed youth in Europe. However, there are again important differences between countries. Long-term youth unemployment varies from less than 10% in Austria and the Scandinavian countries to 46% in Greece and 55% in Italy. In Spain the proportion is 27%, in Germany 22%. In France 15.5% of young unemployed people have been without work for one year or more and in the UK the figure is 11.2%.

Unemployment, however, is not the only problem met by young people on the road to full and stable integration into the labour market. Flexibilisation processes have led to the growth of part-time and temporary work and dead-end jobs, making the labour market more like that of earlier periods in industrial development Everywhere in Europe young people are strongly overrepresented in such forms of atypical and precarious employment. This, together with low youth wages, leads to low incomes that are in many cases not sufficient to secure an independent existence. Another risk is having to work in jobs that do not match the skill levels that young people have mastered during education and training. This kind of underutilisation of skills (which may be the consequence of the fact that young people are often encouraged to stay longer in education) can be damaging in the long run. The cult of 'credentialism' and training raises expectations in young people that may not be met. There is then a risk of some of them drifting into alienation, despair and the adoption of antisocial forms of behaviour. Such risks may be particularly severe in post-communist Europe (see Chapter Six, this volume).

Problems such as these form the core of this book. The book originates in the EU-sponsored programme 'Changing labour markets, welfare policies, and citizenship' (technically, the COST Action A 13), and is the end product of the activities of the working group on the position of youth in the labour market. The purpose of the book is to bring together, from a policy point of view, the results of research on youth and labour markets from several European countries, including some of the mid-European countries that have recently joined the EU. The authors are all active researchers studying aspects of young people's labour market involvement. We focus on what has been the traditional framework of youth studies – the transition from school to work. There is universal agreement that processes of economic and social change have led to such transitions being prolonged and becoming more uncertain and varied. To understand this development better, the traditional labour market perspective is in this book supplemented by a youth perspective.

From a youth perspective, the transition from school to work is seen as part of the wider transition from youth to adulthood. According to youth theorists, modernisation processes (the growing importance of education, individualisation, emancipation and so on) have changed the youth period radically. As a consequence, the transition to adulthood now covers a much longer period and at the same time has become much more complicated. During the course of barely half a century, the steps that are central to the transition – leaving school, starting a working career, leaving home, founding a family – have become less synchronised. Whereas these steps were formerly taken more or less simultaneously, nowadays they are taken successively and in no fixed order. As a consequence, the status of young people in society has become more ambiguous: in some respects they are treated as adults, in others they remain dependent on their families and/or on state contributions.

At the same time, the extended youth period offers the opportunity to develop youth cultures and lifestyles that, among other things, influence the attitude of young people towards education, work and leisure. In some countries, such as Britain and Germany, this has included the development of aggressively violent or ultra-hedonistic youth cultures (with widespread use of drugs, alcohol and casual sexuality), which are of general concern to society. There is clearly a need for further exploration and discussion of these emergent cultures, but this lies outside the remit of this book, since our focus is on labour market policies.

In our perspective, the labour market is still a key to the transition to adult status, but the transition from school to work is not seen as a linear process as it is influenced by other status passages. Elsewhere in the book, the image of 'yo-yo' movements is used to characterise the transition processes: young people can move forwards and backwards between education and work, for example, or try to combine them in different ways. Special attention should be paid to the values and orientations of young people, because they determine the course young people try to follow in negotiating the complexities of the transition period. All in all, the transition to adulthood is a more demanding, complex and precarious process, and parents who have grown up in a more stable work environment often feel at sea in steering their children to success in this 'brave new world' (Beck, 2000) of flexibilisation and insecurity.

At the same time, many researchers argue that a polarisation is occurring, termed by Gill Jones in a recent report 'the youth divide' (Jones, 2002), between disadvantaged young people with low levels of education and training and a well-qualified and well-rewarded élite from privileged and comfortable backgrounds. Youth researchers talk about 'winners' and 'losers', terms they relate not only to education and skills, but also to work values and attitudes – the 'winners' being characterised by modern values like self-actualisation and a risk-assessing and enterprising attitude that enables them to profit from new opportunities in the knowledge-based economy. This book takes a particular interest in the structures of class, ethnicity and gender that contribute to this divide. In particular, ethnicity has been rather ignored within the field of youth research and policy making, although certain minority groups across Europe have been identified by governments as 'problem groups'. In this book Chapter Eight focuses primarily on this issue, but themes of division and diversity are addressed throughout.

The youth perspective also informs our approach to youth citizenship. In the first two chapters of the book, the authors take account of the ambiguities surrounding this concept and the problems in translating it into policy. These ambiguities and problems derive on the one hand from the recent developments in the transition processes mentioned earlier. But they also originate in the recent debate on the reconceptualisation of social citizenship that is connected to the reconstruction of the welfare state. Some theorists have argued that the traditional concept of citizenship as political and social rights should be extended into a more active concept of citizenship as participation (Lister, 2002). According to this argument, political and social rights should enable people to participate fully in the political, economic and social life of society and prevent processes of marginalisation that may end in social exclusion. This concept was the point of departure for the COST programme mentioned earlier (see Andersen and Jensen,

2002). As young people in the present day labour market are especially vulnerable to marginalisation processes, this concept of citizenship is particularly relevant to them.

In fact, welfare policy in most European countries seems nowadays to favour a different interpretation of citizenship. In neo-liberal thinking about the welfare state, but also in the concept of the active welfare state, the idea of citizenship becomes intimately connected to the duties of citizens who claim some form of state support. In particular, social benefits are made conditional on the earlier contributions of claimants to work and employment, and their present efforts to remain or become employable. It is obvious that this concept of citizenship presents problems for those young people who have not yet achieved full and stable integration into the labour market. They cannot fall back upon earlier contributions and have to make the best of their willingness to behave as responsible citizens-to-be, for example by participating in training or workfare programmes. Whereas changes in the transition period generally lead to greater risks, state support (which is most of the time indispensable to independent living) becomes more precarious. As a consequence, young people may become more dependent on family support. It is well known that in Mediterranean countries like Italy and Spain family support has always played an important role, but there are indications that elsewhere too young people have to fall back to a greater degree on their families of origin – in the UK, for example. The interest in this changing 'youth welfare mix' is also apparent in several chapters of the book.

Of course, the specific 'youth welfare mix' varies across Europe. Following Esping-Andersen's pathbreaking study on welfare state regimes (Esping-Andersen, 1990), it has become customary to distinguish different types of welfare states. In this book several chapters use an extended version of Esping-Andersen's typology, which adds to the Nordic social democratic, the Anglo-Saxon liberal and the continental corporatist types a fourth 'sub-protective' type that is found mainly in the Mediterranean countries (see Chapter Two for a more precise description). However, some provisos are in order. First of all, this typology so far does not cover the transition countries in Middle and Eastern Europe, such as Hungary and Slovenia, which are discussed in Chapter Six. Second, it does not take into account the institutional arrangements concerning families and care. Finally, social protection systems are only one part of what may be called 'transition regimes', the institutional frameworks regulating the transition from school to work. Another important element is constituted by the different systems of (vocational) education and training that can be found in the

European countries. These will also be discussed in some chapters of the book. As a consequence, quite some variation in transition patterns and problems might be found between countries belonging to the same welfare regime.

We have already raised the issue of risk, which can be related to Ulrich Beck's influential text, *Risk society* (1992). A central issue of the risk society debate is whether risks in what is seen as an increasingly insecure environment are equally shared by all citizens. A theme that emerges in these chapters is that young people are indeed 'at the sharp end', unfairly exposed to labour market risks in comparison to their more protected elders, many of whom benefit from long service, guaranteed tenure or 'custom and practice' arrangements. Thus young people are at greater risk of unemployment, insecure employment and low pay. For these reasons it is indeed a 'risky business' for young people to invest in property or start a family. Among the young people, however, the risks are not divided equally. As the chapters will show, young minority ethnic people, those from less privileged social class backgrounds and, in some respects, young women, are more exposed, while middle-class men from majority ethnic backgrounds have crucial advantages in terms of economic, cultural and social capital to cushion them against risk-laden labour market activities.

The structure of the book

The next two chapters of the book present an overview of the reconstruction of youth social citizenship that is presently taking place against a background of globalisation and the recalibration of European welfare states towards employment-based social protection systems and a growing emphasis on the duties of citizenship. In Chapter One, Reiter and Craig consider how, as welfare benefits are increasingly made conditional upon contributions from work and employment, obvious problems arise for those young people who want to continue their education, are involved in casual, informal or atypical work, or are unemployed outright. Reiter and Craig argue, moreover, that European youth policies have an individualistic bias, based as they are on an idealised notion of young citizens who are viewed as active and responsible individuals, masters or mistresses of their own fate. This notion neglects the structural constraints operating in the labour market and may backfire by stigmatising the unemployed. As a consequence, the transitions to qualified employment have to take place in an environment where contradictory expectations towards youth prevail (for example, becoming independent by entering the labour market or prolonging education so as to acquire more valuable qualifications). At the end of the chapter, the authors describe a number of tensions and contradictions that arise from this paradoxical situation.

In Chapter Two, Jones discusses current social protection policies for young people in Europe. The chapter provides an overview of social provision in the different countries covered in this book. As the transition to adulthood becomes more complex and extended, it also becomes more imbued with risks and more expensive. There is therefore a greater need for economic support for young people, but the moot question is: who will provide it? According to Jones, this question refers directly to the boundary of responsibility between the state and the family, which is of course strongly influenced by the recent adaptations of welfare systems in general. Here, she shows first that youth policies are based on different constructions of youth as a category, which becomes manifest among other things in different age divisions for different policy measures. She then presents a detailed overview of state provisions for young people across Europe, covering minimum wages, social assistance, unemployment, housing and child benefits, and the funding of post-compulsory school-age education. Overall, there is a lot of ambiguity in the citizenship status of young people, which is sharpened further by the increasingly prevalent restriction of welfare rights for young people. This in turn means that the support of the family becomes more important to young people. The chapter ends with an overview of expectations of parental support across Europe, but the author concludes that more research is needed to get a fuller picture of the role of the family in different countries and for different groups of young people.

The next set of chapters investigate various aspects of the labour market for young people, drawing upon quantitative and qualitative research studies. In Chapter Three, Plug and du Bois-Reymond use the image of 'yo-yo' movements to describe the complex transition patterns that prevail nowadays in the youth labour market. How do they relate to the work values of young people? Some modernisation theorists argue that among the young there is a decline in the centrality of work and a strong shift to 'non-material' work values. By this it is meant that work is prized not just for the economic rewards it brings (pay, good conditions, pension and so on) but for its contribution to self-fulfilment, personal development, service to society and a balance of creative activities. In the chapter Dutch youth research is used to illustrate that by no means all young people hold non-material work values and have 'modern' ideas about the combination of different work-related domains. On the contrary, whereas the importance of gender in determining attitudes appears to have become less, class and ethnic differences still persist. However, European youth research, which tries to identify winners and losers in the transition process, leads to the conclusion that modern values and attitudes towards education and work (including intrinsic motivation, a blurred distinction between work and free time, and a risk-assessing attitude) mark the winners. Evidently these values and attitudes help young people to make the best of the opportunities offered by the emerging knowledge economy. In their absence the chances of achieving a stable integration into the labour market are much lower.

The chapter by Álvaro and Garrido (Chapter Four) turns to unemployed youth and focuses on their efforts to find a job. There is a strong tendency to explain job-seeking behaviour by individual characteristics of a psychological nature (such as the importance attached to work, coping mechanisms and work-related expectations and attitudes). In addition, the intensity of job search is thought to be related directly to its success – in other words, the finding of employment. Álvaro and Garrido studied these assumptions, on the basis of surveys among unemployed youth in Finland, Sweden, Germany, Spain and Scotland (thereby covering the major types of welfare regime in Europe), and found them wanting. Psychological variables have some influence on job search, but do not improve the chances of finding a job; nor are the latter improved by the strategies used in looking for a job. Another important result is the strong and consistent relation between remaining unemployed and economic and social deprivation: although deprivation acts as an incentive for job-seeking activities, it does not in itself lead to success. Both job search and job finding can be explained much better by previous work experience or the length of the unemployment period. Álvaro and Garrido conclude that structural constraints in the first place determine the fate of unemployed youth on the labour market. This can be seen as a refutation of theories and policy assumptions alike that hold the lack of 'will and skill' of young people themselves responsible for their being unemployed.

In the next chapter (Chapter Five), Harriet Bradley discusses in detail the impact of labour market changes on different groups of young people by means of an in-depth study of the youth labour market in a service-based, 'post-industrial' city in the south west of England. Which groups are winning or losing out within the new structure of opportunities created by a service-based economy? The research confirms the view of Plug and du Bois-Reymond that the adoption of 'modern values' helps young people to deal successfully with the changing labour market. However, Bradley argues that a simple division between 'have nots' who are excluded and marginalised and highly educated 'haves' is overstated and fails to capture the complexity of change. Even the 'winners' face problems of job shift and instability. The prevalence of low wages makes it difficult for young people from all backgrounds to achieve independence. Social, economic and cultural capital are increasingly important in helping young people grapple with these problems, and class and ethnic divisions are thereby sustained.

In Chapter Six, the focus shifts to two of the countries that recently joined the EU, Hungary and Slovenia. According to Fóti et al, the present labour market in both countries is shaped by trends that are also familiar in the West European countries: demographic trends, flexibilisation of labour markets, changes in life and family patterns. To these must be added, however, influences emanating from the transition from a planned to a market economy. Overall they have led to rising unemployment, a decrease of participation rates and infringements on social protection systems. The youth labour market has also been affected: in Slovenia youth unemployment is high, in Hungary it is lower, but so is the youth participation rate. At the same time, educational policies in both countries aim at the expansion of secondary and higher education, which temporarily reduces the number of new entrants in the labour market but may lead to new imbalances in the future if job opportunities do not catch up with the rising educational level. The growing importance of flexible work arrangements and polarisation of job options between higher educated and less educated youngsters are visible in both countries too. Social protection measures are meagre and their efficiency is limited. In the last part of the chapter, the authors discuss how these developments affect the position of youth in society at large. They point in particular to the growing social and cultural differentiation among young people.

The next chapter (Chapter Seven) directly addresses the position of one of the vulnerable groups discussed in the previous chapter: youth from ethnic minorities. Craig et al examine the process of entry into the labour market (including educational attainment) for young people of different ethnicities in three countries – the UK, France and Germany – with differing traditions, legal frameworks and understandings of citizenship. Discrimination based on ethnic origin and skin colour is a common feature of national labour markets throughout Europe, and this structures the opportunities that young people have as they leave school. In spite of the differences between the three countries, the evidence suggests that in general many minority ethnic young people are disenfranchised from the benefits of citizenship

– regardless of how it is defined. Ethnicity is clearly a key factor both in shaping individual choices and institutional responses within the context of the youth labour market. This is not to deny that within the broad category of ethnic youth there are important differences: some minorities may do considerably better than others. There is also an important gender dimension. According to the authors, more research is needed to chart these differences. However, they conclude that at present national governments are generally unable to provide effective support for minority young people in terms of educational opportunity at all levels, training and vocational support or access to the labour market. There is also a question of the will to do so.

From the point of view of citizenship and exclusion, a very pertinent question is to what extent labour market marginalisation, in particular long-term unemployment, affects the political attitudes and behaviour of young people. This question is studied by Carle and Hammer in Chapter Eight. Drawing on their survey research, they explore a number of propositions about young unemployed people's political attitudes and behaviour. Has unemployment led to greater political militancy or, by contrast, to alienation from the political system? Have the unemployed lost trust in formal politics? Are they likely to turn to less formal types of political activity? Carle and Hammer present a complex picture. While there is some evidence of apathy among the young unemployed and greater involvement in informal action by the longer-term unemployed, Carle and Hammer suggest that their attitudes to politics are not really very different from those of employed young people.

The final section of the book considers some policy options. Everywhere in Europe vocational education and training is seen as an important instrument to improve the transition from school to work and to prevent marginalisation of young people in the labour market. In this way it becomes an integral element of youth citizenship. Although educational systems differ widely across Europe, almost everywhere efforts are being made to strengthen the vocational element and to bring it more in line with new skill demands and job requirements. This is illustrated in Chapters Nine and Ten, which deal with the Netherlands and Italy respectively.

In the Netherlands, a public system of school-based vocational education existed for a long time side by side with an industry-based system of apprenticeship training that was administered by employers and trade unions. Recently they were brought together within a single system of national standard qualifications. As is argued by van Hoof in Chapter Nine, this reform reinforced the dual and corporatist elements within vocational education by integrating theoretical and work experience training within vocational programmes, and by strengthening the influence of the social partners on the range and content of vocational courses. This should lead to a better correspondence between education and the world of work, and higher skill levels of young people entering the labour market. However, a critical assessment of the initial consequences of these changes for the transition from school to work shows a mixed picture: although the position of vocational education as a gateway to the labour market has been strengthened, still a sizable proportion of youngsters do not enter vocational education at all or drop out without reaching a minimum skill level that qualifies them for the labour market. Moreover, the new corporatist consultation framework seems to favour specialised vocational profiles rather than the broad qualifications that were intended. Van Hoof uses these results to illustrate some dilemmas that come to the fore when vocational education is being used as an instrument both for preventing marginalisation and for upgrading skill levels, especially when industry has a major influence on skill standards.

Italy has always been an example of a country where state policy has strongly favoured general education above vocational education, leading to an inferior status for vocational education. This is mirrored in the educational preferences of children and their parents who generally hold vocational education in low regard. Apprenticeship training has been left to individual firms that restrict training to their own employees and to their immediate training needs. In Chapter Ten, Bianchi argues that this lack of correspondence between state-provided education and the needs of industry, together with job protection measures that favour male adult workers, is a major reason for the weak position of youth in the Italian labour market (Italy is one of the countries in Europe with the highest youth unemployment). However, with the move to more flexibilisation and an active labour market policy in the 1990s, an effort is being made to revalue vocational education by turning it into an alternative for those who do not want to go to university. According to Bianchi, it is the apprenticeship system that forms the core of recently initiated employment policies. A new contractual framework for apprenticeships has been introduced, extending the system to all sectors of industry, strengthening the training component and opening it to older apprentices and those with an education beyond compulsory schooling. This policy of upgrading apprenticeship training and linking it more closely to the educational system follows a model adopted by many other European countries.

Although some financial and organisational problems are evident, the first results of this policy seem promising.

Active labour market policies for unemployed young people are the subject of the final chapter (Chapter Eleven). Here, Malmberg-Heimonen and Julkunen study the effects of participation in special labour market schemes in four countries: Finland, Sweden, Germany and France. These countries differ considerably in their reliance on active labour market policy, Sweden having the longest experience in this respect. The effects studied include not only the integration into work (either temporary or permanent jobs), but also the return to education and participation in another scheme. Moreover, to find out more about the effect of schemes, some particularly vulnerable groups were distinguished: unemployed youth without any work experience, long-term unemployed youth and youth from immigrant groups. Generally it was found that participation in a scheme did not improve the chances of becoming employed. With the exception of Sweden, those who participated in a scheme had higher risks of becoming unemployed compared with those young people who did not participate. The results for immigrant youth and youth without any work experience were somewhat better, which indicates that labour market schemes do in fact have some effect for more vulnerable groups. Another important finding is that there is a group of unemployed young people who circulate from scheme to scheme with diminishing chances of finding a job. Malmberg-Heimonen and Julkunen conclude that outcomes of scheme participation can be positive, but they seem more effective in a country like Sweden with a long history of activation policies.

Finally, in the Conclusion, we draw out some general issues from the findings presented in this book. We affirm that global economic change has brought about the fracturing of youth transitions that have become lengthened and precarious. Young people across Europe are vulnerable to unemployment, insecure employment and low wages. Characteristic responses to these problems include the provision of youth programmes based on principles of activation; the development of dualised systems of academic and vocational education; the encouragement of young people to stay on longer in education; and the greater involvement of families in providing material support for young people through the transition. Following Reiter and Craig (Chapter One), we conclude that increasingly youth policies are framed in a rhetoric of tackling individual problems that, although they may indeed help some young individuals, are hardly adequate to tackle the structural problems of neo-liberal economic systems.

Part One:
The reconstruction of
youth citizenship

This part of the book consists of two general chapters dealing with youth policy across Europe. These set the scene for the various, more specialised chapters that follow. Both point to the way that policy is working to promote new forms of youth citizenship based on notions of independence and self-responsibility. The opening chapter, by Herwig Reiter and Gary Craig, offers a strong critical perspective on current neo-liberal trends in youth policy which they see as becoming dominant across Europe. They argue that these policies rest on certain (not necessarily correct) assumptions about young people's behaviour that have led to the widespread adoption of welfare-to-work policies and more conditions being laid on recipients of state benefits. They explore the tensions between the individualistic ethos that permeates many new youth employment policies and the structural constraints that continue to frame young people's lives. Gill Jones adds to this picture of change with an informative overview of current social protection policies in all the European countries covered in this book. She shows how neo-liberal approaches to state benefits, despite their stress on helping young citizens to achieve financial independence through employment, paradoxically increase young people's independence on their families. This interesting picture of the changing relation between the state, families and young people is elaborated on for specific countries in many of the later chapters.

ONE

Youth in the labour market: citizenship or exclusion?

Herwig Reiter and Gary Craig

Introduction

The work/welfare nexus is still a subject of political dispute and redefinition. So are the criteria for the societal recognition of different kinds of work-related activities throughout the life course as well as the relations between life-course stages. The particular implications for the nature and quality of citizenship of young people exposed to the rules of a youth labour market embedded in a welfare context provide the general frame of reference for the discussion in this chapter, setting the scene for the more specific chapters that follow. The aim of this chapter is to identify the specific tensions and contradictions resulting from such processes of redefinition for the life-course transition of young people into national (and indeed transnational) labour markets within Europe. The different arguments concerning the relationships between youth, the labour market and citizenship throughout the chapter are drawn together in a final discussion of what we call the 'dilemma of youth transitions'. In reviewing the evidence, we point to several key issues relating to the impact of gender and ethnicity on labour market prospects; these, however, are dealt with more fully in subsequent chapters (see, for example, Chapter Seven by Craig et al on 'race' and ethnicity, and Chapter Five by Bradley on gender). The comparative overview of differences between social protection policies for young people across Europe, provided by Jones in Chapter Two, provides an empirical reference point for many arguments made here with regard to the different 'dimensions' of youth citizenship.

The following section frames the issue of youth and the labour market by looking at the current re-evaluation of paid work and employment as the basic feature of individual life. Despite considerable national differences in its actual legal status, work is identified as a major determinant of social citizenship and integration. The second section addresses some conceptual issues related to the changing nature of labour markets and youth citizenship. We briefly discuss the interaction between globalisation and labour markets, reconstruct an approach to citizenship from a youth perspective, and highlight policy choices for the conceptualisation and practical enforcement of youth citizenship in relation to employment. In the third section, some of the contradictions and tensions apparent in the reality of youth transitions to citizenship are discussed. These tensions make the status passage to qualified employment in capitalist welfare societies very difficult for many young people. The concluding section summarises the major dilemmas for the transition of young people into labour markets.

Life-course policies and the obligation to work

Growing up in Western-style capitalist welfare societies at the beginning of the 21st century means entering into a well-organised arrangement of interdependencies. One of the mechanisms of social integration is the life course, which could be described as the process by which the relationship between societies and individuals is mediated (Schwinn, 2001). In the context of the welfare arrangements existing in any particular country, individuals in modern societies are subject to specific 'life-course policies' (Leisering and Walker, 1998). These policies create, shape and institutionalise the range of possible patterns of growing up, living an adult life and growing old. Given the life course as an institution (Kohli, 1986), youth and old age are bound together in different models of 'normal' biographies where employment, family and, as a more recent dimension of 'normal' life, consumption, are the spheres of the major individual contributions to the economic and human reproduction of capitalist societies.

From a normative socialisation perspective, childhood and youth (the latter a relatively recent construct: Craig, 2003a) are the periods of preparation for working life through education and learning. Adult life is characterised by domestic labour (including reciprocal and caring responsibilities) and some 30 to 40 years of active participation within the labour market[1]. These latter are the major preconditions for keeping state welfare systems functioning and for having a third period of life (retirement or 'Third Age'), where the remaining years can be enjoyed without the immediate pressures of physical or intellectual productivity. Social security and institutions of 'risk management' help to moderate threats of discontinuity throughout the life course; and welfare arrangements related to old age, which make it possible to become and to be old, simultaneously have a potential impact on the shape and content of young people's lives (see Figure 1.1).

However, the predominant frameworks of welfare arrangements in 'developed' societies codified in the diagram, and with them the validity of the life course as an institution, seem to be eroding. The changing nature of the labour market, early exit and retirement, the increasing participation of young people in post-compulsory school education, as well as flexibilised and increasingly discontinuous employment relationships, indicate a fundamental change in the middle phase of the life course, the period where it is still expected that we will actively contribute to the maintenance of the welfare system through paid employment. This middle period is becoming shorter, thus requiring a need during this period for an intensification of labour and an increasing pressure of productivity. This 'active' middle period is also becoming individualised and less predictable in its course, so that individuals have to increase their mobility and flexibility to adapt to new challenges; and, of course, these processes affect both youth and old age. For example, the first phases of the life course, childhood and youth, seem now to be extended and individualised (for example, Coles, 2000a; Jones, 2002). However, as will be argued later, this does not necessarily imply being released from the constraints of a certain 'normality paradigm'.

Moreover, the requirements are also changing for what constitutes membership in society. The definition of membership and, implicitly, social citizenship as the "core idea of the welfare state", as Esping-Andersen (1990, p 21) noted, depends on certain welfare regimes and how access to social rights is regulated. Even in the social democratic regime type, where, according to Esping-Andersen's analysis, decommodification (that is, the protection of individuals from the logic of the free market) is a universal principle and entitlement is based merely on citizenship, employment remains the overarching issue in social policy, and full employment is a major policy aim. The 'fusion of welfare and work' is the outstanding characteristic of this regime and individual contribution through employment (or wealth) is a moral obligation: "All benefit; all are dependent; and all will presumably feel obliged to pay" (1990, p 28).

The persuasiveness of such obligations is probably the reason why employment commitment is very high in the most generous welfare states, although an incentive-based economic hypothesis concerning the willingness to work would suggest the opposite (Gallie and Alm,

Figure 1.1: The institutionalisation of the life course by the welfare state

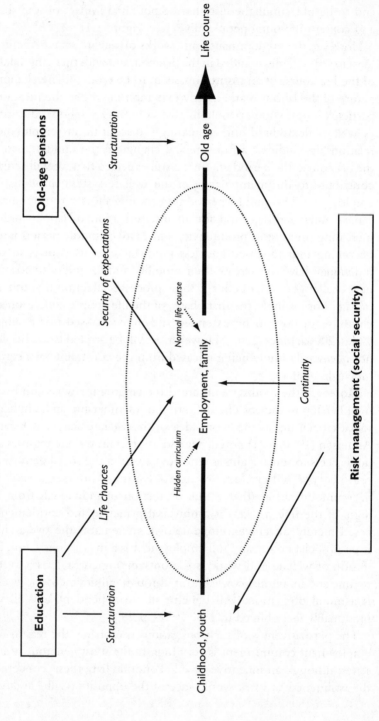

Source: Adapted from Leisering and Walker (1998)

2000). In a comparative study, Hult and Svallfors (2002) found the highest values for employment commitment in Scandinavian countries.

However, the citizenship approach has been widely criticised as not reflecting the value of caring and other unpaid domestic or other work (Lister, 2002). Nor does it recognise the ways in which welfare systems can exclude members of society from citizenship on the basis of 'race' and ethnicity or age (Craig, 2002, 2004).

Recent developments in EU social policy also underpin the continuing central importance of paid work as a route to full citizenship. The 1997 Treaty of Amsterdam, for example, re-emphasises the formal recognition of the primacy of employment. This is accompanied by a shift from 'passive' measures – the unconditional allocation of unemployment benefits – to 'active' labour market policies – the allocation of unemployment benefits under the condition of 'activity', such as participation in training and subsidised work programmes (Lødemel and Trickey, 2001). The latter are required to promote integration into the world of work; they are considered to be the main route out of poverty and, additionally, to help reduce public expenditure. But, instead of fostering social coherence, this approach has resulted in new social divisions and the overall prognosis of such a policy approach is far from optimistic. For example, Hantrais (2000, p 229) writes in her concluding assessment of EU social policy:

> Paradoxically, the active approach to employment policy, with its emphasis on employability and workfare as defining criteria for social inclusiveness, was thus helping to reinforce the divisions within societies between work-rich and work-poor households, and to devalue the contribution made to society and to the economy by unpaid workers, former workers, those unable to work and informal workers. From this perspective, the member states appeared to be opting collectively for an employment-based model of social protection, while reluctantly accepting that provision had to be made through residual schemes at national level to insure sufficient resources for the 'unemployable'.

Youth, labour markets and citizenship

The global context and its impact on labour markets

Due to the ongoing process of the globalisation of the division of labour, the European labour market and its regional and national labour markets are radically changing both in their internal organisation and external performance. The internationalisation of economies is usually associated with processes such as the 'outsourcing' of industrial and manufacturing production and therefore the loss of work opportunities for the less skilled labour force (especially minority ethnic groups and migrants [Craig, 2002]); the increasing importance of the service economy in established capitalist countries; a revolutionary transformation of work and work relations through information and communication technologies; demands for new competencies; flexibilisation of work and an increase in part-time, 'atypical' and other forms ('Macdonaldisation') of precarious work; new and reinforced inequalities; and unemployment- and poverty-motivated migration both between developed economies (Plougmann, 2002) and from less developed ones (Craig, 2003b). The competition between economies along new global front lines increases the pressure on European economies to improve their economic performance through adaptive reactions enabled by policies, usually termed deregulation policies, generally following the example of the aggressive economic policy of the US.

In this context, youth labour markets are even more vulnerable than adult labour markets, and they are more sensitive to the impact of global changes on regional, national and local labour markets. Though differences across OECD countries are considerable, the transition to work remains primarily sensitive to aggregate economic conditions. Youth unemployment rates tend to be higher and more cyclically variable than adult unemployment rates, and rises in levels of adult unemployment are generally associated with disproportionately higher youth unemployment rates. When this happens, certain groups (such as minorities) tend also to be affected disproportionately. Although low skills levels do affect individual employment prospects, skills levels as such have fewer determining effects on the overall youth unemployment rates of a country than on the skills/wage equilibrium and the general economic performance of a country (O'Higgins, 2001). The lowest qualified have higher unemployment risks and are most affected by cyclical changes in economic conditions across Europe. The generally increasing educational levels of the labour force disadvantage labour market entrants without post-compulsory school education in a disproportional way (Gangl, 2002).

Although the relative size of the youth labour force plays a role in the level of youth unemployment, its role is outweighed by other factors such as the aggregate demand for labour or by competition from others prepared to take low-paid work, such as minority ethnic groups. The 'cohort-crowding' hypothesis, which assumes future improvements in youth labour markets due to declines in relative youth cohort sizes, has to be revised. Cross-national comparative analysis and youth unemployment rate projections show that the influence of general improvements within the labour markets on the performance of youth labour markets in particular is much higher than even large reductions in relative youth cohort sizes. Youth unemployment rates are thus more closely related to adult unemployment rates than to changes in youth shares (Korenman and Neumark, 2000).

Altogether, the overall devaluation of less skilled and low-paid labour caused by macroeconomic changes, in the contexts of globalised economies and deregulated labour markets, affects school-to-work transitions and youth labour markets more negatively than adult labour markets. The conclusion of Blanchflower and Freeman (2000, p 55) makes no reference to the impact of any general decrease in youth skills:

> Unless overall rates of unemployment are reduced, there is little prospect for improvements in youth outcomes, even if youth shares of the population continue to fall or remain relatively small, or if the composition of employment shifts modestly toward service sectors that hire relatively many youths.

However the phenomenon of 'globalisation' finally comes to be defined by academics – as an ambivalent element of a post-Fordist modernity or as one of the more recent 'meta-myths' fundamental to the worldwide maintenance of capitalist hegemony (Bourdieu, 1998; Bradley et al, 2000) – it is nevertheless a useful concept to describe the process of increasing cultural and economic interconnectedness that is impacting substantially on Europe and its nation states (Crouch, 2000). Although economic globalisation is generally associated with pressure on national economic policies towards deregulation and privatisation, the specific effects are different for various forms of contemporary capitalism (Crouch and Streeck, 1997).

As Hall and Soskice (2001) indicate, deregulation (generally referring to policies that remove regulations limiting competition and the expansion of the market principle) as an answer to globalised competition is first of all associated with 'liberal market economies' like the US or, within Europe, the UK. Although the 'coordinated market economies', which dominate the EU, tend, on the other hand, to react less radically, the reshaping of the regulatory framework was an important issue in EU social policy throughout the 1990s (Lodovici,

2000). The coordination of the diverse national social and employment policies of the EU leading to the introduction of a general frame of reference is still, however, a long way from resulting in a convergence of policies, and further EU enlargement in 2004 may make this prospect even more distant. With regard to the labour market, the introduction and enforcement of active policies with elements of 'workfare', a focus on employability and recent activation-dominated employment policy strategies have become an integral part of the regulatory arrangement of the EU and its member countries (Hantrais, 2000; Gilbert and van Voorhis, 2001; Lødemel and Trickey, 2001).

As these are key terms in the EU policy framework, we will define them here. 'Workfare' signifies practices that introduce work requirements into welfare and social assistance. Such practices are, for instance, compulsory job-finding programmes or the provision of training for requalification and reintegration into the labour market. They may be complemented by 'non-skilled, low-paid forced labour activities' and they may have a punitive character. Related notions are 'work-for-benefit' or 'welfare-to-work'.

The term 'employability' signifies the positive relation between the individual's skills profile and an abstract or specific set of job requirements. Recent notions are associated with the individual's capacity to achieve meaningful employment. Thus motivation and self-presentation become seen as important skills for those employing labour market entrants.

'Activation', finally, refers to the individual as well as to labour market policy funds and institutions. With regard to individuals, activation implies the motivation or the obligation to participate in active labour market policy measures. It can have the character of a right to active measures. Funds can be reduced and made less favourable and in this sense more efficient; unemployment benefits can be transformed into financial assistance to active measures. The activation of institutions refers to the modernisation of the public employment service with the move away from treating clients as passive welfare dependents (Chabbert and Kerschen, 2001; Gazier, 2001; Rosdahl and Weise, 2001).

Globalisation, economic liberalisation and the changing face of capitalism undermine the autonomy of nation states, redefine the power relations between national politics and markets and require a reconceptualisation of social citizenship. Crouch et al diagnose a 'new triumph of the market over citizenship' on economic, cultural and political levels that is driven by international agencies such as the OECD. They suggest that, for the sake of securing future employability:

More and more policy areas are being declared off-limits to democratic influence and passed to the control of market forces and private business. The task of democracy is reduced to legislating the privatisation and deregulations which make this possible. (2001, p 10)

There seems to be absolutely no reason to suppose that such a decline in national sovereignty and the transition to a new organisation of membership in society in relation to life-course positions will not affect young people substantially. On the contrary, we can expect such trends to affect the future labour force and the youth of today more rapidly than other groups. How then can youth citizenship, and social citizenship particularly, be conceptualised in the context of changing welfare states, and what are the indicators for the new definitions of the status of young citizens in relation to the labour market if it remains as the central platform for social integration? The following sections reflect on these questions.

Conceptualising citizenship: a youth perspective

Mackert and Müller (2000) see the reasons for the revival of the concept of citizenship in the crisis of liberal democratic societies and the 'return', or re-recognition, of 'old' problems such as poverty, exclusion and standards of social justice. The concept of citizenship was revived politically by the left in Britain to react to the attack of Thatcherite liberalism on social security in the 1980s, but started to become an ideological and trendy 'catch-all' concept that easily found its way into more recent EU terminology.

With its roots in the formation of nation states and the establishment of universal membership rights for people in a distinct territorial, political and cultural space, the classical evolutionary notion of citizenship was formulated by T.H. Marshall (1950) in the context of the post-war development of the British welfare state. He conceptualised the development of citizenship as an historical accumulation of rights related to civil, political and social elements. The civil element represents basic individual freedoms and justice; the political element is associated with participation in democratic decision making and the exercise of political power; and the social element includes the right to receive economic welfare and security and to live according to the common standards prevailing in society. The institutions associated with these rights are the courts, parliament and the welfare system.

Particularly during the past 20 years, Marshall's social democratic notion of citizenship has become the reference point for a lively political dispute about the relationship between the citizen and the state. Social democratic, conservative, neo-liberal, civic republican and communitarian positions offer varieties between the extremes of a passive conceptualisation of the private citizen as a holder of individualistic rights (the liberal view) on the one hand, and an idealisation of collectivities of actively participating public citizens (the communitarian view) on the other (Turner, 1990). Recent developments in citizenship theorising are dominated by a common agreement on the superiority of active forms of citizenship to passive forms; by a newly emerging discourse of obligations (Kymlicka and Norman, 1994)[2] that has entered the policy pronouncements of governments; and by a recognition that many groups – including carers, older people and minority ethnic groups – remain excluded from the benefits of citizenship.

The recent discussion about citizenship, stimulated by the debate between the liberal and communitarian camps (Honneth, 1993), has brought a gradual semantic change due to the introduction of a specific notion of 'active citizenship'. Although the term has different meanings according to different political traditions, it broadly implies the revival of the essentially 'unmodern' term 'duty' (Preuss and Everson, 1996, p 547). Hvinden and Halvorsen (2001), for instance, distinguish three traditions. In a 'social liberal' position, active citizenship is connected with the emphasis on duties. In a 'libertarian' conception, the responsibility of active citizens for their behaviour, their decisions and choices in a market situation is stressed. Only in a 'republican' tradition is active citizenship essentially related to the actual use of possibilities for active participation. While all three positions focus on the question of the active role of the individual, the current dominant political connotation of active citizenship emphasises individual responsibilities and obligations towards society, rather than the activation through rights to participation. Lister (2002), for example, laments this redefinition of the relationship between rights and obligations as well as the residualisation of social rights (in other words, narrowing entitlements and encouraging individual provisions through private insurance) as one of the recent key trends in European welfare state reforms.

Youth social citizenship has also to be reconceptualised in the light of this recalibration of European welfare states towards recommodification and the revaluation of a citizen's duties. Welfare citizenship depends on a certain 'normative definition of good behaviour', which, in many countries, distinguishes on the basis of 'contributions' between those entitled to welfare benefits and those excluded from them. Young people, who have not yet had the opportunity to make such contributions, need to show their abstract willingness to contract into the welfare state:

> The policy expectation is that young people should learn social responsibilities before they are granted welfare rights, and even political citizenship should be constructed as the responsibility to vote rather than the right to do so. (Jones, 2002, p 37)

Considering demographic developments in Europe and the increasing numerical imbalance between the young caused by the ageing of the population, the commitment of young people to the idea of the social contract or other and new 'forms of solidarity' between the generations will become crucial (European Commission, 2002, p 12). Due to the shift within education and employment programmes from passive to active policies (Richter and Sardei-Biermann, 2000; Serrano Pascual, 2000), labour market policy measures are engaging with large shares of youth cohorts (Dietrich, 2003). They can be regarded as the provisional arenas where young people's readiness to demonstrate 'good' behaviour and 'contributability' is assessed.

When welfare benefits are generally, though differentially across countries, considered to be a reward for contributions from work and employment, the obvious problems for young people result from their more probable involvement in casual and informal or atypical and part-time work, which fails to give them access to full benefits (Wallace, 2001; Harsløf, 2003). The boom in such forms of employment among youth is less the result of individualised lifestyles than of the economic advantages of such deregulated forms of employment for entrepreneurial interests (aided by, for example, the weakening of traditional labour organisations such as trades unions).

Youth (social) citizenship thus remains largely a second-class citizenship, particularly with respect to the labour market. The maintenance of a youth citizenship by proxy (Jones and Wallace, 1992; see also Chapter Two), with entitlements derived from the parent's status, is counter-productive in the arena of labour markets as it denies young unemployed people, especially in insurance-based models, the status of full citizens. Activation policies without integrative or even qualificatory value (and whose outcome is at least ambivalent, as shown in Chapter Eleven; see also Walther et al, 2002) ignore the macroeconomic determinants of youth unemployment. They also reflect society's expression of a deep suspicion towards young people, rooted in a widespread misperception of them as inherently reluctant, lazy and unwilling. Another aspect of activation policies, the 'massaging' of politically unpleasant youth unemployment figures by temporarily 'parking' young people in transitional labour market measures, also contributes to the undermining (or the continued denial) of their citizenship status.

Governments and politicians tend to be quick to forget that the early citizenship duty of young people (mediated by parents) to go to school and to follow standardised curricula can be conceptualised as an explicit citizenship performance (or implicit for young people in further education). Education systems are structural elements of the modern role of the citizen and, together with schools, represent the objectives and interests of education policies in the development of human resources of a certain kind (Lenhardt, 1984). The ambivalence of compulsory membership in the education system becomes clear when we assess this membership (required by the authority of the state) against future employment chances and risks for young people. In a life-course perspective, the obligation to attend school, an important weapon against child labour, implies the temporary release from the obligation to participate in the employment system on the one hand, guaranteeing a certain standardised preparation for future employment activities.

Given this formal relationship between education, un/employment and youth citizenship, the denial of access to unemployment benefits to young unemployed people without an employment record seems incomprehensible. The entitlement to welfare benefits for young people in the case of unemployment should logically be related to the primary citizenship indicator of participation in the compulsory programme of schooling. From this perspective, a responsible social policy that considers education policy should, from our point of view, be accountable for educational outcomes and their matching with labour market needs. The creation of jobs and the provision of opportunities for vocational training cannot be the responsibility of young people themselves, yet implicitly this effectively underpins most current European labour market policy measures for young people. This appears to be a classic case of blaming the victim, as discussed in Chapter Eight.

If we conceptualise citizenship in a sociological way as a set of mutual expectations between the state and the individual, citizenship rights for young people should be immediately relevant and appropriate to their life-course situation (Coles, 1995). The right to sustainable (vocational) education and qualification could, for example, challenge the 'asymmetrical production of life chances', to use an early definition of exploitation by Giddens (1973, p 130). When citizenship rights for young people remain irrelevant in the context of state provisions during this transitional period, the state, with regard to young people, fails to meet its commitment to contribute to the balance of the mutual expectations indicated through citizenship.

Making new citizens: integration, inclusion and the implicit ideologies of youth policy

The idea of the 'active citizen' is readily accepted in many policy areas affecting young people, including labour market policy and youth policy in general. Relevant policy documents suggest that the ideal of a new kind of citizen is already emerging. The figure of the 'ideal worker' – equipped with favourable skills and social attributes such as flexibility, adaptability, capacity for teamwork and demonstrated loyalty, as Wyn and White (1997, p 41) characterise it – is complemented by the stereotype of the 'responsible consumer' (Wyn and White, 1997, p 48). These notions merge and form the contemporary 'ideal citizen'.

Assuming agency and activity on the part of young people by those engaged in youth work, youth research and youth policy are preconditions for empowerment. On the other hand, considering agency and activity as the major determinants of globally changing patterns of school-to-work transitions, while downplaying or ignoring the change in opportunity structures, reflects complete political naivety, a dismissal of accumulated scientific evidence or the influence of ideology. It is therefore all the more surprising that, despite having access to substantial macroeconomic evidence for the interplay of economic performance and trends in labour markets and education, the OECD experts responsible for the report *From initial education to working life: Making transitions work* (OECD, 2000b) still prefer to choose to explain changing patterns in youth transitions in terms of notions of individualised behaviour, as if 'transition' were a matter of agency alone.

In this report, the transition from initial education to working life is conceptualised as embedded in a life-course status passage of a strictly normative character:

> The transition from dependent student to working life is an important milestone in all young people's journey to

adulthood. As well as the transition to work, young people must establish economic independence, establish an independent household, and begin family formation. Each is a necessary rite of passage in all industrialized societies. (OECD, 2000b, p 26)

At the same time, the disadvantages of a narrow focus on the school-to-work transition are acknowledged and its usefulness doubted as it "tends to perpetuate a front-end model of education" (OECD, 2000b, p 26). The other important focus is the concept of pathways, introduced to capture the trends towards destandardised transitions. As a "metaphor of travel" (OECD, 2000b, p 57), it individualises transitions; it emphasises the preferences and choices of young people (and their parents) as one of the three main groups of actors (besides governments and employers) determining the features of transition systems.

Following a simplistic logic, the report tends to reduce the destandardisation of transitions by drafting 'new' patterns of behaviour among young people. They are, for instance:

- 'working the system' (OECD, 2000b, p 61): that is, swapping between pathways to optimise outcomes;
- 're-dipping' (OECD, 2000b, p 61): that is, returning as graduates of upper secondary education into upper secondary school for vocational programmes because of a shortage of places in tertiary education;
- following a 'holding pattern' (OECD, 2000b, p 11): that is, delaying transition to secondary education to increase the chance of gaining a place in a more prestigious pathway;
- 'double dipping' (OECD, 2000b, p 72): that is, obtaining more than one qualification at the same level;
- 'job shopping' ((OECD, 2000b, p 13): that is, trying out different employers in connection with early career instabilities after initial education in order to 'improve the fit between young people's skills and employer requirements'; and
- 'milling and churning' or 'swirling' (OECD, 2000b, p 78): that is, undertaking many part-time, temporary and poorly paid jobs – the other, negative side of early career instability after initial education.

In this interpretation, changes in transitional patterns appear to be not the outcome of structures and institutionalised pressures, but the result of thousands of individual decisions and choices, and the image of young people is distorted towards that of egoistic and rational consumers of the education system, who are intentionally optimising their chances by prolonging and enriching their educational careers[3]. Taking such a widely influential policy document as an indicator of the general attitude towards changing youth transitions on a political level, it might be expected that the (national) policy measures concerning youth transitions, which follow, would reproduce the trend of individualisation of responsibilities[4].

Another more recent policy document, the potential of which to influence and shape national policies in the frame of the 'Open Method of Coordination' is still to be assessed, is the European Commission's White Paper on youth policy (European Commission, 2001). Though far less openly tendentious and altogether much broader and less binding in its outlines than the OECD interpretation of changing youth transitions, it readily absorbs and integrates a notion of active citizenship as well as the figure of the 'active young citizen' as the ideal of youth. Without having been defined (since this had already been done in a previous European Commission study [Osler, 1997]), 'active citizenship' enters the White Paper at the level of one of four 'key messages'. The other key messages are "expanding and recognising areas of experimentation" (non-formal aspects of learning together with increased mobility and voluntary service), "developing autonomy among young people" and "a European Union as the champion of values" (European Commission, 2001, pp 18-19).

Employment, on the other hand, is recognised as a means for social integration. The close relation between youth policy coordination and the European employment strategy, emerging since 1997, is emphasised within the White Paper in the framework of European actions on the 'youth front' (European Commission, 2002, pp 82-98). In this youth policy context, employment, understood as a 'prerequisite for social inclusion', is clearly recognised as the link between youth, society and the welfare state.

The following excerpts are included in one of the annexes of the White Paper. They are meant to be part of the outcomes of the consultation process for the White Paper proposed by young people, representatives of youth organisations, researchers, administrators and policy makers. They were summarised and included as "proposals addressed to the public authorities by young people and all those who took part in the consultation exercise" (European Commission, 2001, p 32). In fact, passages with the character of proposals by 'the young people' are integrated throughout the whole policy document; this gives the impression that the White Paper intends first of all to reproduce the young people's suggestions and reflections:

Young people are very concerned about the opportunities available to them on the labour market. They feel the best way to social integration is to find a job. Young people would like to have a genuine sense of direction, guiding them to find their place in the world of work in the long term. To have a job means adult status, self-respect, money, independence and the opportunity to broaden one's social contacts. Young people who are cut off from work are losing a vital chance to get new perspectives and to integrate into a wider society. (European Commission, 2001, p 49)

Young people are willing to work, but finding a good job is getting harder. Young people know that their employability, and thus their chances on the job market, increase when they have a good education and skills and when they have spent some time in a school or university in another country. This puts them under growing pressure, and the level of expectations is higher than ever in terms of their mobility, flexibility, competencies and skills. With young people spending more time in education and training, they remain more dependent on their families and public institutions. (European Commission, 2002, p 49)

Pension systems in particular will depend on the willingness and the capacity of young people to contribute to their funding. This will only be possible if young people have access to employment. Thus, intergenerational solidarity – and hence young people's willingness to contribute to social inclusion and to the well-being of their parents and grandparents – is being put increasingly under strain. (European Commission, 2001, p 50)

Apart from breathing the 'spirit of globalisation' by potentially undermining national youth policies, policy documents like these suggest a particular and idealised notion of young citizens. They are viewed as egoistic and active agents, masters (or mistresses) of their fate, as well as aware of their responsibilities and more than willing to sustain the fiction of a social contract. They are thus ambitious and eager to work, concerned about the sufficiency of their qualifications and skills, and ready to update their knowledge and to share the rules and play the games of the market.

What seems to have found its way into policy documents on the highest level within Europe and its member states is not just an ideology in the disguise of a positive vision. It is also a fundamentally distorted general image of youth that hardly corresponds to reality. Take, for example, the idea of 'working the system' in order to optimise outcomes: unless understood as mere opportunistic and unsustainable behaviour, which increases individual risks, it would require a profound understanding of the system, and a prognostic capacity among young people, which educational researchers certainly would like to have but very rarely do (see Chapter Four).

The open method of coordination of national youth policies within the EU, adopted from the European employment strategy as a 'Community instrument', will doubtless contribute to the promotion of such images of youth. However, the problem is not the promotion of a certain image of youth as such – the question is who does this, for what purpose, and how?

Tensions and contradictions: the reality of youth transitions

In her critical assessment of the concept of social exclusion within European social policy, Levitas (1996, p 12) describes the European project to build a 'long-term social consensus' as being driven by a biased understanding of social integration. Based on an analysis of European Commission policy documents, she concludes that "the possibility of integration into society through any institution other than the labour market has disappeared". The 1997 Treaty of Amsterdam, which brought formal recognition of the centrality of work, has probably confirmed her suspicions. Though Levitas' conclusion is radically critical, it perfectly distils the essence of common understandings of integration into a capitalist economy. Labour markets are those subsystems of market economies where individuals can be accessed as resources and become functionally integrated. In the European model of social policy, this is viewed as the desired opposite of social exclusion (see also Byrne, 1999).

These findings are instructive for our discussion of youth un/ employment and citizenship, and show the paradoxical situation that is emerging as the natural environment for the transitions of young people, particularly when we consider the secular trend towards a prolongation of the 'youth transition' (Cavalli and Galland, 1993). Advanced market economies – increasingly knowledge-based service economies – obviously have a decreasing need for young people as a resource for employment, especially when their education does not go beyond the standard provided as general education. High youth unemployment rates can be understood as a signal to stay on in education and to extend the period of full-time education, training and, consequently, dependency.

The consequence of all these tensions is a contradiction that young people have to face in their transition to the status of recognised social citizens. On the one hand, the centrality of employment (and the labour market as its institutionalised entrance point) for social citizenship (including retirement provisions) suggests the need to participate fully in the system of paid work as soon and as extensively as possible. On the other hand, early exit from full-time schooling and further education clearly has negative effects on lifelong employment careers – it is connected to a loss of flexibility and leaves fewer opportunities to acquire recognised qualifications or learn those basic (social) skills and abilities that will be most important for a life within knowledge societies and service economies. Staying on in further and higher education is promoted and higher rates of participation in post-compulsory education are a clear aim of education policies in many European countries (for example, the UK, where the current target of government is 50% participation in higher education, and Finland). Against this, the increase in fees for young people staying on in higher education in some countries (met partly by themselves by taking on flexibilised jobs, and partly by their parents) presents yet another major contradiction. Confused expectations and uncertainties regarding their future biographies are potential problems for young people on the individual level (Reiter, 2003).

The difficulties for welfare models resulting from such inconsistencies are obvious. The hypothesis of the 30:30:30 model – 30 years of studying and training, 30 years of active employment and another 30 years outside the labour market again (Wallace, 2001, p 18)[5] – challenges the structures of welfare and support for young people and of the kinds of societies that are predicted for the near future. In the European welfare democracies, young people's transitions to full (social) citizenship have generally become prolonged and more difficult. The shift in most countries towards a mixed economy of welfare or welfare pluralism with a predominating employment/insurance model at its base (Hantrais, 2000, p 38) reinforces these inconsistent pressures on youth.

Another source of unpredictability results from the deregulation of labour markets outlined earlier in a given society. The realisation of social citizenship is a function of the scope of welfare provisions and the possibility of accessing them. Therefore, the steady withdrawal of state responsibilities and the prevailing political attitude to let supply and demand find their equilibrium are patently irresponsible in that they leave young people to the unmediated whims of the market. This kind of 'economic citizenship' provides little support for young people in their transitions.

Social citizenship is anything but uniform across Europe, so that the transition of young people to social citizenship has many faces. Equally, the preconditions for either social integration or marginalisation and social exclusion are different across Europe (Furlong and Cartmel, 2003; Hammer, 2003b). Nordic countries still have generous welfare provisions for young people, while in the Central and Eastern European countries welfare, and social citizenship in consequence, is at best residual and still, in many cases, in the process of being established (see Chapters Two and Six). The different qualities of social citizenship (even in countries regarded as having the same welfare regime) become obvious when we read Gallie and Paugam (2000) through 'citizenship glasses'. They offer an ideal–typical distinction of sub-protective, liberal and minimal, employment-centred and universalistic unemployment welfare regimes. These reflect, in this order, an increasing level of 'decommodification' – the detachment or protection of the status of individuals from the market logic (Esping-Andersen, 1990) – and provide clear evidence for differences in the quality and form of social citizenship across Europe. As far as the institutional arrangements of welfare are concerned, the quality of social citizenship in the event of unemployment depends on the degree of coverage (ie the proportion of unemployed receiving benefits), the level and duration of financial compensation (ie average expenditure per unemployed person) and the extent of active labour market policies (ie expenditure in relation to Gross Domestic Product [GDP]). Apart from given age limits, the quality of social citizenship is therefore to a large extent the result of country-specific welfare traditions.

With regard to the young unemployed in particular, Bison and Esping-Andersen (2000) note considerable country differences in the generosity of unemployment benefits relative to the average wage among youth. The rates of coverage differ across countries from 19% in France to 75% in the Netherlands. In most countries, the coverage of benefits for young people are lower than the corresponding rates for all workers. Taking individual income as an indicator for the quality of youth social citizenship in the case of unemployment, Bison and Esping-Andersen's (2000) findings paint a disastrous picture. Their target group of research – older youth (20-29) in different countries – lives on incomes that are below 50% of mean individual income (generally regarded as poverty-level income). They suggest that, with the sole exception of Denmark, the economic status of unemployed youth is substantially inferior, and the establishment of a separate living and household seems to be an unrealistic goal for them. The North/South differences are considerable with Italy and Greece at the bottom of the line, where the welfare state seems effectively to be invisible for this age group.

The dilemmas of youth transitions

The transitions of young people to the labour market and to citizenship are characterised by a number of fundamental tensions and contradictions resulting from the complex organisation of the economic reproduction of advanced capitalist welfare societies. In these societies, the life course as a means of social integration is organised according to the individual's capacity to make employment-based contributions. Based on the above discussion, we conclude by highlighting three of these dilemmas.

The first dilemma consists in the mere fact that social citizenship is an undefined idea, as the very concept is ideologically contested and anything but clear (for example, Roche, 1992). On the other hand, and somewhat detached from the conceptual inconsistencies, the national realisations of social citizenship through the emergence of welfare states imply very different qualities of social citizenship in general (Esping-Andersen, 1990; Arts and Gelissen, 2002). With regard to young people, further cuts in the quality of citizenship have to be made for several reasons:

- The social citizenship of young people is essentially different from those of adults (Jones and Wallace, 1992; Coles, 1995; Helve and Wallace, 2001; and see Chapter Two) because the extent of access granted or denied to entitlements varies with age and corresponds to the respective life-course position.
- The mutual relationship between the state and the individual that the concept tries to reflect is asymmetrical by nature. The definition of the criteria for the fulfilment of the implicit expectations within this relation is, in principle, imposed and usually inappropriate for young people, who are indiscriminately assessed according to their capacity to contribute. In the case of unemployment, following engagement in an education system for many years, the non-recognition of the (automatic) entitlement to social rights without preceding contributions turns out to be a form of discrimination

and an implicit expression of suspicion towards the young unemployed.

- The way in which social citizenship is conceptualised and whether or not access for young people requires participation in specific activities affects their status as being closer to insiders or outsiders of a society, just as social exclusion, as a concept and as an empirical problem, has to be understood as a relative phenomenon (Rodgers et al, 1995; Silver, 1995).

A second dilemma for youth transitions results from the trend towards prolonged education. Though skills and human resource development can solve many problems related to the tertiarisation of employment, it cannot serve as a universal remedy for other policies (Crouch et al, 1999). For instance, the European trend towards education policies that strongly facilitate further and higher education (perhaps as a substitute for social policy measures) is in tension with the necessity to prolong the individual duration of employment participation over the life course in order to be able to claim or maintain pension entitlements. It is very unlikely that the increase of human life expectancy will be rapid enough to absorb the effects of both these trends.

It seems inappropriate to pin too much hope on migration to solve this problem, even if it is 'properly controlled', as the corresponding passage in the European Commission's White Paper on youth policy proposes (in other words, through a combination of a Fortress Europe approach alongside a willingness to allow specific groups of skilled workers inside the Fortress [Craig, 2002]) – and even anticipating the dark clouds gathering in the sky above the European Union in respect of these debates:

> The ageing of the population will also make it necessary to call on human resources from outside the European Union in order to make up for labour shortages. Our societies will have to diversify in ethnic, religious, social and linguistic terms. And all this will have to be properly controlled, particularly with regards to young people, if we are to avoid social tensions or negative repercussions for education systems and the labour market. (European Commission, 2001, p 12)

Although, at first glance, high youth unemployment rates suggest an over-supply while concealing future shortages of young people in the labour market, it seems unavoidable that the 'pressure', to use the term generally, on youth will increase. In a worst-case scenario, the period of education prior to employment, even if it might on average be prolonged, will become more oriented towards outcome and 'utilisability'; in addition, it will become more competitive and, at the same time, more uncertain as to its immediate benefits. In particular, despite extensive participation in post-compulsory education, the prospect of an accelerated need to readjust skills and knowledge requirements by individualising educational and skills-related responsibilities (for example, lifelong learning) in relation to changing criteria for access to forms of social citizenship (for example, employability) might further undermine the middle-class concept of youth as a moratorium. This 'pause' has education (in the sense of the German term '*Bildung*') and self-development as two of its most important constitutive elements.

Yet, to give an answer to the question of how far the concept of youth is challenged by changes in employment and education in advanced industrial countries certainly requires a much more profound discussion of these changes in the context of sociological and historical accounts of youth. For instance, it needs to be clarified in what way the loss of socialisation functions assigned to education in the course of its becoming 'more technical and demanding' (identified by Gillis [1974, p 203] even by the 1960s) signifies, in relation to current conditions, a starting point for a continued and intensified phase of development or perhaps even an entirely different form of ideological stance towards the position of young people.

Indeed, it may well be that the recent changes in the employment system and the related problem of the gradual decoupling of education and employment are indicative of those kinds of 'great change' that Marshall had in mind when he discussed the problem more than 50 years ago:

> If it were possible for the school system to treat the pupil entirely as an end in himself (sic), and to regard education as giving him something whose value he could enjoy to the full whatever his station in after-life, then it might be possible to mould the educational plan to the shape demanded by individual needs, regardless of any other considerations. But, as we all know, education today is closely linked with occupation, and one, at least, of the values the pupils expects to get from it is a qualification for employment at an appropriate level. Unless great changes take place, it seems

likely that the educational plan will be adjusted to occupational demand. (Marshall and Bottomore, 1992, p 37)

Moreover, such an analysis would have to be related to a thorough and critical analysis concerning the validity of a life-course model (see Introduction) as a socialisation programme for a 'flexible capitalism' (Sennett, 1998).

A third dilemma refers to the fact that youth unemployment is a highly complex but, at the same time, politicised issue. It is a political and policy battlefield where quick and unsustainable solutions are offered, tending to neglect the fact that the problem, like so many other societal issues, can only be tackled through a careful coordination of different policy areas within a long-term perspective. This must include, at the very least, social, education, labour market and employment policies. A precondition is once again the extensive de-ideologisation of the discourse about youth because the combination of the two terms 'youth' and 'unemployed' involves many temptations to stigmatise a social group that should, in reality, be held least responsible for its chances in the process of transition and within the opportunity structures it inhabits. The debate about a youth underclass is exemplary in relation to debates about youth unemployment; the concept of the underclass fortunately appears, at least within Europe, to be taken seriously in the UK, and there only in the political margins. At the same time, the UK has the most liberal and deregulated market economy in Europe and is the most receptive to the moralising policy ideologies of North American provenance (Bagguley and Mann, 1992; MacDonald, 1997).

Together with the equally dubious idealisation of young citizens in recent youth policy documents, which no doubt intend to be constructive in their primary impetus but in reality articulate narrow public claims towards youth, these distorted images of youth refer to opposite sides of the same coin. It seems paradoxical that young people have become recognised as a significant quantity in the equations of welfare capitalism – in other words, as an indispensable resource with the tendency to dry up – and at the same time, on a discursive level, tend to be excluded from being representatives of an average and 'normal' social reality – that is, people who occasionally search without ulterior motives for jobs. Instead, they are presented as a kind of avant-garde of a new model of citizen, an ideal that unambiguously conveys a certain image of a prospective outsider.

For young people, unemployment is a threat to their right to social citizenship, and the re-evaluation of employment in European welfare economies is heightening this threat. The undiminished importance of paid work as a crucial element structuring the life course applies equally to young people, despite its increasing competition with alternative activities and priorities such as those of leisure or consumption (Bauman, 1998; van Hoof, 2002a). Though the transition to adulthood is certainly more complex and cannot be reduced to the school-to-work transition (Coles, 1995; Jones, 1995), mastering this key transition will grow in importance in the future (Roberts, 2003). The status of unemployment as an indicator for failure in the course of this transition as well as its threatening and stigmatising connotation needs to be 'deactivated' or at least relativised. This can be done, for instance, by finally recognising it for what it is − a necessary and de-individualised aspect of the labour *market*.

Notes

[1] This assumption exaggerates a male life-course model, as the social division of labour is still essentially gendered (Rubery et al, 1998; Rubery et al, 1999). Given the general character of this chapter, this simplification seems necessary. For the same reason, another simplification is related to national specificities.

[2] Marshall (1950) was quite explicit even then about what kind of activity and ethic the work obligation involved:

> It is no easy matter to revive the sense of the personal obligation to work in a new form in which it is attached to the status of citizenship. It is not made any easier by the fact that the essential duty is not to have a job and hold it, since that is relatively simple in conditions of full employment, but to put one's heart into one's job and work hard. (Marshall and Bottomore, 1992, p 46)

[3] It is exactly this priority to stress individual action and to neglect 'impersonal and inevitable forces' that Boltanski and Chiapello (2002, p 19) describe as one of the main characteristics of the model of change in the spirit of capitalism.

[4] Other policy initiatives promoted by the OECD and the European Commission are the encouragement of employability and lifelong learning. In particular, the latter appears to follow the same spirit of balancing skill supply and demand by individualising educational responsibilities. For a substantial critique of the OECD's neo-liberal approach to the relationship

between employment and skills development, see Crouch et al (1999, especially Chapter Two).

[5] Again, this reflects a male model.

TWO

Social protection policies for young people: a cross-national comparison

Gill Jones

Introduction

The transition to adulthood has become more complex, more extended, more expensive and more imbued with risk. The different strands of transition (education to employment, family formation, housing and household transitions) each require increasing financial resources. Whether in education, training or the labour market, young people are generally not able to take economic responsibility for themselves: the costs are too high and their incomes too low. This means that they may need to seek economic support either from their families or from the state. As youth has been extended, the need for economic support has become greater, and the question of who will provide it more acute.

This last question will be answered differently in different European countries, since the roles of the state and the family in providing social protection vary. This chapter starts by identifying some of the problems policy makers have to confront in considering support and protection for young people as a specific group. It then explores the national variation in young people's main transition events, and considers the scope for differing constructions of need. It then seeks to define the boundary of responsibility between the state and the family in relation to young people in need of economic support. It does this first by examining state provision with regard to key elements of policies affecting young people's incomes (wage policy, National Insurance, social assistance, housing benefit and support for post-compulsory education). Then, it considers the legal and moral frameworks of family support. Though primarily based on recent research on youth policies in the UK (Jones and Bell, 2000; Bynner et al, 2004), the chapter examines cross-national variation with a range of other European countries. Its ultimate purpose is to set out an agenda for European cross-national empirical research.

Age and dependence

Policy structures designed for the wider population are not easy to apply to young people who are somewhere between the statuses of dependent child and independent adult. It is difficult for policy makers to grapple with the concept of 'youth'. If 'youth' is socially constructed, and varies over time, by gender and culturally, then how can policy makers cope with the extreme variability of circumstances in which young people live? The simplest solution to the problem of defining youth in policy and provision is to use the criterion of age. Thus, many policies are age-structured, but they can be based on quite crude assumptions about the significance of age.

An example is in the UK's Income Support (IS) system, which has always included age dividing lines as a basis for determining need. The 1985 Green Paper, *The reform of social security* (DHSS, 1985), spelled out the basic age divisions (defining benefit levels) for claimants as 16, 18 and 60, adding that "for many young people there is a further structural dividing line at age 21". The practice of age grading was defended (and an arguably more meaningful distinction between householders and non-householders was abolished) on the basis that 90% of all Supplementary Benefit claimants aged over 25 were householders, while a "clear majority of claimants under 25 were living in someone else's household". Thus, the Green Paper concluded: "It is clear that at the age of 18 the majority of claimants are not fully independent, and that the great majority of claimants above the age of 25 are".

This statement contains some very simplistic assumptions about homogeneity within age bands, about clear division between dependence and independence, and about capacity for dependence (raising the question of who is responsible for 'dependants'). Age-graded welfare provisions in the UK now define young people as independent at the age of 25, when adult levels of IS become available. Until then they are deemed to be able to receive economic support from their parents (or carers). In practice, this may make them very vulnerable.

Although welfare policy in the UK has abandoned the criterion of whether or not a young person is in an 'independent' household, it has retained a clear distinction between students, trainees and those in the labour market (whether or not they are unemployed). This is in contrast to education, training and employment policies, which are increasingly concerned with *breaking down* the divisions between these statuses. Being in education seems to equate (in welfare policy terms) with dependence in a way that being in training or employment does not. Thus, as we shall see, parental responsibility is clearer where young people are in education. In contrast, 16- to 17-year-olds outside education and training receive little support in the UK: they do not generally qualify for welfare benefits or (until 2004) the National Minimum Wage (NMW), and therefore need to be able to depend on their families for economic support. These examples suggest that structures of economic support for students and of social protection for unemployed young people are based on different policy constructions of youth. They deny the possibility that young people may have several economic statuses simultaneously, such as combining their studies with part-time work. They also ignore the fact that much of the work in the youth labour market is low-paid and insecure, and provides limited scope for independence (see also Chapter Five). The EC White Paper on youth policy (discussed at greater length in Chapter One) commented that many young workers in Europe do not earn enough to be financially independent of their parents, and quoted research indicating that 20% of young people with a job said they still received most of their income from their parents (European Commission, 2001, p 42).

In practice the concept of a simple transition from dependent childhood to independent adulthood is fraught with problems. Children are not necessarily dependent, but may have to take responsibility for themselves and others; adults may not achieve 'independence' in policy terms. The period of youth may be characterised by 'inter-dependence' between young people and their parents (Jones, 1992), increasingly recognised as an important element of social cohesion. Young people may have caring responsibilities for their parents or siblings (Dearden and Becker, 2000), help in a family business, or make a financial contribution to the household.

Not only are patterns of transition very complex, but they vary by social class, gender and ethnicity. Policies based on normative beliefs drawn from the behaviour of white middle-class men, for example, will not hold good for other groups. A recent summary of research on young people (Jones, 2002) shows the extent of division among young people in the UK. There is polarisation between an (albeit heterogeneous) majority engaged in extended transitions to adulthood, and a working class minority whose 'fast-track' (Bynner et al, 2002) transitions lead to social criticism and targeting by policy makers.

Rather than see transition to adulthood as unitary and orderly, it is now more realistic to think of separate strands of transition, including from school to work, from child to parent, from single to married (or partnered), and from living in the parental home to living independently (Jones, 1995). While these strands of transition appear to have been closely linked a generation or so ago, the linkage has become looser. People are less likely to leave home in order to marry, less likely to marry before having a child, and so on. The result is that young people can be independent in relation to one strand of transition but not another. Young people can be living in independent housing but not have an independent income, or living with their parents but in a well-paid job.

There is thus an increasing need to take a holistic approach both to the study of young people and to policy development. Anne-Marie Guillemard (2001) stresses the importance of incorporating a life-course (rather than age) perspective to understanding the links between labour and welfare. She suggests that the welfare state, based on age thresholds, effectively standardises the life course into three phases, of education (childhood), work (adulthood) and rest (old age), thus accentuating the differences between these states rather than the relationships between them. Kohli (1986) calls this a 'tripartition' of the life course. What we see now, according to these commentators, is a destandardisation of the life course. The result, according to Guillemard, is a 'crisis of normativeness' in which people's lives have come adrift of policy structures. I argue, in contrast, that policy structures have always been adrift, in the case of young people, and that 'youth' has never been successfully incorporated into policy thinking.

With all these caveats, we have to think again about how need and dependence are constructed in youth and how systems of social protection should respond.

Youth transitions in Europe

Studies of cross-national variation in patterns of transition to adulthood show a broadly north/south divide, between the Scandinavian countries and the Mediterranean ones (for example, Jones, 1995; Iacovou and Berthoud, 2001). Iacovou and Berthoud's analysis of the European Community Household Panel identified a middle group of six countries, comprising the UK, Belgium, France and Germany, where patterns tended to be 'northern', and Ireland and Austria, both of which were more similar to the 'southern' pattern.

Patterns of entry into the labour market varied considerably across Europe. In the UK, there was a strong working-class pattern of early entry into employment, at the minimum school-leaving age, and the wage was once seen as the key to adulthood (Willis, 1984). Despite encouragement to young people to stay in education, the UK still has the lowest age at which 50% are in employment (along with Austria and Ireland, and in contrast to Spain and Italy)[1]. However, with the extension of education, and loss of the better jobs in the youth labour market, more young people are deferring their entry into the labour market. This is not necessarily a matter of choice: 16-year-old school leavers in the UK are now considerably disadvantaged by a combination of labour market and state welfare factors that assume that all under-18s should be in education or training (Bynner et al, 2002). This may put them at greater risk than their peers elsewhere in Europe. According to Iacovou and Berthoud (2001), the UK has the lowest education staying-on rate (65% at 17 years) in the EU, while Finland, the Netherlands, Belgium, France and Germany have the highest (over 95%). The formal school-leaving age varies in its significance: although set at 15 (Austria, Germany and Italy) or 16 (Netherlands, Norway, the UK and, currently, Hungary), several countries have compulsory post-school education or training beyond these ages. Employment may still play a significant part in young people's lives, however. Iacovou and Berthoud (2001) found the highest proportions of students with part-time jobs in the Netherlands, followed by the UK and Denmark.

Alongside the extension of education, there has been a trend within all European countries for family formation to be deferred by all but a minority. The process of household formation has also been subject to change, but the patterns are complex. Where young people still typically leave home in order to marry (and the median age at marriage is rising), then the age of leaving home will also rise. Italy is a case in point here, although the link between the ages of leaving home and marriage is weakening. But young people seem to be increasingly leaving home for other reasons, such as to study or take up a job, and in these circumstances the age of *first* leaving home may become lower. We must be cautious about inferring too much from national statistics giving mean or median ages of leaving home, especially when meanings of 'leaving home' may vary. The proportion of young people who are living in the parental home may mask the complexity of leaving and returning. Students may see themselves as 'living away from home' rather than as having left it. In northern European countries (UK,

Denmark, Netherlands, Germany and Austria), young people tend to leave the parental home earlier, often for reasons other than marriage (but may return again). There has been an increase in the proportions that have returned home, and then left home for a second time for a different reason (Jones, 1995). In southern European countries (Spain and Italy), young people may remain in the parental home until well into adulthood, only leaving in order to set up a marital home.

Just as doubt is cast on the possibility of clearly distinguishing between education and work statuses, or the degree of independence associated with each, so should we question the significance of leaving home as a 'marker' of economic independence. First, living in independent accommodation may be associated with economic hardship. Iacovou and Berthoud (2001) found that the poorest group were under-20s who had left the parental home, unless they were living with an employed partner, and that earlier independent living may be offset by higher levels of material disadvantage (see also Jones and Martin, 1999, on ownership of consumer durables in young people's households). According to these factors, young people in northern countries would be most at risk of poverty. Second, we should not assume that in countries where young people remain longest in the parental home they do so out of choice, or are better off there. The EC White Paper reported that 70% of young people in Europe said they lived with their parents because they could not afford to live alone (EC, 2001, p 42). In Spain, though 53% of 25- to 29-year-olds lived with their parents, only 11% expressed a preference for doing so (Álvaro and Garrido, 2000). Third, we should question the general assumption that young people are dependent while in the family home and independent once they move out (the basis of the now abolished householder/non-householder distinction in UK welfare policies). Housing costs, for example, are not necessarily incurred only when young people have left the parental home. In the UK, young people living with their parents tend to pay them 'board money', an almost universal arrangement for those who have left full-time education (Jones, 1991). European data on board money are scant, but it seems that board money is paid in Germany and Norway and may be becoming more common in the Netherlands. Payment of board money is associated with poorer families in Italy and Austria. Thus, we cannot estimate without further empirical research the extent to which parents who provide a room in their home for a young adult are actually subsidising them *or being subsidised by them* – this is a key concern when estimating need for social protection.

European welfare systems

Systems of social protection involve a complex relationship between the state and the family that varies between nations, and changes over time – both historical time and over the life course. Typically, nations vary in the extent to which states take responsibility for social protection of those in need. There has also been fairly rapid change in welfare regimes obliged to respond to wider socioeconomic and demographic trends. In order to compare systems of social protection for young people, we need a framework. This is provided by Esping-Andersen's (1990) typology, modified by Scheepers et al (2002, pp 188-9):

• Social democratic (universalistic regimes) – Sweden, Norway, Finland, Denmark and (possibly) the Netherlands. The system is based on decommodification (in other words, breaking the link between labour power and living standards), and the aim of social policy is to reduce the power of the market and take responsibility for social care. This produces highly individualised independence-from-kin networks (Scheepers et al, 2002).

• Liberal – UK, Ireland. The system is based on a low level of decommodification. The market is considered to be the arena for the distribution of resources. Scheepers et al (2002) argue that this type of regime produces a high degree of independence from the state and forces people to rely on their families and friends in times of crisis (such as unemployment). Strong social networks are needed for the system to be effective.

• Conservative corporatist (sub-protective regimes) – Belgium, France[2], Germany, Austria, Luxembourg. The regime is shaped by the Church and the traditions of family support are upheld, with minimal interference from the state. The family is thus the dominant focus of solidarity.

• Latin rim – Spain, Italy, Portugal and Greece are argued by Scheepers et al (2002) to represent a different group, characterised by an underdeveloped social security system and a high degree of familialism. Care is and always has been the responsibility of the family, the Church having a strong influence.

• Central Europe – Slovenia and Hungary represent a different group (outside the basic typology), which has been undergoing transition from state control to marketisation, but where there may be a strong underlying degree of familialism. They may therefore contain characteristics of other systems.

Broadly speaking, the second half of the 20th century saw a trend in many European countries from traditional protection systems operating largely in the private sphere through family and kin networks to state welfare systems. However, these are now under pressure. Welfare states have increasingly had to cope with demographic and social change, which has created an imbalance between contributors and beneficiaries of state systems. The EC White Paper on youth (2001, p 9) commented on the impact of demographic change and the need for new social protection frameworks:

> This quantitative imbalance between old and young will bring about a qualitative change in relations between generations. The financial pressure on social welfare systems will be only one aspect of this challenge. Indeed, we will have not only to invent new mechanisms for solidarity between young people and their parents or even their grandparents, but above all to organise, to everyone's satisfaction, the transition between generations in societies undergoing profound change. (EC, 2001, p 9)

Welfare systems have thus had to adapt to new circumstances. Benefits have become more conditional, in a trend described by Lister (2000) as recommodification. Where welfare states were once based on Universalist principles, increasingly the benefit system has been targeted to families or communities. Means testing plays an increasing role, undermining individual rights within families (by stressing dependence). Lister (2000) indicates that traditional Bismarckian and Beveridge models of social insurance are being modified in ways that undermine principles of equality. In Central Europe, too, there is pressure to adopt a residual safety net model of provision, as the role of social insurance is being questioned and means testing becoming more important (Clasen, 1997, cited in Lister, 2000). The renewed emphasis on the family both as the recipient of benefit and as the primary safety net assumes that family systems remain strong. With more partnerships breaking down, and with complex patterns of relationship among divorced and remarried parents and their children, systems of obligation and reciprocity may be far less clear.

The circumstances of young people in these policy configurations have barely been examined in research. The report from IARD, the Italian research institute, (2001a) used a typology of models of youth policy drawing on Gallie and Paugam (2000), but in practice close to that of Esping-Andersen. This focuses on: the *universalism* of social democratic systems; the *community-based* policies of the liberal regime of the UK; the *protective* emphasis of conservative corporatist systems; and the *centralised* sub-institutionalised model of the Mediterranean countries. If, as I have indicated, many of the characteristics of 'northern-type' transitions – early home leaving, earlier entry into the labour market – are associated with risk of poverty, then it is important to see how northern states (variously emphasising the role of the state, the market and the family) might meet this challenge. If, on the other hand, patterns of transition in southern-type states rely heavily on family support to mitigate risk, and welfare policies are based on families, then it is equally important to check the extent to which family support is really available. As Holdsworth and Morgan point out:

> Just because family is based on 'stronger' kinship ties and takes greater responsibility for the welfare of family members in the south, we should be cautious in assuming that the family is somehow more important in the south than the north of Europe. (2002, p 5)

The IARD study concluded that young people's incomes are most strongly supported by the state in Nordic countries, mainly based on the labour market in the UK, relying on the family in Mediterranean countries, and based partly on the market and partly on parents in most mid-European countries (IARD, 2001a, p 43). Whatever the source, young people's incomes are under threat. The youth labour market is increasingly characterised by low-paid and insecure work, and state systems of grants, while benefits and allowances are being eroded and families are increasingly breaking up.

State support for young people across the EU

Young people are, as indicated, a heterogeneous group. Policy structures sometimes ensure that part of the heterogeneity derives from age differences. Access to incomes from the labour market, the state and the family may vary by age. In some countries, the age of majority confers adult rights, while in other countries there is an age structure for achieving social citizenship. Here we consider specific policy structures that determine the level of economic dependence expected at each age, in the different countries, and ultimately (and perhaps implicitly) define the role of parents in providing social protection for young people. Several questions arise, concerning the relationship between age, economic independence and social citizenship.

- Do young people under the age of 18 have individual rights, or do they derive rights through their families?
- Are entitlements age-structured and, if so, is this consistent?
- What arrangements are there for cases where young people's families are not willing or able to support them?
- When does adulthood, in terms of social citizenship, occur?

Minimum wage

Low rates of pay in the youth labour market have already been commented upon. The minimum wage is a device for reducing poverty, but it has not been universally adopted across Europe, and there is debate about whether or not a national minimum wage (NMW) increases unemployment. Differential applications of the minimum wage are likely to affect parent–child relations among earlier school leavers and in poorer families in particular.

Norway, Germany, Austria and Italy have no NMW legislation, although in Austria the level of *Lehrlingsentschaedigung*, an allowance for apprentices in the dual system, and explicitly not called a wage, is fixed through collective bargaining. A minimum wage system has however been piloted in some Italian cities and may be extended nationally. In some countries (Hungary and Slovenia), the minimum wage is at the same rate for workers of all ages over 18 years, while in others (UK, Netherlands and Spain) there is a special age structure of transitional rates affecting young people. In the UK, the NMW did not originally apply to under-18s on the basis that they should be in education or training (but was extended down to 16- to 17-year-olds in 2004), and there is a transitional rate for 18- to 21-year-olds before the adult rate applies at 22 years. The rationale for the transitional rate is to prevent employers being deterred from employing young people. In the Netherlands, an age-differentiated system of minimum wages starts at the age of 15 years. Thus, 15-year-olds are eligible for 30% of the adult rate, rising each year until the adult rate becomes payable at 23 years. In Spain, young people under 18 years of age receive a lower rate (85%) than those aged 18 and over. The Netherlands and Spain (and from 2004 the UK) are thus the only countries where under-18s have wage protection through the NMW.

Unemployment benefit

In all countries, unemployment benefit (UB) is based on a national insurance system that requires individuals to make a certain level of contribution before they become eligible to benefit. New entrants to the labour market – and thus particularly young people – are clearly disadvantaged in this respect, as they will not have been able to contribute to employment insurance. Where young people are eligible, they may still only be entitled to a lower level of benefit, or for a shorter period of time. The result is that many young people without jobs are not in receipt of benefit. In Spain, for example, only 12.5% of unemployed young people under 25 received UB in 1999, and 10% received welfare benefits, which are age-graded. The system in Spain and elsewhere assumes that young people in the labour market are economically dependent on their parents. Although they may nominally be entitled to the same benefits as adults in the Netherlands, Norway, Germany and Austria, in practice they are not.

Each of the countries has complex eligibility criteria. In the Netherlands, for example, claimants must have been employed for 26 of the last 39 weeks; and claimants who have not worked for four out of the previous five years (in other words, most unemployed young people under 23 years) are only entitled to 70% of the minimum wage for a period of six months. Benefits are wage-related, and previous employment and income are thus taken into account. In Norway and Italy, benefits are similarly wage-related. In Germany, marginal work, freelance work, self-employment and German BEAMTE (career public servants appointed by the state for very special functions) are not counted in relation to eligibility for UB, but rates vary according to marital status rather than age.

In several countries, however, there have been recent changes from passive to active employment policies – that is, from welfare to work. In Italy, with the reduction of passive policies, new active employment measures are being adopted for young people, targeted at the 19-32 age group. These include labour grants for unemployed young people aged 21-32 years, a one-year placement plan (PIP) for 19- to 32-year-olds, involving training and employment and a grant, and Mobility PIPs, which are aimed at encouraging mobility to other areas (see also Chapter Ten). In Hungary, there has also been a shift from a 'passive' unemployment policy (from 1991) to active policies aimed at integrating young people into the labour market in the face of high youth unemployment levels. Since 1996, there has been no UB for school leavers (defined as under-25s, or graduates under 30 years of age) as they are expected to participate in training or an employment programme (PEP) although, if they subsequently became unemployed, they could be eligible for UB (Fóti, 1997, 2000).

However, active policies can misfire. In Spain, there have been particular problems associated with temporary contract schemes introduced in the 1980s. These initiatives offered incentives to employers to take on young workers through work experience contracts (for those with qualifications) and training contracts (for those without qualifications), but employers abused the system. The temporary contracts became virtually the only way that young people could enter the labour market (84% of under-19s and 69% of 20- to 24-year-olds entered the labour market in this way). In 1996/97, temporary contracts were abolished and incentives offered to employers in relation to permanent contracts instead, but these do not apply to under-18s. In Slovenia, the unemployment rate among young people under 26 halved between 1988 and 1998, but most new jobs were similarly temporary. In the UK, provision for under-18s was withdrawn in 1989 and replaced with a 'training guarantee'. The New Deal for 18- to 24-year-olds now offers employment and training options to young unemployed people, as well as an allowance. UB was replaced by a Jobseeker's Allowance (JSA), for which over-18s are eligible if seeking work or training. Research in the UK indicates that there are many young people who fall out of this system ('NEET' – not in education, employment or training), and new initiatives, such as the Connexions Service, are being directed at them (Bynner et al, 2004).

Social assistance/security

Social assistance arrangements thus become particularly important for some young people left vulnerable despite these arrangements. Welfare benefit arrangements vary between countries that take a familial approach and those with more individualised systems of welfare. Generally, parents are held to be responsible for the welfare of their children until such time as they can begin to claim social security, but the systems contain gaps. The age at which young people can claim social security in their own right varies between countries (18 in Norway, Austria and the UK; 21 in Spain and the Netherlands), but it does not necessarily confer on young people the right to adult rates of benefit. Furthermore, students may be treated differently from others. In Germany, Italy, Hungary and Norway there are no transitional rates for young people, who thus receive adult rates if they are eligible for social security.

In the UK, social security is age-structured: IS is available to over-18s, with rates varying by age (18-21, 22-25) until adult rates become payable at 25 years. The expectation is that 'NEET' young people are living at home and being subsidised by their parents. Under-18s who can prove that they are forced to live away from their parents may be eligible for JSA Severe Hardship Payments, and similar arrangements exist in some other countries, including Austria. In Norway, the Child Care Agency is responsible for helping under-18s in difficulty, while at 18 the responsibility passes to Social Assistance.

In the Netherlands, 21 is the age of entitlement to welfare benefit (compared with 23 for the adult minimum wage). Interestingly, rates of social security depend on marital status and living arrangements rather than age, and are based on the minimum wage; single independents get 50%, lone parents 70% and couples 100%. Parents are held to be financially responsible for young people under 21 years, but where someone under the age of 21 cannot be dependent, they can receive benefit equivalent to child benefit.

Housing benefit (HB)

Young people living in the parental home may, as indicated, wish they could afford to establish independent homes of their own. Support for leaving the parental home may take the form of subsidised rents or rates, housing benefits, or special tax and mortgage arrangements. It can be difficult for single young people to gain a secure foothold in a housing market where costs can spiral up or down, and where most housing is owner-occupied and designed for families. In the UK, young people are over-represented in the private rented sector of the housing market, although there is also a relatively high level of home-ownership compared with the rest of Europe, where rented accommodation may be the norm. Single young people may develop strategies for entering the housing market, such as through sharing accommodation with their peers, but this is a minority practice and an urban one (Jones, 2001; cf Heath and Kenyon, 2001). Ways in which young people in need of independent housing can be helped include through HB (as is the case in the UK and the Netherlands), or through tax relief for first homes (as in Italy), or preferential schemes for young first-time buyers (as in Hungary). In Norway and Germany, HB is part of social assistance. In the Netherlands, 18- to 23-year-olds living independently may be eligible for HB if their rents are below 300 Euros per month. In the UK, access to HB has become more restricted. Students lost the right to HB in 1990, and recent reform of HB arrangements means that young people can only claim the local market equivalent of a single room in a shared house. In general, there is little support for young people wanting to live independently, and an assumption that they can continue to live with their parents.

Child Benefit (CB)

CB is one mechanism for decreasing child poverty and it is a universal provision for families with dependent children in the UK, the Netherlands, Norway and Germany. In Italy there is no CB, only a tax reduction for parents. In Spain, Child Support is means tested, as are family allowances in Hungary (which were universal until 1995). Family benefits in Slovenia are targeted to vulnerable groups and means tested.

Perhaps the most interesting question relates to the age of the children in respect of whom parents are eligible for payment. There is no particular problem in respect of under-16s, who are clearly defined as dependants. In Norway, all parents receive CB until a child is aged 16 years, with lone parents receiving a double rate, but no benefit thereafter. In Spain, parents are entitled to means-tested child support in respect of dependent young people under 18 years of age. In some countries, though, parents receive CB for older children living with them if they are still in education or training. In the Netherlands, parents receive benefit for 16- to 18-year-olds who are either in education, unemployed or disabled. In contrast, in Germany, dependence extends well into adulthood: CB is paid to parents in respect of all young people under 18 years, but also to those aged up to 27 years when they are in education or training.

In the UK, there seems to be some uncertainty in policy thinking about whether benefits should be paid to the parent or the child, in respect of 16- to 17-year-olds. Thus, CB is payable to parents of all children under 16 years of age, and to parents of 16- to 17-year-olds in full-time education; at the same time, new (since 2004) means-tested Education Maintenance Allowances (EMAs) are now payable directly to 16- to 17-year-olds to encourage them to stay in education (Bynner et al, 2004).

Post-school education funding

Finally, in an age in which young people are increasingly encouraged to stay longer in education, including higher education, who pays? The trend is for state support for post-16 education to be withdrawn and for governments to expect that parents will subsidise, paying tuition fees and living expenses. There may be state subsidies for students from poor families, as in Italy. In the Netherlands, over-18s in education can receive a study grant, and higher education students can receive financial aid from the government up to the age of 30 (recently increased from 27). In Hungary, around 23% of 18- to 22-year-olds enrol in higher education, and numbers are increasing. Fees were reintroduced after transition but have since been partially abolished again. There are no tuition fees for the first diploma (and free tuition to this level is a major part of government policy). There is also a scholarship system but this does not cover all a student's living costs, which have to be partially met by the student or his/her parents. In the Netherlands, levels of government study grants are means tested on parents' incomes. Government student loans have become less popular recently, and students are increasingly taken on paid work, while their parents are providing more money in the form of gifts or loans. While financial autonomy was once the preserve of those in full-time work, this is increasingly expected of young people in education. In Austria, most higher education students receive some parental support, supplemented with income from jobs.

While the debate about tuition fees has now extended into mainland Europe (*The Guardian*, 13 October 2003), in the UK the system of student finance is under review again, in an attempt to widen access to higher education to poorer students. Following an era when many of the provisions for students, such as IS during the vacations and HB were abolished, and student maintenance grants were replaced by student loans (currently repayable once the student has left the course and is earning over £10,000 per annum) in the early 1990s, the current high levels of student debt and drop-out from courses have forced a rethink. Higher education grants of up to £1,000 per annum were introduced for poorer students in 2004. In other words, it is becoming recognised that not all parents are willing or able to pay for their children's education.

Social citizenship

The underlying theme of this chapter is young people's access to social citizenship, envisaged by T.H. Marshall (1950) to contain the right of individuals to the prevailing living standard in a society, implemented by the state through the education, health, housing and social welfare systems (see also Chapter One in this volume). Just as Lister (1990) has questioned whether women could ever achieve citizenship while they remain dependent on men, so young people cannot arguably be citizens as long as they are treated as dependent on their parents. It is only through economic emancipation (particularly through labour market participation, but also through welfare systems) that young people can enter a direct relationship with the state as citizens. But the situation is not at all clear cut.

The ambiguities of young people's relationship with the state are evident in a range of UK policy fields. Some policy structures treat them as individuals, others as dependants. Table 2.1 shows instances of such status ambiguities (Jones and Bell, 2000). Thus, higher education students are 'empowered' by student loans, which treat them as individuals, but disempowered both by dependence on their parents to pay tuition fees and by the means testing of the fee. Again, EMAs – an attempt to cater for the transition needs of young people – are paid to the individual, but (unlike training allowances) means tested on parents' incomes. There are similar anomalies in other UK policy areas that result in very unclear messages being sent to young people and their parents about what is expected of each. Overall, there has been a clawing back of welfare citizenship from young people but, oddly, a simultaneous interest in their political participation. It is unlikely that political citizenship (and in the UK there were debates about reducing the voting age to 16) could conceivably soften the blow of the withdrawal of welfare and social citizenship. Those who are excluded from economic structures are unlikely to want the right to vote.

Family support

The relationship between the state and families is very complex. Some have argued that the state welfare system actually weakened intergenerational relationships within the family by removing some of its basic roles. This argument assumes that kin systems of obligation and reciprocity, which form the basis for social solidarities, will break down if the 'nanny state' takes over (though the welfare state is itself based on reciprocity). Similarly, Ulrich Beck suggests that the welfare state has *allowed* family ties to be loosened and processes of individualisation to occur (Beck and Beck-Gernsheim, 2002). In contrast is Kohli's (1999) more optimistic view. His study of the family–state relationship explored whether it 'was one of replacement, substitution or crowding out', or whether state and family interacted to complement one another (as Attias–Donfut and Wolff [2000a] indicate). He concluded that, contrary to policy assumptions, public old-age security systems created scope for new links between adult kin generations (in other words, state systems could enhance family ones). When, as we have seen, adult incomes are withheld from young people by the state, the key to their citizenship may be held (supposedly on their behalf) by their parents or carers.

Table 2.1: Citizenship and dependency status ambiguities

Dependence	Independence
Post-16 education and training	
The means testing of EMAs assumes dependence on parents.	EMAs may be paid direct to 16- to 18-year-olds, although some think they should be paid to parents.
Levels of training allowance and EMA exclude housing costs and assume dependence on parents.	Training allowances are not means tested and are payable to young people.
	Training Credits treat 16- to 19-year-olds as responsible consumers able to select the most appropriate training package for their own needs.
	Youth cards will treat young people as independent consumers.
Workers	
Minimum wage legislation treats young people (under 22) as dependent or semi-dependent on their parents.	Employment protection has been removed from young people, treating them as adults rather than children (ie not vulnerable).
Welfare	
16/17-year-olds are excluded from benefit on the basis that they are dependent on their parents, some of whom may receive benefit for them.	16/17-year-olds can pay into the NI system, but cannot benefit from it until 18 years of age.
18- to 24-year-olds are on lower rates than adults on the basis that they can be semi-dependent on their parents, who receive no benefit for them.	18- to 24-year-olds contract, as adults, to seek work under the JSA, New Deal and so on.
Higher education	
In assessing tuition fees, the government treats students as dependants (parents are means tested). The student is required to depend on his/her parents or spouse to pay tuition fees.	Student loans. The student is personally liable for repayment, which is based on his/her income only. The student both enters a contract with a lender and begins repayments as an independent adult.
Housing and transport	
Subsidised transport treats those in education as dependent.	Subsidised transport treats those in training or low-paid work as adults.
If they were living with their parents, the family could be housed because it contains dependent children.	Young people are entitled to local authority housing if they are seen as vulnerable. Age is not usually a criterion of vulnerability – ie, they are treated as adults.
Young people are deemed in social security terms able to live with their parents.	Young people do not have a legal right to live in the parental home but can only live there as licensees of their parents.
	Foyers, in requiring a contract to be signed by residents to confirm that they will seek employment, treat young people as adults.

Source: from Jones and Bell (2000)

Legal framework of parenting in the UK

The family–state relationship in the UK is not explicit in law, in part because governments have been reluctant to interfere in family life. Despite the changes that have occurred in youth and in families, the policy frameworks for parenting remain hopelessly inadequate. The extension of dependence in youth is not matched by any legal construction of parental responsibility (Jones and Bell, 2000). It seems unlikely that many parents realise that they are now expected to take responsibility for their children for the first 25 years of their lives and to stand by to provide economic support where necessary.

The Beveridge Report took the approach that the state should support parenting rather than take it over. The welfare state was based on a dependency assumption (in other words, that young people were dependent on their parents), like the Poor Law that preceded it (Harris, 1989), but during the 1970s welfare policies were increasingly recognising the individual needs of young people (Jones and Wallace, 1992). Under the Conservative governments of the 1980s, the state role in welfare provision for young people was withdrawn, on an assumption that families would once again fill the gaps in provision: a return, in the rhetoric of the time, to 'traditional family values'. The policy change was based on a fear that the welfare system was undermining the family, as one right-wing academic indicated:

> Young people need the support of their families and the family is seriously weakened as an institution if it loses its responsibility for young people. But genuine family responsibility for young people is make believe unless at least some of the costs of their care are shifted back from the state to the family. (Marsland, 1986, p 94)

The logic is flawed, however. As Dean (1995) has pointed out, there is no family tradition of caring for young people, as opposed to children, because 'youth' did not exist when the welfare state was set up, and so care could not be 'shifted back'.

The restructuring of the welfare state in the UK since the 1980s has included a shifting of responsibility from the state onto the family, in a 'privatisation of welfare', but has not spelt out either what parental support should look like or who should undertake it. The legal framework for understanding the notion of parental responsibility (on which the dependency assumption depends) focuses on children and is more sketchy in respect of young people[3]. The 1989 Children Act locates the obligation to care with parents rather than the state, but defines parenting only as a broad duty to care and maintain (Cretney and Masson, 1997). Although it recognises that parenting responsibilities may change according to the stage of development of the child (note that age is not the main criterion here), it does not explain this. Although parents in England and Wales apparently have a legal responsibility towards their children until they reach the age of 18, they are not *required* to care for a child over the age of 16 years. This lack of a clear legal framework leaves many young people dependent on a system of moral obligations.

Expectations of parental support across Europe

In different European countries different approaches are taken to defining parental responsibility. Some reveal more ambiguity than others. In some countries (Norway, Netherlands, Germany and Austria), there is a clearly defined legal framework while in others, as in the UK, parental responsibility is based on individual interpretations of moral and traditional systems of family obligation. In some circumstances, there is an age limit for parental responsibility (18 in Norway, 21 in the Netherlands, 26 in Italy, 27 in Germany); in others, responsibility ceases on completion of education or training (Austria, Hungary).

In Norway, parents are legally obliged to maintain their children until the age of 18 years (when they can claim welfare in their own right), although the social expectation is that they will maintain them until the completion of upper secondary education at 19 years, or later if they remain in education.

In the Netherlands, parents are legally expected to maintain their children financially up to the age of 21 years. However, the social expectation is that support goes on, especially when a young person is studying. Given that full adult levels on NMW and welfare benefits are not payable to young people until the age of 23, there is a potentially problematic situation for those aged 21–22 years.

In Germany, parents are expected to maintain their children until the age of 27 years, and at least until they have finished vocational education.

In Austria, the civil code obliges parents (or grandparents where parents are not 'able'), to provide alimony or maintenance for their children. There is no defined upper age limit, the criterion being the ability to earn one's own income, as indicated by the conclusion of professional training or apprenticeship. There is an obligation on the part of the child to make successful progress in studying. If parents default, claims by over-18s are settled in court, those of minors settled out of court. Parents can be prosecuted in court if they fail to maintain a dependent child.

In Hungary, there is no legal obligation to maintain children, but there is a social expectation that parents will do so until the completion of their children's education. Policies are directed towards families rather than individuals, thereby assuming dependence.

In Spain, there is a strong sense of moral responsibility and social pressure for parents to provide extended support to their children until they leave home at around 30 years. Youth policies are built on an assumption that young people can be dependent on their parents and thus extend the period of transition to independent adulthood (Álvaro and Garrido, 2000).

Traditionally, in Italy parents maintain their children for a long time, especially if they are students. Male workers are legally expected to maintain their families (their wife, if she is unemployed, and children until they are 26 years of age; they receive small subsidies for this (*Assegni Familiari*).

A recent court case in Italy, reported in *The Guardian* (6 April 2002), is relevant. The Court of Cassation ordered an estranged father to continue paying maintenance of 775 lire a month to his 30-year-old son until the latter was able to find a job that satisfied his aspirations. The ruling indicated that a parent's duty of maintenance did not expire when children reached adulthood, but continued unchanged until the parents were able to prove that their children had either reached economic independence or had failed to do so through 'culpable inertia'. The ruling has been criticised as a 'loafer's charter', and for confirming the status of the family as a social safety net, but it has also been praised as being innovative in its precision. In ever more litigant societies, it seems likely that similar cases will be brought by children against their parents in other countries. Indeed, in the UK, a daughter successfully sued her separated father and forced him to pay school fees for the school of her choice, near her mother's home rather than his. While governments may resist interfering in family life, it may be preferable for definitions of parental responsibility to be clarified through legislation rather than left to individual judgements in courts of law. It is individuals in the poorer families, having least recourse to the law, who may have the greatest need for protection.

Need for more research

There is a need, however, for more research to examine the differential impacts of existing legal and moral 'structures' on family life, before new 'standardising' structures are imposed. In contrast to studies of family obligations towards older people (for example, Finch and Mason, 1993; Millar and Warman, 1996), there is little recent research on the 'parenting' of young people (Attias-Donfut and Wolff, 2000b; Holdsworth, 2003; Jones et al, 2004). The main UK studies of the economic relationship between young people and their parents were undertaken in the 1980s and focused on the effects of unemployment (Hutson and Jenkins, 1989; Allatt and Yeandle, 1992). Research on the parenting of young people is more likely to concern parental authority and control than economic responsibility (Coleman, 1997). There is a need to explore the implications of policies such as those described in this chapter for family relationships. In the case of the UK, the contrast between the assumptions of policy makers that young people can be dependent and the support practices of parents could not be more vivid. Smith et al (1998) found that many parents of homeless young people in England saw their responsibilities ending at 18 years, the equivalent age being 16 in Scotland (Jones, 1995). While age-based policies are based on white, middle-class normative ideas (Jones and Bell, 2000), patterns of parental support have been found to vary according to family structure, social class, ethnicity and the gender of the child. Financial support from parents may depend on both willingness and ability to pay (Jones, 1995), and access to family support affects how young people make decisions about the transition routes they will take to adulthood (Jones et al, 2004).

Cross-national variations in patterns of family support are rare. Recent cross-national European overviews (EC, 2001; IARD, 2001a) have only hinted at the kinds of cross-national variation that occur. However, Holdsworth and Morgan's recent (2002) qualitative study of family support in Spain, Norway and the UK showed that, despite a high level of uniformity in support beliefs across the three countries, there was variation in what they call 'action strategies', because of cultural differences in the desirability of different outcomes. Thus, for example, Norwegian parents may assist with setting up an independent home, while Spanish parents place higher value on maintaining a standard of living. What happens therefore when the aspirations of young people and their parents differ? It is now vital to study in all of the countries reviewed here how young people cope when their parents do not support them, and whether the current state safety nets for young people are adequate in a world described by Ulrich Beck as the 'risk society'.

This chapter has focused on cross-national variation in models and expectations of state and family support for young people in need of social protection. It has highlighted some of the problems faced by policy makers, as well as the problems caused by policy structures for young people who are seeking independent citizenship. In so doing, it develops some of the dilemmas discussed in Chapter One (in particular, the problem of the 'normality paradigm' adopted by policy makers; the effect of the policy fusion of welfare and work on young people's access to citizenship; and the dangers of over-stressing individualisation and choice when youth is negotiated within a complex framework of labour market, education and welfare structures). It has added a further dilemma: how can young people who are moving from dependence to independence – in other words, a dynamic and changing (as well as varied) group – be catered for? Policy makers have yet to sort this one out.

Notes

[1] These findings are based on young people living in households, and therefore exclude those who live in student accommodation, which is commonly the case in the UK.

[2] In France, the social security system (developed on Bismarckian principles after the Second World War) created a general public system, but failed to incorporate the public assistance system, thus reinforcing the stigmatisation of the poor in a way quite alien to the original concept of citizenship as involving solidarity and equality. The more recent development of these two opposing trends has led to an increased tension between the social citizenship model and the individual freedom model of social insurance in France (Bouget and Brovelli, 2002).

[3] There are different legal frameworks in England and Wales and in Scotland: cross-national variation within the UK has further increased since devolution.

Part Two:
Changing labour markets:
inclusion and exclusion

This section of the book moves to look at the situation of young people within and outside the labour market. It deals with the excluded and marginalised, but also examines the terms on which young people are included in the labour market, highlighting insecure and non-standard employment, dependency and low pay.

The six chapters in this section draw on research employing a variety of methods: quantitative, qualitative, secondary and documentary analysis. Two chapters (Four and Eight) draw on the survey carried out in Europe by Torild Hammer and colleagues: Álvaro and Garrido discuss job seeking and motivation among the unemployed, while Carle and Hammer consider the political effects of unemployment. Chapters Three and Five draw on qualitative work in the Netherlands and the UK. Both are concerned with investigating who are the 'winners and losers' in the changing economic circumstances of the 'New Europe' and with exploring changing labour market trajectories. Chapters Six and Seven deal with two particular groups of young people whose situation causes considerable concern. Chapter Six considers the position of young people in two of the ex-Soviet societies that are now part of the enlarged Europe – Hungary and Slovenia – while Craig et al in Chapter Seven deal with the particular disadvantages faced by minority ethnic youth in Europe.

The chapters highlight national differences but also point to many common features in young people's labour market situations across Europe.

THREE

Young people and their contemporary labour market values

Wim Plug and Mancula du Bois-Raymond

Introduction

As the previous chapters have stressed, the transformation of the labour market during the past few decades has been the subject of many discussions. In the Netherlands as well as other Western European countries, processes of globalisation and the rise of information and communication technology have changed the functioning of the labour market. New professions have come up and existing ones have changed profoundly or vanished altogether, and organisations require new attitudes from their workers (de Beer, 2001). The job for life seems to be past perfect; instead, employees should commit themselves to lifelong learning to keep up their level of *employability* (European Commission, 2000; van Hoof, 2001).

Transitions between education and work have changed from – at the most – one-off experiences to regularly returning 'yo-yo' movements between situations of employment, unemployment, education and care. Young people may find themselves in situations of multiple status at the same time (blending areas of life) in, for instance, combining work, schooling and care. A smooth and successful transition from education to work is far from self-evident any more. Given the transnational nature of these processes, changes with regard to the functioning of the labour market and related transitions appear to be taking place in most European countries, albeit in different tempi and with diverse outcomes (EGRIS, 2001; Walther et al, 2002; du Bois-Reymond and Lopéz Blasco, 2003).

With the shift from an industrial to a service economy, there would supposedly also take place a change from an industrial to a knowledge-based information society. This development would be accompanied by accelerated processes of individualisation and destandardisation of the youth life course, an increase of expressive values at the expense of instrumental values (Vinken et al, 2002)[1] and a decline in the centrality of work within the life course in comparison with domains such as free time, family, the care for children and personal relationships. In short, there is a tendency away from a work ethic to what we might term a combination ethic, stressing a balance of values and priorities (Breedveld, 2001; du Bois-Reymond et al, 2001; te Poel, 2002). Other discussions point at new skills that would be necessary in this changing labour market and social context, within which insecurity and flexibilisation have become a permanent part of the life course (Dieleman, 2000a). All these discussions pose a common question as to whether a new type of employee is coming into being (de Korte and Bolweg, 1994; van Hoof, 2002b.)

What do these modernisation processes mean for the social integration of different groups of young people? Continuing and deepening inequalities in opportunities and risks will in the first instance hit those young people in the Netherlands and Europe already lagging behind, in particular the less educated ones – often originating from lower class milieus and of non-Western origin (Kieselbach, 2001; Keune and van Horssen, 2002). Moreover, opportunities and risks will be redistributed – for instance, by the choice to follow training courses that will lead to possibly obsolete future occupations and, consequently, potential unemployment (Dieleman, 2000b; Walther et al, 2002). Besides these 'losers', there are those who are considered to be the 'winners' of modernisation: young people who follow middle or higher educational routes and carve out new individual routes of schooling, work and free time, adapting flexibly to the new demands of the labour market (Hogewind and Dijkstra, 2001; du Bois-Reymond et al, 2002).

The *central question* of this chapter is what kind of labour market-related values present-day Dutch young people espouse. We will interpret these data in the light of the above-sketched debate on labour market changes, in particular the redistribution of opportunities and risk. We also investigate how the Dutch outcomes relate to developments in other European countries and what they imply for transition policies and further research.

We expect to find a broad spectrum of differentiated clusters of labour market values among Dutch young people, reflecting processes of both *continuity* and *discontinuity*. In this expectation, we take up a middle position in the ongoing modernisation debate that oscillates between these two extremes (Beck et al, 1994; Furlong and Cartmel,

1997; Rudd, 1997). The *continuity* position states that, although major changes in education and the labour market have taken place, these developments have not altered young people's life courses to such an extent that a new value system with regard to labour market-related domains has evolved. According to this supposition, labour still takes up an important role within the life course, especially in the male one, and there is no general tendency towards an increase of non-material work values. The *discontinuity* position on the other hand states that major social and economic changes in post-industrial societies have brought a decline in the centrality of labour in relation to other life domains and new value patterns. Young people no longer adhere to material values or the traditional ethics of work as a duty, but are directed to non-material work values such as self-development, emphasising self-actualisation in the domains of free time, family and children at the expense of labour. Thus, young people's motivation for labour market participation will not be confined to economic needs or a sense of obligation but will be seen in a broader perspective of reflexive self-development.

In the next section we discuss recent developments in the Dutch and European youth labour market in relation to changing demands for young people. We continue with a review of available research on the subject of labour market values, and present a typology of Dutch young people's work values originating from our own research. Finally, we return to the research questions and give some suggestions for an integration policy for young people.

Education and labour market trends: new demands for young people

Since the recession of the 1980s it has become evident that within the global economic system, with its centrality of information and communication technology, changes in the labour market are increasingly difficult to predict (Esping-Andersen, 1999a). Consequently, objective risks of social marginalisation as well as subjective feelings about the insecurity of the future are mounting among the young. To deal successfully with permanent labour insecurity, young people need to be flexible, possess broad skills that are useable in different contexts, keep up their knowledge and learn to cope with temporary unemployment. These issues can be put under the joint header of *employability*, within which a high individual educational starting level and continuous learning during the remainder of the life course are seen as being of major importance (European

Commission, 1995, 2000; Glastra and Meijers, 2000; Coffield, 2000; SER, 2002; Onderwijsraad, 2003a). The acquisition of these skills is also a major hedge against labour market risk.

In the Netherlands the educational participation of 15- to 24-year-olds increased from 41% in 1977 to 54% in 1998; between 1970 and 1995 the average age of young people in full-time education increased from about 16 to 20 (Ministry of Health, Welfare and Sport, 1998). In other EU countries similar changes are to be observed, although not necessarily to the same extent. In 1998, three quarters of 18-year-olds and almost half of 20-year-old young people in the EU were in education (SCP, 2000).

While the educational participation of females has caught up with that of males, in the Netherlands as in most other European countries, the differences between young men and women with regard to educational choices and types – general education and 'soft' directions (relatively many women) versus vocational education and 'hard' directions (relatively few women) – remain considerable. Moreover, young people who have parents with low educational levels have not profited from the educational expansion to the same extent as young people from middle and higher educational levels. The share of young people who leave education without any diploma at all has remained stable at around 10% since the 1980s. A non-Western ethnic background aggravates all this (SCP, 1998; OECD, 2000a).

An important consequence of the increased educational participation has been that in the Netherlands the share of young people who participate full-time in the labour market has decreased and fluctuated between 40% and 45% since the end of the 1980s (44% in 2000) (CBS, 2001). Although during the past couple of years youth unemployment has been restricted mostly to those (non-Dutch) young people who are the least qualified[2], economic recession has recently set in; unemployment figures have gone up and now also affect young people with higher credentials[3]. High youth unemployment rates are to be found in other European countries as well, as discussed in the Introduction.

Within secondary and tertiary education, more and more Dutch young people hold part-time jobs. Recent surveys showed that 79% of school pupils and about 75% of the higher education students had a sideline job (Steijn and Hofman, 1999; NIBUD, 2002; see also Chapters Five and Six). Moreover, a relatively large share of employed young people had a temporary contract. In 1999, about 27% of all Dutch working young people had such a contract, a percentage more than three times as high as that of the total working population (8%).

Often these jobs involve elementary or low-skilled work in retail and catering services (CBS, 2001). According to the Italian research institute, IARD, the number of European youngsters with these kinds of atypical contracts has increased significantly during the past few decades (IARD, 2001). Further research should make clear what kind of influence such atypical contracts (as well as 'double status positions', such as work and care, work and schooling) will have on young people's successive labour market careers.

Finally, Dutch research shows that young men as well as young women try to arrive at a balance between labour and care, combining job and care tasks. Partly, this has been a consequence of the recent labour scarcity or the demand that young mothers remain *employable*, but at the same time the young mothers themselves want to be more than only mothers and housewives (du Bois-Reymond et al, 2001; te Poel, 2002).

New values with regard to life domains?

Youth sociologists suggest that more individual freedom of choice and higher professional expectations lead to a shift in value patterns among youth, from a sense of duty to a need for self-development and from material motives to non-material ones (Vinken, 1997).

In the case of the Netherlands, there is little research to provide evidence for such a recent overall value shift. Various major youth studies carried out at the end of the 1980s and the beginning of the 1990s demonstrated a high degree of continuity in respect of the importance attached to intrinsic work aspects among young people, just as in the case of other age groups. Young people found interesting and varied work the most important aspects of their jobs, slightly more often than good colleagues and a pleasant working climate. Extrinsic aspects (good salary, employment conditions, career possibilities and so on) were mentioned less often than intrinsic ones (social contacts, working climate, variation). For the higher educated, interesting work is more important than for the lower educated, who stress good working conditions and material rewards (van der Linden and Dijkman, 1989; ter Bogt and van Praag, 1992). A recent youth study by Vinken et al (2003) reported similar results with regard to the importance of a good working climate. In the case of Dutch *young* people, the researchers found analogous outcomes.

Research among unskilled youth shows that they consider learning to be a necessary evil, that they are orientated towards working at a relatively young age and that earnings are important for 'real life', taking place during free time. In general, young people complain that school – especially vocational training – does not connect to their lifeworlds (Veendrick, 1993; Plug and du Bois-Reymond, 2003; Onderwijsraad 2003b).

Concerning gender, ter Bogt and van Praag (1992) show that there are only minor differences between young men and women with regard to the centrality of work: men have a slightly higher work ethic (more directed towards work) than women (more directed towards care). The different life domains are relatively well balanced among Dutch youth. Free time, with its possibilities of social contacts and self-development, scores higher than among other age groups. The domain of family takes up a more important role when people grow older, mainly at the expense of free time. Later on in life, this development is reversed, and work becomes more important again.

At the beginning of the 1990s, the young and the elderly considered, to roughly the same degree, that material well-being was not life's most important issue (ter Bogt and van Praag, 1992). Diepstraten et al (1999, p 153) do observe a generational difference, but this is only between the generation that grew up during the Second World War (more material) and the one that grew up during the 1960s (more non-material). Moreover, this difference turned out to be mainly the result of increased educational levels and not the result of belonging to a particular generation. In comparison with other countries, Dutch society as a whole is relatively more supportive of non-material values and this is largely independent of age.

Concerning the comparison of the outcomes of Dutch youth research with those of other European countries, we encounter a major problem. While data for whole national populations do exist, data that can be systematically compared in this area – the labour market values of young people in European countries – appear to be almost unavailable. On the basis of the 1999 European Value Study (EVS), it was found that family is given the highest priority in the lives of Europeans, more than that of other domains such as work, leisure and friends. The EVS data reveal that work generally takes up a less central position in Dutch people's lives and that they attach more importance to social contacts and leisure than inhabitants of other European countries; also, Dutch people find good colleagues important, more so than interesting work, good rewards and a good working climate (Halman, 2001; van Hoof, 2002b).

We interpret these data as follows. There are no indications that young people more often hold non-material views than adults. These values were already supported more strongly in the Netherlands than in other European countries and it seems that the importance attached to these values is still growing – for all people. This is in line with Hofstede (1998), who argues that Holland is known for its 'feminine culture', with a large degree of individualisation, informality and the need for communicative skills in and outside work (see also SCP, 2000).

While the meaning of work has become less central to people during the past 20 years in the Netherlands, paradoxically its centrality as an activity within daily life has not decreased in importance (SCP, 1998; van Hoof, 2002b), including for young people (Vinken et al, 2003). From this it can be concluded that, although work as a structuring principle of daily life remains unabatedly high, work has decreased in importance to people in comparison with other life domains such as free time, family and the care for children.

During the past few decades, Dutch people have begun to perform more tasks simultaneously and spend considerably more time on paid work, studies and household and care tasks (Ester and Vinken, 2001). On balance, more tasks are performed within the same time budget, especially since females participate more in the labour market while the male participation rate has remained fairly constant. In practice, therefore, the 'art of combining' continues to be primarily a task of females (Keuzenkamp and Hooghiemstra, 2000).

In conclusion, in the Netherlands the importance attached to work may be considered to be unabatedly high, not only for older but also for younger people. However, work as a life domain has to compete more and more with other domains and, consequently, the centrality of work has decreased overall, not only for young people. Today's young people regard the combination of work and private life as of more importance than in the past, while at the same time parents already socialise their children to spend their free time 'productively' (Zeijl, 2001). The increased significance that is attached to leisure and care tasks has not been accompanied by a diminution in working. On the contrary, the filling in of free time has bonded with the 'productive world' (be it paid or unpaid activities). This has led to less free time in the traditional sense of the word and a blurred distinction between work and leisure, and this has been followed by increasing time pressure, among young people as well as adults.

Labour market values of Dutch young people: a typology

To contribute further to the discussion on young people's work values, we present a typology of young people, the empirical basis for which is a research project carried out between 1988 and 1997. The respondents, 120 young people, were between 15 and 19 years old in 1988. We took into account gender, social class and educational background; ethnicity was not a selection criterion as such[4]. The respondents originated from the city of Leiden and its surroundings.

The aim of this longitudinal project was to gain insight into the effects of social changes on the life course of young people, in particular with regard to increased choices and risks (du Bois-Reymond et al, 1998). We asked the respondents four times in nine years about subjects related to their transition period from youth to young adulthood. Special interest was given to their education and labour market trajectories, their ideas about being young and adult and their attitudes concerning the division of care and work tasks between partners (du Bois-Reymond et al, 2001; te Poel, 2002; Plug et al, 2003).

More particularly, we asked them about their opinions and attitudes towards work. In doing so, we acquired a retrospective picture of their labour market orientations and were able to analyse their impact on their life course up until then[5].

The point of departure was a broad division between, on the one hand, expressive and non-material aspects and, on the other, instrumental and material aspects. The following aspects were considered to belong to the former group: self-development and autonomy, intrinsic motivation towards education and work; intention of lifelong learning; intrinsic ambitions with regard to a career; a blurred distinction between work, learning and leisure; and no age limit to working life. The group characterised by these orientations would not mind working abroad and would react flexibly if confronted with new labour market demands. Many of them would be attracted to being self-employed and would prefer non-hierarchical labour relations and a family model in which the mother continues to work (part-time) while the father takes up some of the care tasks.

Instrumental, material work aspects involve: the attitude that making money comes first; an extrinsic motivation towards education and work; no further ambitions with regard to jobs; a relatively strict separation between work and free time; eagerness to retire early. Working abroad and being flexible are not valued by members of this group; neither do they want to run the risks of self-employment. The roles connected to family formation are traditional: he the breadwinner, she the (future) mother and housewife.

Our typology concerns the biographical information from 85 respondents who were interviewed in 1997 for the last time and were then between the ages of 24 and 28. The typology is based on HOMALS, a principal components analysis for nominal data that is a useful technique for explorative qualitative research[6]. We found the following three clusters:

1. a lower social class, *male model*, involving extrinsic ideas about work-related domains and standard biographical views of a gender-specific allocation of (family) tasks (instrumental/material labour market orientation);
2. a lower and middle social class, *female model*, involving traditional or partly modernised ideas about work-related domains and family tasks (partly expressive/partly instrumental labour market orientation);
3. a higher-class, *gender-neutral model*, involving intrinsic ideas on work-related domains and egalitarian views with regard to the division of (family) tasks (expressive/non-material labour market orientation).

Young males from lower social milieux

Young men in this group suffer the most from the restructuring of the labour market, at present and in the future (see also Chapter Five). In general, they have a working-class background and have followed an educational trajectory that, according to current standards, is considered to be too short to provide them with reasonable labour market opportunities. They did not enjoy school and it served a limited purpose: learning an occupation and becoming economically independent as soon as possible.

The restricted occupational possibilities narrow their room for choice. These young men often change jobs out of necessity or would like to because they do not enjoy the work or the working climate. Work is not by definition something that provides satisfaction. If possible, they are eager to quit working before their official age of retirement. Nico (26 years of age, administrator) states: "I really hope, I am very honest about that, to work until I am 55 and then to be able to quit and enjoy my old age". Dennis (25 years of age, assistant at a firm for tree cultivation) shakes his head at the prospect of working and learning until retirement: "Look, you have worked your whole life and then you wouldn't be able to enjoy for example the last seven years of your life?! Hell, that's not what I am working for!". For these employees, work is a nine-to-five job, from Monday until Friday, period. Then there is Jan (28 years old), with no more than a pre-vocational qualification; yes, at first he did have ambitions, to join the navy for instance, but there he was rejected because his Dutch language skills were insufficient. After further attempts to become a security officer and a driving instructor at the Department of Defence, he started working in construction as a bricklayer:"It's like that. I can't do anything else".

The ideas of these young men concerning the division of tasks between men and women fit the traditional standard biography completely.

Young females from working- and middle-class milieux

This model fits young women who find themselves between tradition and modernity. In comparison with the male model above, these young women display greater diversity in background and more ambivalence. First, there is a relatively large diversity in educational and occupational careers: these respondents have achieved various levels of education, from low to high, which can be regarded as an articulation of today's female educational emancipation. Concerning their occupations, these young women are not sure about their previous choices and the ones they still have to make. This attitude is also expressed in their ideas about parenthood: most of them still follow the traditional model of being a housewife and mother, but at the same time they realise that this gendered model does not really correspond with the present trend. They feel a certain pressure to legitimise their traditional wishes or come to (cautious) alternative solutions. Their life course is characterised by a selective modernisation.

Often these young women have more or less rolled into their present jobs. They want work to be varied and highly value a pleasant working climate. Learning and pursuing continuing education are of less importance while work and leisure are two different worlds. There is no impulse to be self-employed or to work abroad and they do not want to work their whole lives; they aspire to have time for childcare and also for self-development. They adhere to more than one work and care model: a number of them want to continue to work part-time when children have arrived. Others wish to work full-time at first, then raise children full-time and eventually, *when the youngest attends school*, start working again, part-time or full-time.

In contrast with the less-educated young males of the first model, it seems that the young women are more reflexive about their wishes and choices. They appear to think about alternatives before making final choices. Their outlook towards work is strongly influenced by their ideas about parenthood, and these may be traditional or rather modern. Work and schooling are subordinated to the life plan of founding a family. An example is Hilde (25 years of age, pre-vocational education, secretary), who tells us that she would prefer to stay at home with the children until they go to school. After that she would like to start working again. Her husband-to-be holds a similar view.

Young males and females from higher social milieux

This cluster represents young men as well as women who, in accordance with their social and economic background, generally followed long educational trajectories and obtained high levels of qualification. They have made intrinsically motivated educational and occupational choices and do not view work and career as being restricted by age. To them work is life: free time and work are partly or wholly interwoven and the most important work aspects are freedom, independence and taking responsibility. Occupations are or need to be brought into accordance with their wishes. Self-employment and working abroad are serious options and they permit themselves an *open-minded* attitude: they know that they have built up enough educational capital.

Their high qualifications imply a relatively high income and in that sense money is not an explicit issue. Others take up the position that 'as long as there is enough to live on', any money is good. But sufficient freedom, not having to do routine work and not having to submit to the demands of a boss are considered to be more important. Often these young people originate from 'negotiation' households. Their parent–child relationships are identified by relative equality in communication and conflict resolution through compromise[7] and they are equipped with good communicative skills.

Much importance is attached to self-development, be it during their study, their work or in their leisure. Lea (26 years of age) finished two academic courses and after that spent time in the US following a postgraduate course. While studying, she participated in various commissions and was engaged in social matters. However, she did not continue her educational career with a highly qualified and well-paid job. Instead she is playing with the idea of starting up her own firm, organising educational exchange programmes together with two girlfriends. However, she would not want to put all her energy into this, as she is also thinking about doing a PhD or travelling for a year.

Most of the young people in this group are still vague when it comes to family building and all the problems connected to it. In their minds it is still a long way off and everything can change in the meantime. In all probability they will choose a more or less egalitarian model in which the female will continue to work at least part-time and the partners will divide the tasks within the family.

Considering the three models, one might wonder where the young men from the middle social classes are located. The HOMALS analysis does not provide us with a clear and separate cluster in relation to the other groups. This is in agreement with the modernisation tendencies in the labour market that we described earlier: (young) men from this background are a highly varied group with regard to their educational and occupational choices and their views on work values. Besides, the term 'middle class' indicates a growing segment of the population that has unclear boundaries both at the upper and low ends. These respondents originate from parents who have realised a highly diversified mix of life trajectories: from the small and medium-sized self-employed to middle management civil servants, and from both parents working to mothers having always stayed as housewives.

Middle-class young men hold education and employment views that may be either instrumental or directed to self-development. They may occupy a nine-to-five job and be satisfied with that (in contrast to their working-class peers) or they may want to quit working and retire early (similar to their working-class peers). Although our research shows that more men than women support the breadwinner model, it is especially the men in this diverse group who are under pressure from their similarly well-educated partners. The latter do not want just to give up their job for children and the former would like to take part in the care of children, provided that this will not damage their occupational careers too much. Still, the often-mentioned 'one-and-a-half model', whereby the male works full-time and the female part-time, definitely fits this group.

Conclusion

In this chapter we have discussed a number of issues concerning young people and their relation to the labour market. It involved the analysis of changes in educational participation and new developments in the labour market, in the Netherlands as well as in other European countries. Related to that, we enquired into young people's current work values. In this section we want to examine these outcomes in relation to the discussion about winners and losers of modernisation.

We found by no means that all young people hold non-material work values and have 'modern' ideas about the combination of different domains, as has been put forward by various writers on social change. Likewise, we do not find evidence of a wholescale conversion of young people to embrace the culture of employability, flexibility and lifelong learning. Young people continue to differ in their labour market values and their attitudes towards learning, working and other life-course domains, within as well as between countries (see Chapter Six for a value typology that relates to Hungary and Slovenia). In particular, class and ethnic differences remain persistent; the importance of gender appears to have lessened (see also Chapter Five on the UK). In one of the European projects[8] we are involved with and that is still in progress, we appear to be seeing similar results (see Karsters et al, 2004).

What do these outcomes mean in relation to the discussion about the 'losers' and the 'winners' of modernisation? Our research project reveals that, in terms of the new demands with regard to learning and working of young people, those who are on the lower rungs of the stairs are at the greatest risk of 'falling off'. These are young people – relatively often from non-Dutch origin – who dislike school-based learning, have low educational credentials or none at all and who adhere to labour market values that do not correspond with the present – and possibly future – unfavourable labour market situation (see also Doets et al, 2001; ROA, 2003). These outcomes are similar to those discussed in Chapter Five.

In another European project[9] in which we are participating, we are investigating differences between failure and success by interviewing two contrasting groups: potential or actual modernisation 'losers' – young people who are not able to tune their education and labour market careers to the demands of today's knowledge society – versus young people who use the increased opportunities of the knowledge society to the optimum. In spite of many differences between the involved countries, our preliminary results show that the labour market values of losers in *all* countries correspond with each other, and the same holds for the opposite group of winners. In every country involved in the research[10], the winners express ideas about learning and work that involve, among other things, intrinsic motivation, a blurred distinction between work and leisure, and diverse and resource-rich networks. In general, they have a risk-assessing attitude and their educational routes often divert from the institutional educational and vocational system. They view their future as open and in positive terms. In contrast, the losers express ideas about learning as a necessary but unpopular obligation and they are extrinsically motivated towards work. Their educational trajectories are mainly standard, low-level institutional routes. Leisure and work are clearly separated life domains. Their networks may be extensive but are resource-poor and their attitude towards risk taking is unproductive. They perceive the future to be externally imposed and closed (du Bois-Reymond et al, 2002; du Bois-Reymond and Stauber, 2003).

Transition policies in both the Netherlands and other European countries have been regularly criticised for often being ineffective, out of touch with today's education and labour market demands and with the individual's needs and wishes, and for putting too much emphasis on forced participation in training schemes (Furlong, 1999; Lødemel and Trickey, 2001; SCP, 2003). Transition policy that aims to meet the demands of the post-industrial society must have an integrative character by taking into account that there exist different labour market values among different groups of young people, leading to different chances and risks. To contribute to this discussion, we would like to consider briefly two policy strands: Transitional Labour Markets (TLMs) and Integrated Transition Policies (ITPs). Both acknowledge the individualised life courses of the younger generation and propagate a better fit between changing life phases and situations with changing labour market developments.

The concept of TLM assumes that the boundaries between different life domains are opening up for mutual transitions. New institutional arrangements are needed to offer security and support to young people in transition; otherwise the demands of flexibility lead to high risks for this age group. TLMs must provide a *flexibility-security nexus* – in other words, a well-balanced combination of flexibility and security (Wilthagen, 2002). Applied to the situation of young people, TLM would provide better possibilities of making flexible choices for one or the other life domain, while some form of security would continue to exist during the transition period.

The concept of ITP originated from an earlier European project in which we participated and in which we studied *misleading trajectories* (Walther et al, 2002; du Bois-Reymond and Lopéz Blasco, 2003). ITP stands for an integrated and co-ordinated approach to policy and starts from the perspective of the individual. Attention is paid not only to labour market demands, but also to the individual motivation and previous and present experiences of young people. Flexibility in support and active participation are indispensable in doing this.

In conclusion, youth and labour market research – including our own – suffers from the fact that there is relatively little *comparative* knowledge about European young people and their life plans, attitudes and values. Future research agendas should produce such knowledge, not only for scientific reasons but also for policy reasons, and at a national as well as a European level.

Notes

[1] Expressive values emphasise immaterial orientations as autonomy, self-development, responsibility and other non-material notions. Instrumental values refer to more or less traditional and material orientations as a good income, a steady job and fixed working hours (Vinken et al, 2002, p 84).

[2] The drop in youth unemployment in the Netherlands can hardly be attributed to a boost in full-time jobs for young people: it is mainly the consequence of other developments. One important process with regard to the latter has been that full-time and fixed labour market positions have increasingly made way for part-time and temporary labour market situations, often in the context of daytime education.

[3] The youth unemployment rate stood at 7.3% in 2001 and has increased to 11.3% during the period June–August 2003 (15- to 24-yearolds). The unemployment rate among the total labour force (15- to 64-year-olds) went up from 3.4% in 2001 to 5.4% during the same period (CBS website: www.cbs.nl).

[4] Six of the 120 respondents in 1988 had a non-Dutch background. In 1997, during the final research round, there remained three out of a total of 85 respondents.

[5] The expressed opinions and attitudes of the respondents with regard to work therefore do not necessarily imply that these will remain constant in the future.

[6] The outcomes of HOMALS analysis are interpreted with the use of a two-dimensional graph, in which the relationship between categories of variables is visualised by the mutual position of points (ie the different categories). Clusters of points represent the fact that certain categories are often mentioned together in the answering patterns of respondents. For a comprehensive methodical account, see Plug et al (2003).

[7] For the origin of this concept and a more extensive discussion, see de Swaan (1982).

[8] 'Family and Transition in Europe' (FATE). Research project within the 5th Framework Programme of the European Commission. Coordinated by the University of Ulster, Northern Ireland.

[9] *Youth Policy and Participation (YOYO). Potentials of participation and informal learning in young people's transitions to the labour market. A comparative analysis in ten European regions.* Research project within the 5th Framework Programme of the European Commission. Coordinated by IRIS e.V., Tübingen (D) (www.iris-egris.de/yoyo).

[10] The involved countries are former West and East Germany, the Netherlands, the UK, Ireland, Denmark, Romania, Spain, Portugal and Italy.

FOUR

Youth unemployment and job-seeking behaviour in Europe

José Luis Álvaro and Alicia Garrido Luque

Introduction

For quite some time youth unemployment has been a much–debated issue in the European Union. Although long-term unemployment brings the risk of economic and social marginalisation for everyone who is affected by it, the idea that young people, who are only beginning their transition to adulthood, can become marginalised in the labour market is particularly disturbing. In the five European countries that are included in this chapter, rates of youth unemployment are above general unemployment rates in all cases, and are twice the general figure in the majority of cases (Finland, Sweden, Scotland, Spain and Germany). Young Spaniards are one of the most seriously affected groups, with 23.1% of them unemployed – that is, more than double the percentage of the general unemployed population in Spain. In the Scandinavian countries too, youth unemployment rates are twice as high as those in the general population. Thus, 11.4% of young Swedes are jobless, while the figure for Finland is 21.7%. The UK also has a youth unemployment rate (12.3%) of more than double the figure for the general population. Only in Germany are the youth and general jobless figures similar, at 9.8% and 8.9%, respectively (see Table 0.1).

We have chosen these five countries as the object of study because they can be considered representative of the different European regions to which they belong, and of the different welfare models, which will inevitably influence unemployment rates. Thus, Finland and Sweden represent the social democratic welfare state model, according to the typology developed by Esping-Andersen (1999a), with a generous system of assistance for young people. The two countries differ, however, in their levels of youth unemployment. The liberal model, characteristic of Britain, is more stimulating for the private sector, though it also has a stable system of state benefits, albeit less extensive than that of the social democratic model. Germany represents what Esping–Andersen calls the continental type of welfare states, which focuses on the income protection of those who are included in the labour force, but does not extend this protection to the same extent to new entrants. Finally, the conservative model, characteristic of southern Europe, would be represented in our research by Spain, a country with high unemployment rates at all levels of its population, and especially among its youth, and in which the family plays a fundamental role as a substitute for the state in the social and economic welfare of young people. In this book Chapter Two by Gill Jones spells out in detail what these different models mean for the rights of young people.

In the policy debate on youth unemployment, the individual characteristics of the unemployed are often held responsible for their reduced chances of finding employment. We might even say (following Reiter and Craig in Chapter One) that the policy thinking on youth, unemployment and citizenship has a strong individualistic bias. Often it is their lack of skills that is seen as the most importance cause of unemployment. But motivational deficits (such as a lack of effort in finding jobs, a low commitment to work and so on) are also sometimes strongly emphasised. From this point of view, a study of job-seeking behaviour of unemployed young people, as is presented in this chapter, is of great scientific interest and policy significance.

The data for this chapter come from the Youth Unemployment and Social Exclusion in Europe (YUSE) study. In this comparative study, surveys were conducted in each of the above-mentioned countries. Representative samples of young people aged between 18 and 24 who had been continuously unemployed for at least three months were drawn from national unemployment registers. They were sent postal questionnaires approximately six to 12 months later. In Finland the net sample consisted of 1,736 young people, in Sweden 2,518, in Scotland 817, in Spain 2,523 and in Germany 1,918 (see Hammer, 2003b, for more details). Thus, the results discussed in this chapter refer to the employment status of these young people at least half a year after they were unemployed.

We start with a discussion of the theoretical approaches that are generally used in explaining job seeking and job finding. Next we present our results on job-seeking behaviour and continue with an analysis of the present employment situation of our respondents. Finally, we relate the results to the main theoretical issues of the chapter and point out some very important policy implications.

Job seeking and insertion into the labour market

One of the objectives of the present study is to analyse the factors affecting job-seeking behaviour. Among the different psychological models most commonly used for explaining this behaviour is the motivational model of expectancy-valency. This model has a long tradition in organisational psychology (Vroom, 1964), but has only recently been applied to the study of unemployment. More specifically, the model has been used to explain both the consequences of unemployment for mental health (Álvaro, 1992; Garrido Luque, 1992) and job-seeking behaviour (Vinokur and Caplan, 1987; Aramburu-Zabala, 1998). We can summarise this theoretical model in the following way: "The general approach of the theory starts out from the assumption that the performance of an action is determined both by the expectations of successfully carrying it out and the subjective values associated with the consequences deriving from that action" (Álvaro, 1992, p 16).

The model takes into account the consequences of actions in instrumental terms – that is, the relationship between costs (behaviours involved in obtaining a job) and benefits (the consequences deriving from obtaining a job). The expectation that a desired result can be obtained is determined, according to the theory, by previous experience. In relation to job-seeking behaviour, we understand that expectations can be considered as beliefs that certain types of behaviour will be effective in the achievement of certain ends, such as insertion in the labour market. Likewise, in accordance with the theory, we can predict that low expectations of finding employment are associated with feelings of lack of control, despair and pessimism, and that high expectations are associated with feelings of control and optimism (Feather, 1992). In the present case, job-seeking behaviour would be associated with the unemployed person's perception of the labour market.

According to Jahoda (1982), obtaining a job provides the person with a manifest function, which is access to economic resources, but also a series of latent functions, such as the structuring of time, the performance of an activity, the linking up of individual and collective goals, the development of interpersonal relationships and, finally, the achievement of status and an identity. Commitment to work – the consideration of a job as an end in itself, beyond its manifest function – may be considered as an indicator of the way the person values work. Commitment can be understood as a reflection of the valency or importance given to work and, therefore, as a motivational factor in the quest for a job.

Research on the relationship between attitudes towards work and job-seeking behaviour has a long tradition in the psychological study of work. Many authors have already indicated the existence of an association between the two, and subsequent research has confirmed their results, with regard to the observation that commitment to work is associated with job-seeking behaviour (Feather and O'Brien, 1987; Ripoll et al, 1994; Wanberg et al, 1996). With respect to the nature of the relationship between expectations and job-seeking behaviour, there is less of a consensus. Thus, for example, while authors such as Ullah and Banks (1985) found an association between expectations and job seeking, and Taris et al (1994) suggest that perceptions about joining the labour market predict job-seeking behaviour, others, such as Ripoll et al (1994), do not find a clear association between the two variables. Other researchers, such as Aramburu–Zabala (1998), point to the need to extend the theory to include factors such as pressures from outside for people to seek work, self-efficacy, and attitude to job seeking.

In accordance with some of these previous studies, it might be expected that expectations of finding work determine job-seeking behaviour. That is, the higher the expectations of young people that they will find a job, the greater the motivation, and therefore, the harder they will try to find employment. Similarly, the valency or importance attributed to work should have a positive effect on job-seeking behaviour. Thus, the greater the commitment to work, the greater the probability that the person will undertake actions aimed at finding a job.

Obviously, in addition to expectations and attitudes with regard to work, other factors have been taken into account in the explanation of job-seeking behaviour, among which is the person's psychological well-being. It was in the 1930s, in the classic Marienthal study, that Jahoda et al (1933) showed that looking for a job is affected by attitudes towards unemployment and by psychological well-being. For example, apathy leads to the inhibition of efforts to change one's employment situation. However, more recent studies (Feather, 1992) suggest that job-seeking behaviour is more intense in those who show a more negative emotional reaction.

Social support from parents and friends is another variable that has been considered in studies of youth unemployment (Álvaro, 1992). Expectations of finding employment may be increased by the support received from others. A sense of failure and lack of control could be reduced through social support, which in turn may help the person to maintain his or her job-seeking behaviour (see Feather, 1992). Nevertheless, the actual need to find a job may be greater for those who are socially and financially excluded or marginalised.

Finally, another factor that should certainly be taken into account is length of unemployment. Length of unemployment may be related to a fall in expectations of finding a job and in the value attached to work, which may reduce job-seeking behaviour.

The second part of the current study refers to inclusion/exclusion with regard to the labour market. Studies of job-seeking behaviour are based on the assumption that there is a direct relationship between motivation, behaviour and results. Two types of explanation can be applied to the study of the exclusion of young people from the labour market. The first is based on the human capital theory, according to which lack of work experience is a determining factor in exclusion from the labour market (Fallon and Verry, 1988). Work experience would be considered in this economic theory as a part of human individual capital that provides the capacity for successful labour market insertion. As Plug and du Bois-Reymond argue in Chapter Three, many employers prefer young employees who are already attuned to a work environment. Moreover, participation in employment training programmes may help young people to find work by virtue not only of the information, experience and training, but also of the beneficial effects on their subjective well-being. In line with this economic theory, other authors (such as Hammer, 1998) have proposed two more concepts, those of cultural capital and social capital, to account for the probabilities of young people entering the workforce. The first of these, developed by Pierre Bourdieu, refers to the set of knowledge and practices obtained through the educational system and by way of cultural transmission from parents. This form of capital guarantees specific competencies that influence a person's career. The second construct refers to the social support, both instrumental and emotional, deriving from social relationships, and may determine general achievement and specific achievement in relation to labour market insertion.

A second type of explanation of the differences observed in the integration or exclusion of young people with regard to the labour market refers to aspects focusing on the individual characteristics of young unemployed people. Individual differences in motivation for actively seeking work, and in the number of strategies or methods used for insertion in the labour market, would, according to this model, constitute fundamental variables in relation to insertion in the labour market. Lack of commitment to work and problems with subjective well–being are also factors that have normally been taken into account in explaining the differences between young people who find jobs and those who remain unemployed.

Job-seeking behaviour

In presenting our results we start with a description of differences in job-seeking behaviour. Job-seeking behaviour was measured in two different ways. First, interviewees were asked whether they were engaged in looking for a job. In addition, they were asked to indicate the methods they used in looking for a job. The number of methods was used as a second measure. Table 4.1 summarises the answers to the first question.

First of all it becomes clear that in all countries most of the young people currently unemployed were actively looking for a job. Percentages varied from 71% in Germany to 90% in Scotland. Much lower percentages were found among those who had returned to education or who were participating in a training scheme, in particular in Finland and Germany.

There are also considerable differences between those who are looking for a job and those who are not, according to the variables supposed to influence job search. As Table 4.1 shows, the total time for which a person has been unemployed (measured in months) is significantly related to job seeking in the five countries studied. In all of them, we found that as the period of unemployment increases, the greater the possibilities that the individual will seek work. As this period increases, economic needs and social deprivations due to the lack of a wage will certainly grow, and this may encourage the person to look for a job as the solution. In the case of Finland, for example, the mean time unemployed for young people who do not seek work is 20 months, while for those who do seek work it is 26 months. The same occurs in Spain, where the group of young people seeking work presents an average unemployment period of 38 months, while this falls to 32 months for those not seeking work.

The results further indicate that in all the countries unemployed young people show a tendency to look for work as their economic deprivation increases. Deprivation was measured by asking about a number of items, both economic, such as main meals or clothing, and social, such as going to the cinema or out with friends. We asked whether the respondent had sometimes to do without them due to a lack of money. Thus, for example, in Germany, those responding that they are seeking work present a considerably higher average of material

Table 4.1: Responses to the question 'Are you seeking work?'

	Finland		Sweden		Scotland		Spain		Germany	
	Yes	No	Yes	No	Yes	No	Yes	No	Yes	No
Unemployed (%)	81.7	18.3	85.4	14.6	90.6	9.4	79.2	20.8	71.3	28.8
Occasional/irregular (%)	45.9	54.1	76.7	23.3	50.0	50.0	59.0	41.0	100	0.0
Training scheme (%)	24.9	75.1	57.5	42.5	67.6	32.4	47.7	52.3	24.8	75.2
Education (%)	8.0	92.0	15.8	84.2	35.1	64.9	39.3	60.7	6.1	93.9
Total time unemployed (mean)	26.2	20.2	19.9	15.6	26.8	23.4	38.0	31.6	20.8	14.5
Material deprivation (mean)	0.6	0.5	0.6	0.5	0.6	0.4	0.2	0.1	0.4	0.2
Social deprivation (mean)	2.6	2.1	2.8	2.2	3.0	2.6	2.2	1.3	2.3	1.6
Parental support (mean)	2.1	2.2	2.8	3.0	2.6	2.6	4.0	3.5	2.7	2.5
Friends' support (mean)	1.7	1.9	1.8	2.1	1.7	1.6	2.3	2.2	1.9	2.0
Work commitment (mean)	23.3	22.5	24.7	23.1	23.6	21.6	25.1	23.8	24.8	24.1
% who think they will be working in a year's time	66.0	34.0	70.7	29.3	88.0	12.0	63.4	36.6	49.3	50.7

or economic deprivation (0.40) than those not seeking work (0.20) (values range from 0 to 1). As regards social deprivation, once again, in all countries, there is a relationship between the fact of seeking work or not and the level of social deprivation. It should also be pointed out that social deprivation in all the countries is much higher than material deprivation. The countries in which job seekers and those not seeking work most differed in social deprivation were Spain and Germany. In Spain those seeking work presented a mean of social deprivation of 2.20, while the figure for those not seeking work was just 1.34. Germany showed similar results, with the job seekers presenting a mean of 2.35 and the non-seekers 1.56.

Relating job seeking to support from the family and friends (in both cases measured with an identical scale with a number of examples of support such as providing money, giving advice on various matters and showing affection), we found the mean scores to be quite similar in all the countries analysed. In the cases of Spain and Germany, parental support is somewhat greater among those seeking work. This is reasonable if we consider that it is precisely these two countries that have the highest proportion of young people still living in the family home of origin – 78.1% in the case of Spain and 50.7% in Germany. In the Scandinavian countries, on the other hand, a far lower percentage of young people live with their parents. In Finland the figure is 33.8%, while in Sweden it is just 24.8%. The support of the people with whom these young people live may influence their job seeking, since it tends to be these close people who maintain them or help them financially in case of need.

As we mentioned earlier, many psychologists state that job search will be influenced by attitudes to work (in particular, work commitment) and by expectations that jobs can be acquired by one's own efforts. Therefore we looked for differences in work commitment. We measured this concept by means of a well-known scale consisting of six statements concerning the importance of work or a job for the respondent (Warr et al, 1979). In line with these theories, we find small but consistent differences in work involvement between currently employed and unemployed young people. Both groups differ much more clearly in the expectation that they will be working in a year's time, with those looking for a job having much more optimistic expectations than those who are not.

This presentation of differences already shows that for an explanation of job-seeking behaviour we need to take into account factors other than the values, attitudes and expectations of the unemployed youth. In particular, the total time that someone has been unemployed and the degree of deprivation s/he suffers seem to be important for explaining job-search activities. It is also remarkable that social support does not differentiate between employed and unemployed. To validate these preliminary conclusions, we conducted a more sophisticated analysis in which we analysed the effects of the variables discussed simultaneously and controlled for background variables like age, gender and education. This was done by means of a logistical regression analysis. In the next section we summarise the main results.

Factors influencing job seeking

First, we considered the influence of some sociodemographic variables. It is gender that maintains the closest relationship with job-seeking behaviour. In all the countries considered (except Spain), it is young men who more actively seek work. The differences were significant in three of the countries analysed: Finland, Scotland and Germany. In Spain, however, we found differences between genders in the opposite direction to those of the other countries, with women more actively seeking a job, even though these differences did not reach significance. No significant differences were found for either age or educational level. Job-seeking behaviour was thus found to be independent of both of these factors.

Second, and with respect to work-experience variables, the analysis confirmed our preliminary conclusion. In all the countries considered, job-seeking behaviour was associated with the length of time unemployed – the longer the period of unemployment, the more intense the job seeking. Likewise, it is those with the least work experience who most actively seek work. Participation in training programmes only proved to be a factor contributing to the search for work in the Nordic countries, though there was a difference between them: while in Finland, the more the interviewees participated in such programmes, the more they sought work; the opposite was true in Sweden, with participation in training programmes leading to a reduction in job-seeking activity. This result is probably an effect of the unemployment rates in the two countries. Finland, as we saw, has the highest rates of youth unemployment of all the Nordic countries, and this may explain why the active search for work is found independently of being on a training course. In general terms, it can be stated that the most significant variables in job seeking are those related to experience in the labour market. Lack of work experience and long-term unemployment are associated with more intense job-seeking behaviour.

With regard to social and economic deprivation, the analysis confirmed that this was an important factor explaining job-seeking behaviour. In all the countries analysed, the higher the levels of social and material deprivation, the greater the motivation to seek work. Contrary to what was expected on the basis of earlier research, it was not found that social support influenced job-seeking behaviour. Unemployed young people who seek work do not differ significantly from those not actively seeking work with regard to the social support received from family or friends.

In this analysis we also paid attention to the coping behaviour of our respondents: we classified responses as either emotional or problem-solving (where people tried to find rational ways of handling their situation). In relation to their responses to the experience of unemployment, coping with the experience of unemployment by way of emotions has a positive effect on motivation to seek work – that is, the greater the emotional response to the experience of unemployment, the greater the likelihood that the young person will be actively looking for a job. However, problem-centred coping responses only proved to be significant in the case of Germany, where they were associated with a reduction in the active search for work.

Finally, we turn to the psychological variables. We also found in this more rigorous analysis that the expectations of finding employment and attitudes towards work are significantly associated with the active search for work in almost all the countries analysed. Moreover, the higher the importance-valency attributed to work, the more intense the job-seeking behaviour. In the case of Germany, this association, though in the expected direction, did not reach statistical significance ($B=0.13$; $p=0.27$). Likewise, expectations of finding work influenced job-seeking behaviour. In the cases of Scotland and Spain, however, this association was not statistically significant at the 0.05 level, even if it came close for Scotland ($B=0.37$; $p=0.06$). In the light of these results, it can be stated that, in the majority of the countries studied, the theory of expectancy-valency is useful for predicting individual behaviour aimed at labour market insertion.

We finally turned our attention to the psychological well-being of the young people included in our study. This was measured by means of 10 statements from the Hopkins Symptoms Checklist. We found an association between this variable and job seeking. Thus, our results confirmed those of other studies that showed how negative emotional responses to the situation of unemployment and psychological deterioration are associated with more intense job-seeking behaviour (see Feather, 1992). At the same time, young unemployed people seeking work have a perception of less control over the employment context. In the case of Germany, there are no data for this aspect, as the interviewees were not asked about their feelings of control over the unemployment situation.

In summary, we can conclude that various factors influence job-seeking behaviour. First, and in view of the association of the variables described, the young people who most actively seek work are those with the least work experience, the longest time out of work, the greatest economic and social deprivation, and the highest levels of psychological deterioration, who cope with unemployment by way of emotions, and who perceive least control over the situation. Moreover, we can also conclude from these results that the higher the expectations of finding a job, and the value attached to work, the more motivated are the young people to look for a job. Thus, the sociostructural variables determine a more intense search for work on the part of those young people who are most excluded socially and from the labour market, and whose reactions to unemployment are centred more on the emotions. These variables can be considered as indicators of the need to find a job, while the valency of employment as regards work as a value, and the perception of the ability to find a job, are also associated with a more active search for work.

As for the association observed between job-seeking behaviour and negative emotional reactions, as well as feelings of lack of control, these may act as both effects and causes of job-seeking behaviour. Lower psychological well-being and stronger feelings of uncontrollability may lead to more intense job-seeking behaviour, but it is also possible that negative emotions and feelings of uncontrollability are consequences of frustrated attempts to secure a job.

Explaining (un)employment

After the analysis of job-seeking behaviour, we turn now to the theme of job finding and try to explain why some of our respondents remained unemployed and others were employed at the time of the interview. We used the same variables as in the previous sections, but added the number of job-seeking methods to find out whether job finding is influenced by the intensity of job-search activities. We start with a description of the different situations of employment/unemployment in each country, and how they are experienced by young people.

According to the data of the present study, we can see that there are clear differences between the employment records of young people who obtained work and those who remained unemployed. Thus, as

Table 4.2 shows, in the case of the Scandinavian countries and Scotland, those young people who found a job had roughly six months more previous work experience than those who remained unemployed. In Germany and Spain, these differences increased to almost eight and 16 months, respectively. As regards the total time they had been unemployed in their working life, those who remained unemployed had a longer record of previous unemployment than those who found a job.

There are also differences between employed and unemployed young people with regard to social and material deprivation, with higher levels in the jobless group. Family support provided to employed and unemployed young people is similar in all the countries studied, except for Spain, where support for unemployed young people is considerably higher. This can be attributed to the fact that in Spain the family subsidises protection for the unemployed, which in other countries is the sole responsibility of the state.

Young people may use different coping strategies when faced with the situation of unemployment. The differences between the young people who remained unemployed and those who found a job with regard to strategies centred on emotions and strategies centred on tackling the problem are significant in both cases in two countries, Scotland and Germany. With respect to their job-seeking behaviour, the number of methods used is greater in the case of the unemployed in the majority of the countries studied.

The young people interviewed showed a high level of commitment to work in all the countries, with no significant differences between employed and unemployed, except in the case of Finland. As for mental well-being, the differences are significant in all the countries, so that it can be stated that unemployment is associated with lower levels of mental well-being. Also, those who are unemployed present significantly lower levels than those who are employed in perception of control of the situation.

Young people's expectations of finding a job within a year in the countries studied depend, to a large extent, on their current employment situation, as can be seen in Table 4.2. Thus, for example, percentages of young people who see themselves working are higher in the employed than in the unemployed. Likewise, the percentages of young people who consider that they will be unemployed in a year's time are greater among the unemployed than among those with a job.

Table 4.2: Differences between employed (Em) and unemployed (Un) young people

	Finland		Sweden		Scotland		Spain		Germany	
	Em	Un	Em	Un	Em	Un	Em	Un	Em	Un
Position in the labour market										
Total time employed (mean)	18.7	12.5	27.5	22.6	25.3	19.2	32.7	16.7	20.1	12.5
Total time unemployed (mean)	17.3	27.5	11.8	20.7	15.2	26.9	22.3	38.4	14.9	21.7
Deprivation										
Material deprivation (mean)	0.4	0.6	0.2	0.6	0.4	0.6	0.1	0.2	0.2	0.3
Social deprivation (mean)	1.7	2.5	1.4	2.7	2.2	3.1	1.1	2.1	1.6	2.2
Social support										
Parents' support	2.1	2.0	2.9	2.8	2.4	2.6	3.2	3.9	2.5	2.7
Friends' support	1.5	1.7	1.9	1.8	1.8	1.6	1.9	2.2	2.0	1.9
Coping responses										
Adaptive strategies	13.0	13.2	12.1	12.3	10.2	10.6	10.1	9.9	10.6	10.1
Emotional strategies	16.9	16.0	18.1	18.2	20.5	19.6	18.8	18.4	18.9	17.3
Number of methods	3.9	3.8	3.9	4.3	4.4	4.5	5.4	5.9	4.3	4.0
Psychological variables										
Work involvement	24.3	22.4	24.5	24.3	24.0	234	25.1	24.9	24.9	24.5
Mental health	1.5	1.6	1.5	1.7	1.5	1.7	1.6	1.7	1.4	1.5
Perception of control	2.3	2.1	2.3	1.9	2.8	2.5	3.3	2.8		
% who think they will be working in a year's time	68.6	49.5	74.3	56.4	71.8	65.3	86.0	62.6	69.0	60.2

Factors influencing insertion in the labour market

This description of differences between employed and unemployed young people already points to some factors that may influence integration or exclusion in the labour market. Most remarkable is the fact that the importance attached to work and the number of methods that are used in looking for jobs (which can be seen as an indicator of the intensity of job search) do not seem to be related to the employment status. In order to study the effects of the variables included in the study more precisely, we again carried out a logistical regression analysis. This analysis confirmed our tentative findings concerning both motivational variables.

Unemployed young people, compared with those in work, reported having used more job-seeking methods; these differences were significant in the cases of Scotland and Spain. Therefore, we reach the paradoxical conclusion that the intensity of job search does not improve the chances of becoming employed! Only in the case of Germany were those who used more methods more likely to be employed. The explanation for this probably resides in the fact that the greater number of job-seeking methods is a consequence of the situation of long-term unemployment experienced by a large proportion of these young people, as we saw earlier. They may change the ways they look for work as the ones they try prove unsuccessful.

With regard to commitment to work, which we saw was another of the significant factors for explaining job-seeking behaviour, we found that it did not contribute to the explanation of the employment situation, with no significant differences in the value attributed to work between the employed and unemployed. Only in the case of Finland did we find that young people without a job attributed less importance to work. Finally, it should be noted that unemployed young people show greater psychological deterioration than those who are employed, as well as a reaction to unemployment centred on more emotional responses and feelings of less control over the situation.

If these variables do not influence the chances of finding employment, are there other variables that do have a positive influence? Beginning with gender, age and education (the sociodemographic variables), we found that, except in the case of Spain, where the women in our study had a greater probability of being unemployed than the men, in the rest of the countries it was the men who were more likely to be unemployed. Therefore gender influences employment status. As far as age and education are concerned, they were not found to affect the probability of being unemployed, except in the cases of Germany, where older subjects were significantly more likely to be unemployed, and Spain, where those with university education had more probability of finding a job.

Not surprisingly, work experience variables have an important influence. We found that time spent in paid work and length of unemployment had significant effects on employment status in all the countries considered. The less the work experience and the longer the time spent unemployed, the greater the likelihood of being unemployed. Similarly, low participation in training programmes is associated with higher probability of being unemployed. Moreover, it was found that social and material deprivation is negatively related to the chances of finding employment in all the countries considered, while social support received from family and friends does not discriminate between the employed and the unemployed and therefore is not a variable that influences the chances of finding a job.

In sum, it is not so much individual behaviours in terms of motivation to work that most affect the probabilities of insertion in or exclusion from the labour market, but rather accumulated work experience and social and material deprivation. This conclusion is reinforced by the fact that the unemployed young people, compared with those in work, do not show significant differences with respect to the number of hours they would be prepared to work, but are nevertheless prepared to work for a lower wage than those who already have a job.

Conclusion

One of the objectives of the present chapter was to identify the influences on job-seeking behaviour. Among other things, we aimed to determine whether the theory of expectancy-valency was useful for explaining motivation in the search for work in the five countries involved in our research. We saw that a person's expectations about his or her future situation in the labour market influence that person's efforts to find a job. Similarly, attitudes with respect to the value of work, its centrality for the unemployed person, are influences upon the young person to actively seek work. In conclusion, we can state that job seeking is significantly associated with expectations of finding a job and with the value attributed to work, over and above its instrumental function. These results can be considered as confirmation of the motivational theory of expectancy-valency.

We should add that the differences between unemployed people according to their motivation to seek work are defined not only by the beliefs and values associated with work, but also by the feelings towards the unemployment situation itself. Those young people who tend to respond emotionally to unemployment, and whose mental health is most affected negatively by it, are most active in looking for work. Nor should we forget that material and social deprivation is greater among those seeking work than among those not actively seeking work. If, moreover, we take into account that low levels of work experience and having spent a long time out of work also result in more active job seeking, we can conclude that it is young people with higher levels of social exclusion – due both to their smaller social capital, and their greater social and material deprivation and psychological deterioration – that most actively look for a job. It is in this context of exclusion that we should interpret the role of the values and beliefs associated with work as explanatory factors in job-seeking behaviour.

Psychological research on job-seeking behaviour assumes that this behaviour is related to success in finding work; it would be the most motivated young people who had the best chance of obtaining employment. However, as we can conclude from our results, motivation in the search for work is not a factor that determines workforce integration. Indeed, in all the countries included in our analyses, with the exception of Germany, the intensity of job-seeking – determined by the number of methods used – is not a factor that contributes to success in the labour market insertion of young people; in countries such as Spain and Scotland it is actually a negative factor. Thus, it is not motivational aspects that determine a person's chances of being employed. Nor are the values attached to work related to the unemployment situation. With the exception of Finland, in no country studied was the fact of being unemployed significantly associated with young people's attitudes and values in relation to work. Thus, being unemployed cannot be explained by a lack of commitment to work, by a lack of a central role for work, by lower motivation for work or to a lower value attributed to work among unemployed young people in any of the European countries considered.

However, if the variables mentioned do not influence the employment situation of young people, quite the opposite is true with respect to variables that reflect work experience. Thus, for example, it should be stressed that participation in training programmes has a significant influence on the unemployment situation of young people. In all the countries analysed, participation in employment programmes was associated with lower probability of being unemployed. This result is consistent with the finding that work experience is a variable influencing the employment situation of young people positively, whereas the length of time spent unemployed has a negative influence. In the case of Spain, we should add that educational level has a highly significant influence – that is, the higher the educational level, the greater the probability of avoiding unemployment. However, in the other countries this effect was absent.

Two other factors were taken into account as possibly influencing unemployment: social and economic deprivation. Here the same type of pattern can be found in all the countries analysed. Unemployed young people in the five countries studied (Finland, Sweden, Scotland, Germany and Spain) have a greater experience of material and social deprivation than those with jobs. A possible explanation for this result is that unemployment is an effect of young people's social and material deprivation because it reduces the motivation to seek work. Nevertheless, as we remarked above, this explanation can be discarded, since the young people with the highest levels of deprivation are also those who make the most effort to find a job. Obviously, it cannot be ignored that, despite the efforts of this group, the prolonged situation of unemployment will affect their situation of material and social deprivation.

From the results we have just discussed, some conclusions of a theoretical nature can be drawn. First of all, the theories cannot be isolated from the reality under study. Motivational psychological models such as that of expectancy-valency may be useful for explaining individual behaviours, such as the search for work. However (as argued by sociological explanations), it is the situation of the labour market, interacting with sociostructural factors such as those related to education (for example, in Spain), or with work experience and length of time unemployed (in the rest of the countries studied) that significantly affect the chances of being unemployed. This does not deny the role of individual variables in the explanation of processes of inclusion/exclusion in relation to the labour market, but it does place the emphasis on social determinants.

From a policy perspective, the conclusions of this study indicate people's capacity to undertake action for changing their situation; but they also indicate that such actions and their results should be interpreted within the framework of models emphasising social determinants of behaviour and of the relationship between behaviour and its results. In the present study, job seeking reflects the capacity of young people to take decisions and initiatives guided by values and beliefs. Nevertheless, it is eventually sociostructural factors, such as the situation of the labour market, educational level, gender, length of time unemployed, work experience or social deprivation that impose limits on their labour market position and that determine, also, their social integration as citizens. Young unemployed people, according to the data from this study, are trapped in a vicious circle, since they are the most disadvantaged economically, socially and in terms of employment, those who display most motivation to find work and, at the same time, those with the highest probability of being excluded from the labour market.

In sum, without excluding the weight of motivational factors in individual success in the labour market, nor of the attitudes and values associated with work, it is sociostructural variables, such as previous work experience, participation in youth training programmes and length of time unemployed, that most affect the (un)employment situation of young people. In general, neither the number of methods or strategies used for seeking work, nor the values associated with work, nor availability for work – see the case of Spain – contribute to the explanation of the unemployment situation of young people. We shall have to look more closely at the personnel policy of employers and the criteria they use in selection processes to find a better explanation.

In the light of these results, we can conclude that psychological/ motivational variables contribute to explaining individual behaviour in relation to job seeking, but their contribution to the explanation of the unemployment situation of young people can only be interpreted correctly by taking into account the set of sociostructural variables that predict young people's integration in the labour market.

The emphasis on finding psychological models through which to explain job-seeking behaviour derives from an individualist conception with regard to the determinants of young people's insertion in the workforce, as Reiter and Craig argue in Chapter One. Individual behaviour and its effects on the context can only be understood as a part of the structural restrictions that any context – in this case the labour market – imposes. It is for this reason that knowledge of the factors that determine the unemployment situation is a key to the success of youth employment policies implemented by employment authorities.

We can conclude that our data can be interpreted as a strong refutation not only of individualistic theories of youth unemployment but also of policy models that suffer from an individualistic bias.

FIVE

Winners and losers: young people in the 'new economy'

Harriet Bradley

Introduction

There has evolved in Europe a popular rhetoric of winners and losers linked to the changing labour markets of the 'new economy' of Europe and the advanced capitalist economies. This chapter picks up this idea, already explored by Plug and du Bois-Reymond in Chapter Three. While it is commonly stated that major social and economic changes are under way, involving the advancement of some groups and the decline of others, there is little systematic empirical evidence concerning such changes. For example, two major chroniclers of such change, Richard Sennett (1998) and Ulrich Beck (2000), have spoken of the tide of insecurity and demoralisation resulting from 'flexible capitalism' and of the 'Brazilianisation' of European labour markets, with increasing numbers of people confined to temporary, insecure and subcontracted jobs, but they have provided little hard data in support of their claims.

This chapter explores the notion of winners and losers in relation to the changing labour market situation of young people. The major group who are 'losing out' are those totally excluded from the labour market, especially those labelled in Britain as 'NEET' (not in employment, education and training). But since unemployment and exclusion are explored elsewhere in this volume (see, for example, Chapters One, Four and Seven), another focus here is on difference and disadvantage among those who are within the labour market. How are young people being affected by flexibilisation and the end of a 'job for life'? Are there common labour market disadvantages faced by all young people? Are the changes overturning fixed and persistent disadvantages of class, gender and ethnicity? In other words, this chapter poses the questions 'On what terms are young people *included* in the labour market?', and 'Are the terms different for different groups?'.

To answer these questions, the chapter draws particularly on primary data from a study of young adults (aged 20-34) in one local labour market, that of Bristol, a service-based 'post-industrial' city in the south west of England. The Bristol survey provides data on different aspects of young adults' labour market experience and various indicators of labour market success or failure.

This chapter will seek to address the key question of which groups are seen to be winning or losing out within the structure of opportunities in the new service-based economy. It has been argued, for example, that young men are losing out to young women who have recently started to outstrip them in school examination results (Bradley et al, 2000). Walby suggests that young women are growing up in a new 'regime of gender' that frees them from expectations of a domestic future (Walby, 1997). Crompton and Sanderson (1990) had previously alerted us to younger women's increasing use of the 'qualifications lever' in order to compete more equally with men in the labour market. Gallie et al (1998) point to changes in the relative position of women and men in terms of job stability and job security. They argue that men are experiencing a decline in job stability, *especially young men*. This is contributing to a convergence between men and women in their experience of employment, accompanied by a sharp rise in women's commitment to the labour market. This indicates that the 'feminisation' of work has possibly led to diminished gender difference in the labour market trajectories of young men and women. So, are women now winners?

Similarly, it is argued that previous patterns of racial disadvantage in Britain are changing in the face of upward social mobility among some sections of Britain's minority ethnic population (Modood et al, 1997). Chapter Seven in this volume discusses the situation of young minority ethnic people in Europe and points to widespread disadvantage in every country under consideration. Research into ethnicity is more developed in the UK than in many other European countries, partly because official statistics on ethnicity are more readily available, sponsored by governments that have long defined 'race relations' as an important policy issue. In recent studies, such as Modood et al's Fourth National Survey of Ethnic Minorities in Britain, the focus has been particularly on differences within ethnic groups. Indians and Chinese are seen to be 'winning', while Pakistanis and Bangladeshis remain among the losers. Young British Muslim men suffer most from unemployment. Some young middle-class Asian women, both Pakistani and Indian, appear to be using education and qualifications to gain access to high-status jobs, although less well-educated young Muslim women are more likely to face restrictions in the kind of jobs to which they have access and that are considered suitable for them (Holdsworth and Dale, 1997). African-Caribbean boys have been particularly prone to school failure and subsequently are vulnerable to being absorbed into delinquent or criminal inner-city subcultures, while their sisters have shown more determination to benefit from education and make their way into stable employment.

Education is a key issue here, as evidence points to sharp polarisations between the labour market position of those possessing high levels of education, especially degrees, and those who do not (Hills, 1996; Bynner et al, 2002). Furlong and Forsyth, in their study of Scottish young people's transitional patterns, distinguished a number of clusters, with highly educated young people attaining greater labour market success. Other research highlights the continued influence of class in a successful trajectory from school to university to stable employment (Bates and Riseborough, 1993; Roberts, 1995; Forsyth and Furlong, 2000); Ball, 2003). Ball provides a detailed account of how middle-class parents, especially mothers, actively construct their children as 'clever', by the use of private tuition, monitoring the children's social contacts (social capital), involving them in appropriate cultural activities and so forth. Middle-class parents also use their knowhow (cultural capital) to manipulate the school and university systems, and they know how to negotiate with teachers. They can use their economic capital to buy a private education that insulates their child from contact with 'undesirables'. By contrast, working-class children and parents face many barriers – economic, cultural and social (Forsyth and Furlong, 2003, Furlong and Cartmel, 2004). With the end to free access to higher education, debt is a major deterrent. Young people from disadvantaged backgrounds tend to drop out of higher education more frequently, attend less prestigious institutions (with consequences for their job prospects) and often report feeling uneasy in a university context (Furlong and Forsyth, 2003). As a result of all this, the class gap in education is widening: Roberts (2001) shows figures to the effect that 80% of middle-class children entered higher education in 1996 as opposed to 15% of the skilled working class; in 1991 the figures were around 55% and 10%. But where young people from disadvantaged backgrounds do succeed in education they have at least the chance of rivalling their middle-class peers: as indicated above, girls at the moment seem more attuned to the importance of educational success.

This chapter, then, will draw out aspects of young people's experience within evolving labour markets. It starts by discussing the ideology of 'winners and losers' and its consequences for social policy, especially in relation to young people, and it then uses the Bristol case study as an example of such changes. One hypothesis is that increased labour market inequality is bringing about a polarisation between, on the one hand, privileged young people with high levels of education and of social and cultural capital and, on the other, young people from disadvantaged social backgrounds who are at risk of exclusion and poverty. There is some evidence for this hypothesis. However, it will be pointed out that even some apparent 'winners' face problems of insecurity and low income, making it difficult for them to accomplish full transitions to adulthood in terms of financial independence, starting a family and securing decent accommodation.

Winning and losing: the divisive effects of capitalist industrialism

The discourse of 'winners and losers' has become an increasingly common feature in the reportage of contemporary society. The idea that processes of change bring winners and losers is particularly popular in the media, where in the UK it may be applied to virtually anything, from university financing to supermarket trading to family incomes after annual budgets. It is found in many contexts, but is often employed to highlight qualitative changes in the 'experience of inequality' wrought by social transformations. Sassen (1994) asserts that the move towards an information-based global economy contributes to the increasing labour market polarisation in so-called 'global cities'. Crompton (1997) and Sennett (1998) point to 'employment flexibility' – contributing to labour market 'individualisation' – as the cause of increasing material inequality: "... in a situation where there is increased competition and individualism, there are going to be *losers* as well as *winners*" (Crompton, 1997, p 131, emphasis added).

One of the most striking examples of the use of this discourse is in the work of Zygmunt Bauman, who in a series of publications (for example, 1998, 2001) has described what he sees as consumerist capitalism in terms of a growing polarisation between a highly socially and geographically mobile elite of young professionals, managers and media types, forever jetting on aeroplanes to business meetings in the capital cities of the world and enjoying an increasingly glamorous leisure-based lifestyle, and an excluded sub-proletariat, no longer needed for production and flawed even as consumers, who are confined to the 'excluded places' of inner-city ghettos or jobless housing estates on the peripheries of cities. It is this group, named by Bauman the

'New Poor', that the young unemployed and unqualified are destined to join.

While Crompton (1997) links the discourse to the increased competition and individualism that has been seen to be characteristic of 'late' capitalism or modernity, there is an argument that it is in the very nature of capitalism as a mode of organising social production and reproduction to produce marked inequalities between differently located groups. Thus, Marx and his followers saw social polarisation as an inherent tendency within capitalism; in particular, the creation of a reserve army of labour or surplus labour population was seen as necessary for capitalism to achieve the necessary flexibility to ride out the booms and slumps of the business cycle. In this sense, unemployment is the product of capitalism and industrialism (pre-industrial societies being more characterised by underemployment). Neo-classical economists recast this idea as a 'natural level' of unemployment in the economy (about 2-3%). Perhaps the most notable development of the second half of the 20th century was the tendency for most advanced industrial nations to experience prolonged periods when unemployment rates rose high above this level, and this has particularly been the case for young people. As we have seen in previous chapters, youth unemployment has become defined as a major social problem of contemporary European societies. This is particularly so in the case of young men, even though across the EU they are less likely to be unemployed than young women (14.8% compared with 17.1% in 2002), given the belief that young men's frustrated energies and desire for 'respect' and status will easily lead them into crime, drug use and other antisocial behaviour.

In the perspective we have been discussing, such problems are endemic to capitalist industrial societies and the existence of 'winners' and 'losers' is inevitable. However, there is a twist in the discourse that links it to the ideology of meritocracy. In this version individuals bear their own responsibility for becoming either a winner or a loser – anybody can make it if they work hard, make the most of the chances given to them. As Devadason et al point out (2001), the language of winning and losing draws on sporting and competing imagery: sporting contests are premised on the assumption that 'losers' in some sense deserve to lose, while 'winners' have justly earned their victories. This is where, as Crow and Rees (1999) point out in their critical article '"Winners" and "losers" in social transformations', the usage of this discourse becomes problematic: "Language of this sort has the capacity to suggest that there is a moral as well as a material side to the relationship between 'winners' and 'losers'".

Thus losing becomes seen as the result of individual weakness and failure, not of structural positioning, while winning (whatever methods may have been used to attain success) becomes per se admirable, and different starting points in the race (if we continue our sporting metaphor) are ignored. There is a danger, then, in using this framework that we may contribute to the stigmatisation of those identified as losers. Thus, for the Bristol study we made it clear that we did not view 'winning and losing' as characteristics of individuals, but as a process whereby the workings of the capitalist labour market construct certain groups as 'winners and losers'.

In their essay Crow and Rees (1999) identify a number of other problems with the discourse of a more substantive nature. First is that this framework glosses over the existence of intermediate groups that may in fact be more numerous and socially significant. Bauman's work can certainly be criticised on this score: most people in Europe are neither 'yuppies' nor neo-proletarians, but ordinary families making do and doing all right. Jenkins (1983) made a similar point when he criticised youth studies for concentrating on 'lads and ear'oles' at the expense of 'ordinary kids'. A second issue is that of time and fluctuations. For young people, occupancy of a low-paid, insecure job may be only a 'stepping-stone' to greater things. People's positions alter dramatically over the life course. Finally, judgements of what is 'success' and 'failure' are typically made in a top-down way and reflect middle-class norms and values of achievement. The young people themselves may have very different views about what constitutes success – for example, when we asked the Bristol young adults that question, 'just being happy' was a common answer.

The two strands in the winners and losers discourse, those of structural requirements and individual responsibility, are interestingly reflected in the way social policy has evolved to deal with issues of employment and unemployment. American sociologist Seymour Lipset (1960) commented that the problems thrown up by capitalist industry, including poverty and unemployment, had been effectively solved by welfarism. Similarly, the post-war British welfare state was founded on the idea of a 'safety net' to help people deal with structural unemployment and issues outside their control. The benefits payment system reflects the idea that the state must step in to help when circumstances rule out the possibility of self-sufficiency. But against this, and co-existing with it, there has been a strand of moralising that tends to 'blame the poor' for their own poverty: a discourse of fecklessness, irresponsibility, parasitism and scrounging (which Deacon [1976] has labelled 'scroungerphobia'). This has lain behind, for example, the debates around the notion of the 'underclass' and is discerned in New Labour thinking in contemporary Britain. For example, at the core of the development of the new universal Connexions programme is the notion that motivation is the crucial factor in getting young people out of the NEET category, despite the lack in many areas of suitable jobs for young people to take up. The core of the Connexions strategy is the provision of a personal adviser (PA) for every young person aged 13-19 so that their needs can be assessed. Where the young person is at risk, the PA will help them develop a plan of action and then monitor its progress, using a set of standardised assessment techniques. In effect, Connexions tries to turn all losers into winners, in the face of that strand of the discourse that asserts that there will always be losers.

This tension will affect the various programmes of labour market integration discussed in this volume. Any realistic programme must surely take on board the limits to individual responsibility by assessing what lies behind the construction of 'losing' and 'winning' groups. Data from the Bristol study and other sources show that winner and loser groups are clearly related to existing structures of class, gender and ethnicity.

Losing out: the young unemployed and excluded

Who, then, are the losers? Table 5.1 presents a labour market profile of the young adults surveyed in the Bristol study. The researchers

Table 5.1: Employment status profile of respondents (in relation to previous week before interview) (%)

	Women n=599	Men n=501	Black/Asian n=128	White n=951	All n=1,100
Full time work	27	52	29	40	39
Self-employed	4	7	4	6	6
Part time work 8-29 hrs per week	21	4	14	13	13
Part time work less than 8 hrs per week	2	–	0.8	2	1
Government training	–	0.3	–	0.3	0.3
Temporarily absent from work	3	1	2	3	2
Long-term sick	2	3	–	3	2
Registered unemployed	7	7	6	7	7
Unregistered unemployed	2	2	2	2	2
Caring for family/ not seeking work	18	1	14	9	10
Full-time student	13	21	26	15	17
Part-time student	1	0.2	0.8	0.7	0.7
Other			0.8	0.9	

interviewed 1,100 adults through a household survey carried out in 2001 in four demographically contrasted zones of the city, covering some of its most affluent and its poorest parts. In addition to the household survey, 40 in-depth interviews were conducted with a wide social mix of young people (identified by agencies, employers or through personal links), which fed into the development of the survey. Subsequently, 80 more interviews were obtained with a sub-sample of survey respondents, selected on the base of gender, education level, zone and ethnicity.

The table shows that men and white people are most likely to be in full-time work. Nine per cent of the respondents were unemployed, a figure just below the national average. However, only 59% were in the labour market, with another 18% being students. Ten per cent reported themselves as being at home or looking after the family, with another 4% describing themselves as long-term sick or temporarily absent from work. This 14% may well cover a considerable amount of concealed unemployment.

Surprisingly, there are virtually no gender or ethnic differences in levels of reported unemployment, which is a divergence from national trends. This may reflect the differing fortunes of differing ethnic groups, as discussed earlier, but it is also probably an artefact of sampling; experience suggests that deprived minority ethnic people are more unwilling to take part in this kind of research for fear of reprisals. However, class appears to be the major factor influencing unemployment. Of those from managerial backgrounds, only 3.6% were unemployed compared with 8.4% of the intermediate group and 12.1% of those from skilled/unskilled manual backgrounds. If we add on the other three categories (sick, temporarily off work, at home), the difference is compounded to 12.2%, 23.2% and 40.9%. This links to a current concern of the British government, that the tightening up of rules of entitlement to unemployment benefit (revealingly re-presented as Jobseeker's Allowance) has pushed many out-of-work people into the take-up of long-term sickness or disability payments. We also noted very high area differences, with 16% unemployment among those living in a deprived, white working-class area and a mere 1.5% registered unemployed in the affluent middle-class zone. Thus, we suggest that labour market exclusion is structured by a mix of class and location. Those from the UK's 'excluded places' with manual backgrounds are much more at risk. The agencies we interviewed also tended to link long-term unemployment to multiple disadvantage: in other words, people who are working class, but are also single parents, often suffer from mental or physical illness or disability, have drug or

Table 5.2: Experience of unemployment among respondents who have completed full-time continuous education by age group (%)

Have you ever been unemployed?	20-24	25-29	30-34
Yes	55	52	54
No	45	48	46

alcohol problems or are ex-offenders. This would be confirmed by some of our qualitative interviews, in which those who were unemployed often referred to difficulties such as poor mental and physical health, family breakdown or disrupted schooling.

While this suggests that unemployment may have become a problem of a 'hard core' of young adults who are not yet 'work-ready' in the term currently popular among agencies dealing with unemployment, the picture becomes more complex if we consider those who have ever experienced being unemployed. As Table 5.2 shows, over half our respondents have experienced unemployment.

The median for the longest spell of unemployment experienced was eight months, the mean 21.88 months. About 10% of all our respondents had experienced a period of unemployment of three or more years; it is particularly significant that there was no marked decline in the experience of unemployment among the youngest age group despite the improved economic situation in which they were entering the labour market.

We have seen that unemployment was not higher among the minority ethnic respondents: however, their participation in full-time work was significantly lower than among whites. They were more likely to be found in the categories of caring for family/not seeking work and full-time students. This may well indicate a considerable degree of concealed unemployment as the result of workfare policies that push young black people off benefits and into dependency on the family. It is also likely that some in the former category may be involved in the hidden economy.

Ethnicity, class and residence in a deprived location are then strong indicators for labour market exclusion in the UK. Data from the EU show similar effects. While it is hard to obtain comparable data for all EU countries, given the diversity of minority ethnic groups between countries and the variability of minority ethnic groups' labour market positions within countries, there are strong suggestions that they do less well in all nations. Eurostat data for 2002 show than non-EU non-nationals in the age group have higher unemployment rates in all countries for which data are provided except Greece. In some cases the rates are shockingly higher – for example, 51.5% in Belgium, 36.7% in France and 27.3% in Sweden.

Insecure inclusion: a growing cohort of 'shifters'?

Unemployment, however, is not the only marker of labour market disadvantage. A key feature of the young adults' experience was what economists call 'churning', or moving between a number of unskilled and insecure 'dead-end' jobs. We identified a group of our respondents as 'shifters' who moved around between a number of jobs that might be seen as typical of an evolving youth labour market: jobs in bars, catering, retail, call centres, finance sector offices and so on. Plug and du Bois-Reymond describe how in the Netherlands, too, such 'yo-yo' trajectories are increasingly common (see Chapter Three). Often such jobs were acquired through employment agencies, of which there are many in Bristol. Furlong and Cartmel's study of disadvantaged young men highlights the role of agencies, which, in helping young people find jobs, effectively trap them in a sequence of short-term jobs (2004). The role of employment agencies in constructing a low-wage precarious youth labour market should not be underestimated.

The Bristol data show that shifting between jobs is associated with levels of education. Forty-seven per cent of those leaving education between the ages of 16 and 20 had held five or more jobs compared with 27% of late leavers. The difference persisted when controlled for age. There was again a strong link with occupational class. Twenty-seven per cent of those from managerial and professional backgrounds had held over five jobs as compared with 39% from manual backgrounds.

However, it is important to note that these class and education effects are not the whole story, given that over a quarter of the children of professional and managerial fathers had held five plus jobs, as did 34% of those who attended higher education. Job insecurity is not confined to the working class; moreover, while some of it is unwanted, there is also a degree of voluntary shifting. Crompton and Sanderson (1990) speak of the shift from 'bureaucratic' careers (developed within a single organisation) and 'portable' careers (involving moves between jobs and organisations) (20). Today's young professionals may well follow this route. Others may deliberately choose to work in low-paid 'flexible' jobs. One respondent, Kieran, described how he had thrown in his Business Studies course, entered into straight after leaving school, and spent many years moving between jobs, as he saved up money for spells of world travel in Australia, India and Thailand, before settling in his thirties into a vocational degree. Another young man, Gillon, had made several false starts in a number of courses and programmes and was still drifting around in low-paid jobs, his real interest being in becoming a writer. Lucy also had a creative bent, and had switched from Business Studies to Media Studies: having graduated she had moved between a number of low-paid (even non-paid) jobs in the magazine and music industries, before becoming self-employed as a DJ's agent. Du Bois-Reymond and her colleagues in their study of Dutch young people found a similar group of highly educated people with precarious and fragmented trajectories that they categorised as 'high opportunities, high risk' (du Bois-Reymond et al, 2001).

Seventeen per cent of the black and South Asian Bristol survey respondents reported their jobs as not secure compared with 9% of the white group. This confirms the greater precariousness of minority ethnic labour market involvement, commented on above. Across Europe, minority ethnic young people who escape unemployment are likely to be found in the least desirable jobs in the flexible labour market.

Insecure futures: young adults and the low-wage economy

As we should expect, the 'winners' in the labour market were the obverse of those who suffered in the labour market. They were much more likely to be white and male, from managerial and professional backgrounds. Education is a key variable. Across most dimensions of advantage (job stability, occupational status, income, promotion and so on), the survey showed that those with higher levels of education fared better.

As we noted earlier, other research has clearly shown the link between educational success (especially participation in higher education) and labour market success. This has had important policy results. Across Europe, young people are being encouraged to make further investments in education and training. Most activation schemes, many of which are discussed in this volume, are based on the premise that education is the key to solving youth unemployment.

However, things are not so simple. As we have stated, we interviewed many graduates who were in insecure and precarious jobs, who had experienced unemployment and who had not settled into a secure career, even in their thirties. Interestingly, Dutch data on young people collected in yearly surveys show that in the Netherlands graduates are more likely than those who have taken vocational courses to be on

Table 5.3:Young adults' yearly incomes by gender and ethnicity (%)

		Women n=549	Men n=466	White n=889	Black/Asian n=111
Low	Under £12,000	72	53	62	75
Medium	£12,000-£19,000	19	26	23	18
High	£20,000+	9	21	15	7

temporary contracts one year after completing education: 50% of university graduates, as compared with 31% of vocational graduates and a mere 16% of those completing vocational education (ROA, 2003). The chapters in this book on Slovenia and Italy provide other examples of how graduates may face precarious situations in the labour market (Chapters Six and Ten).

But the most striking finding from the Bristol study was the low level of pay across the whole sample, as shown in Table 5.3. Sixty-three per cent of the young adults were earning less than £12,000 a year. The very lowest-paid group was black and South Asian women of whom 80% earned less than £12,000, while the percentage of white women and black and South Asian men in this wage band were very similar, at 72% and 71% respectively; the percentage for white men was 51%.

Other research also highlights the presence of low pay among young workers (Dex et al, 1999) and suggests that the age-based pay gap is widening. In 1979, 16- to 17-year-old men in full-time work could expect to earn 63.6% of the wage rate of adult men. By 1995, 16- to 17-year-olds were earning 33.9% of the adult wage rate and 18- to 20-year-olds 48-9%. In 2001 the average gross weekly wage for full-time workers was £444 (£490 for men and £366 for women). Bison and Esping-Andersen (2000) found that those aged 20-29 constitute a low-wage workforce in all countries except Denmark, and this is at its worst in the Latin Rim countries. The survey in Bristol, a fairly affluent city, revealed that 81% of the young workers earned less than £444. Moreover, nearly half of them (48%) were living on less than £12,000 per year; this reflects the mix of activities people in this age group are doing: low-paid jobs, part-time and casual work, studying and training, relying on benefits. All this suggests that young people find themselves in a precarious economic environment, which certainly makes it difficult to settle down and start a family. The Bristol earnings were way below the level needed to procure a mortgage in the south of England. Recent research commissioned by the housing charity, Centrepoint, revealed that up to 52,000 young people aged 16-24 were homeless, with many sleeping rough on the streets, 'couch-surfing' (sleeping on a succession of friends' sofas) or living in unsuitable bed and breakfast accommodation (York University Centre for Housing Policy, 2004). Local councils' hostel provision (itself very basic) is quite inadequate to deal with the scale of the problem.

As Table 5.3 shows, women and minority ethnic young people are more likely to be low-paid than white men. This reflects the fact that, as discussed earlier, women and ethnic minority youth are more likely to be working in non-standard, insecure jobs. But another factor comes into play in the case of women. Despite the advances of feminism in the post-war period, young women across Europe continue to be constrained by their domestic roles. Thus we found that the young women we interviewed would continue to sacrifice their careers to their childrearing responsibilities, just as Plug and du Bois-Reymond found in the Netherlands (Chapter Three). Out of 297 women and 100 men with children, 150 women had stopped working, but only nine men; 94 women had shortened their hours and 35 had changed their jobs (compared with 17 and six men, respectively). Twenty-two women said they had missed out on promotion (one man) and 74 could only work at certain times of the day (17 men). Bringing up children was ranked by women as their top priority, while men put career and earning a living first. By and large, the young women wanted to stop working or only work part-time when their children were young. Thus the gender skew in life chances remains very strong.

Facing up to flexibility: adaptable generations?

We have shown that even the young employed are included in the labour market on unfavourable terms, facing precarious employment, non-standard contracts and low pay. Yet curiously, we found that overall our young respondents were not distressed by their circumstances. Generally, they considered that they were doing better than their parents; and, asked to rate their progress so far on a scale of 1 to 10, the mean was 8.1 and the median 7. They were even more optimistic about their future prospects, rating them at 9.5 (mean) and 9 (median)!

Plug and du Bois-Reymond argue (Chapter Three) that young people who espouse 'modern values' are more likely to be winners in the 'New Economy'. Indeed, we found that many of our young respondents were quite reconciled to the conditions of flexibility. They did not lament the end of the 'job for life' (many even welcoming this):

"Nowadays people change jobs much more than like 20 years ago and it makes it difficult to plan ahead". (Andre, engineer)

"I don't think there is a job for life ... I think, say I was doing one job now, when I get to 40 or so I wouldn't want to actually be doing the same job as I'm doing.... It does get monotonous." (Bill, warehouseman)

"I wouldn't want to stay in one job. You want to go and experience different things." (Angelique, unemployed)

The young people were also prepared to retrain and learn new skills to further their employment opportunities. Indeed, when asked about what they saw as their likely futures, one fifth (21%) expected to retrain or study for a new occupation, with another 14% anticipating a major occupational shift.

Thus we conclude that this generation shows an extraordinary ability to accommodate the vagaries of the contemporary labour market. Roberts (1995), writing on the basis of work carried out 10 years ago, concluded that young people were responding pragmatically to flexibility in the labour market. Our young adult respondents, however, had gone further. They seemed to embrace flexibility for the freedom and dynamism it offered, despite the barriers it placed in the way of 'settling down'.

Conclusion

On the basis of the evidence of the Bristol study and other research reported in this volume, we can conclude that the processes of winning is strongly influenced by structures of class, gender and ethnicity. The young winners in the 'New Economy' tend to be white middle-class men. Young women, minority ethnic youth and those from manual backgrounds are likely to be losing out. Education is a key factor, and those with degrees are likely to be doing better, while educational achievement is still very strongly linked to class (Fenton et al, 2001).

However, in this chapter I have argued that it is not only the excluded unemployed who face labour market disadvantage. The polarisation thesis is too simple. Apart from a small professional elite, most young people are entering a precarious labour market and a low-wage youth economy. They are included in the labour market on unfavourable terms. Many earn salaries or wages that are not easily accommodated with home ownership and establishing their own independent households. Dependency on families is a continued reality for many. In this sense we can state that change has created more young losers than winners. However, we can also say that this is a surprisingly adaptable generation that faces up to precarious transitions with energy and ingenuity.

Note

The research reported in this chapter was funded by the Economic and Social Research Council (ESRC) of the UK: ESRC Grant no R000238215. Research team: Steve Fenton, Harriet Bradley, Jackie West, Will Guy and Ranji Devadason.

SIX

Young people in the labour market in Hungary and Slovenia: problems and perspectives

Klára Fóti, Martina Trbanc and Miroljub Ignjatović

Introduction

Economic, political and social systems in post-socialist countries have undergone major transformation as a consequence of transition from a planned to a market economy and of a democratisation process. The complexity of these systems, however, derives not only from the changes themselves, but also from the combination of the transition process and some more general trends in the world economy, such as increasing competitive pressures caused by globalisation and structural changes in the sphere of work. The latter include higher pressure on competitiveness and efficiency, flexibilisation of work arrangements and employment relations, and a shift from industrial to service sector jobs. Recent demographic trends (declining birth rates, ageing of population and changing family structures) have also contributed to the complexity of transformation in the countries of Central and Eastern Europe (CEE).

These processes have also influenced young people in these countries in ways similar to their peers in Western Europe. Several youth researchers in the CEE have pointed out that, as the building up of a market economy advances, the youth situation in the region follows West European patterns more and more closely (see, for example, Gábor 2002; Wallace and Kovatcheva, 1998). Not only does this apply to the transition from education to work, but also to those other features that characterise young people's position in society. Data show that, similar to trends in Western Europe, time spent in schools has become longer, secondary and tertiary education is undergoing expansion, and transition from education to work has become more prolonged and difficult. Compared with their West European peers, however, young people in CEE countries often find themselves in a more difficult position, since labour market entrants in particular were adversely affected by the economic changes accompanying the transition process to market economies. This was already visible in the early 1990s when youth unemployment increased. Later on, when the economic situation began to stabilise, flexibilisation of employment relations mainly affected young people, leading to higher insecurity of employment in their case, to individualisation of risks and other consequences. Not only has the young people's position changed in the risky post-socialist period, the general perception of youth as a social group has changed too, which has implications for public (welfare) policy directed towards them. With economic and political liberalisation, youth as a social category became deconstructed in policy making, which meant that the generous and systematic (and controlling) youth policy of the state socialist regime was rejected for both economic and ideological reasons (Kovatcheva, 2001). Various fields of youth policy have become divided between different ministries and their departments. This means that policies rarely focus on youth as a distinct social group. Instead, welfare policy concentrates on the most vulnerable groups within youth (for example, ethnic minorities, the Roma population, young drug addicts, drop-outs from regular education, and young unemployed people, especially the unskilled). Although in all CEE countries state agencies responsible for youth do exist, youth policy is far from systematic. Instead of supporting young people in the most important transitions (school to work, forming one's own household), in most CEE countries increasing family support is implicitly expected or even encouraged.

The aim of this chapter is to present those major changes young people have been confronted with in Hungary and Slovenia since the beginning of the period of economic transformation. This issue will be examined in the broader context of societal transformation, and the focus is on the educational and employment situation of youth.

Tendencies and conclusions outlined in this chapter should not be generalised for all CEE countries. Although there are many similar features among them, both in terms of economic developments and social policy responses, diverging trends can be described as well. Both in Hungary and Slovenia some market elements were already present at the beginning of economic transformation, whereas this was not the case in most other countries of the region. In addition, when the transition process from a planned to a market economy started, the post-socialist countries opted for different types of reform decisions (for example, shock therapy versus a more gradual approach). The influence of external factors (international organisations such as the World Bank or the International Monetary Fund [IMF], and the role of foreign capital) also varied. Similarly, social policy arrangements evolved in a diverging way, anticipating the emergence of potentially different welfare regimes in the future. Moreover, although most countries of the region have already joined the European Union, the accession process is still under way in the cases of Romania and Bulgaria, a fact that further differentiates these countries.

Economic and labour market developments in Hungary and Slovenia during the 1990s

In the early 1990s both countries suffered a huge loss of their immediate neighbouring markets, which led to an economic collapse. Hungary lost its former Council of Mutual Economic Assistance (COMECON) market, whereas in the case of Slovenia, after its split from the other Yugoslav republics, its presence on their markets declined dramatically, while the country also lost its position on many markets in Eastern Europe. As a consequence of the contraction of foreign and domestic demand as well as other factors, such as low productivity, old technology and over-employment, industrial output fell, causing collapses of giant state-owned enterprises. The non-viable production facilities had to be closed down and industry went through a deep and rather painful process of restructuring. This meant various things: downsizing, subcontracting, shutdowns, technological change, and shifts to more demanding markets. In both countries heavy and labour-intensive industries were most hit. Employment effects were obvious: in 1993, when economic crisis was most severe in both countries, the unemployment rate went up to 9.1% in Slovenia, whereas in Hungary by that time it had already reached a two-digit level of 11.9% (according to the Labour Force Survey). Registered unemployment was even higher, namely 14% in Slovenia and 13.2% in Hungary[1]. Compared with the very low unemployment rates in the late 1980s (for example, 2.2% in 1988 in Slovenia), the increase was really huge.

It should be noted that the growing imbalance in the labour market led not only to unemployment, but also to a sharp fall in the population's participation rate in economic activity in both countries. The previously very high activity rates (which were typical for all state socialist countries, and applied not only to men but also to women) have fallen to a level comparable to most West European countries (see Table 6.1). Reasons for such a fall of activity in the population in the early 1990s lie in a combination of massive voluntary withdrawal of older workers from the labour market (facing uncertain futures and taking advantage of generous retirement conditions at the time), and governments' policies against unemployment. Examples of the latter are the pre-retirement and early retirement schemes (as well as the disability pension schemes) used extensively both in Slovenia and in Hungary as 'soft' methods of workers' lay-offs.

In both Slovenia and Hungary the economic recession was most severe in the early 1990s: between 1990 and 1994 the average annual GDP growth rates were negative (−3.3% in Hungary, −1.7% in Slovenia[2]). 1994 was a turning point, when the GDP growth turned to (and stayed) positive: between 1994 and 2000 the average annual growth rate was 4.3% in Slovenia and 3.6% in Hungary (United Nations Economic Commission for Europe, UNECE). Towards the end of the 1990s employment started to increase in both countries and its structure started to change; currently the share of employment in services exceeds 50% both in Slovenia and in Hungary.

The economic transformation has obviously brought major changes to the sphere of social welfare as well. This and the deep economic recession that accompanied the beginning of economic transition narrowed considerably the scope for manoeuvre in fiscal and social policy, although requirements for increasing expenditure, especially for welfare provisions, became evident[3]. In both countries there has been a general consensus on the state's role in providing a social safety net for the most vulnerable groups (ie unemployed people, poorly skilled workers, elderly people, poor families and so on) Nonetheless, in Hungary the ideology of establishing a 'minimum state', in order to let market forces come into play, was strong. Initially, this approach was a reaction to the ubiquity of the state characteristic of the period of the planned economy, but the approach persisted later. In Slovenia, on the other hand, both in public opinion and in political and policy considerations (regardless of the government coalition in power), the concern to prevent a too quick and radical economic and social differentiation has remained present all through the transition.

Because of the heavy burden of external debt payment in Hungary, austerity measures were introduced in March 1995; the measures, often called the Bokros package after the finance minister of the day, came as a piece of shock therapy. Although the package was able to achieve its main objective − in other words, 'state bankruptcy' was avoided − it seriously cut back many of those social policy provisions, inter alia disbursements to families (and also in the area of health service), that had previously been based on a general consensus. In addition, net real wages decreased considerably at that time. It is true that, as a result, productivity increased and the competitiveness of Hungarian firms improved, but the package also hit hard in the sphere of social welfare, which had been under-financed even before the austerity measures were introduced. Foreign capital, however, continued to flow in and even increased, which can be attributed partly to privatisation. Foreign investment contributed to the recovery of the Hungarian economy to a large extent and it plays an important role in employment, providing about 25% of all jobs, according to estimates. However, in Hungary there are still huge disparities between the various social groups in their living conditions. The benefits of the recent economic growth do not seem to have reached the most vulnerable groups, although the labour market has been showing signs of improvement.

In Slovenia, the gradual reforms continued all through the 1990s. At the beginning of the economic transformation, the government was somewhat hesitant about foreign investment and the legislation stayed relatively rigid until the late 1990s. The result of that, but also of other factors, such as the geographical proximity to war areas in the Balkans, the legacy of a common state (Yugoslavia) with less stable countries, and the fact that Slovenia is a small country (and a small market) with relatively high labour costs (compared with other CEE region countries), was that foreign investment in Slovenia remained relatively low all through the 1990s and only somewhat increased in recent years. However, despite limited foreign capital inflow, Slovenia managed to keep its economy growing through the second part of the 1990s, with the current economic situation being relatively stable (investments, productivity and real wages are increasing). Similarly to the economic reforms, the reforms of social policy were also very gradual and delayed until the second part of the 1990s. The level of social rights did not change considerably during the transition period and the basic social security arrangements remained untouched, but there were many changes in the conditions for being entitled to certain rights (for example, more strict conditions, more control, social assistance tied to the activation of the working-age population), as well as in the implementation of social rights. The provision of social and public services became more diversified (involving not only the state, but also private providers and different organisations). Privatisation of services hit the areas of social care (childcare and care for elderly people) and health (private doctors), while the reform of social housing in the early 1990s and the pension system reform in the late 1990s seem to have had the most far-reaching social consequences. From the beginning of the transitional period, social policy in Slovenia was strongly connected to employment policy, with emphasised active employment policy measures that were initially more demand-oriented (subsidies for employers and financial help to employers), and later became more supply-oriented (mostly measures and programmes to increase the employability of the unemployed).

As can be seen from Table 6.1, unemployment declined in the second half of the 1990s and by 2002 it stabilised at a relatively low level in both countries. Despite recent improvements, however, labour markets are facing severe difficulties. The share of the economically active in the working-age population remains at a low level, around 60% in both countries. Although unemployment figures are favourable, unemployment is of a structural nature and to a large extent long term. In both countries it is concentrated in certain regions. The core of registered unemployed people are those who are difficult to employ, for different reasons but mostly because of their low levels of education and qualification, insufficient skills, long absences from the labour market, older age and so forth. Such unemployed people are, on the one hand, most difficult to activate with any employment measures, whereas on the other hand there are not many jobs available for them and/or the jobs available are unstable, poorly paid and subject to difficult and unfavourable conditions.

In Hungary, the female unemployment rate has always been lower than the male rate since unemployment emerged. This can be explained partly by the fact that the fall in women's activity rates has been greater than men's, contributing largely to the decreasing total participation mentioned already (at the beginning of the economic transformation women were more inclined than men to chose early retirement schemes

Table 6.1: Participation rates and unemployment rates in population (general) and among young people (15-24 years) in Slovenia (SI) and Hungary (HU), 1993-2002

	Participation rate in general population		Participation rate in population (15-24 years)		Unemployment rate in general population		Unemployment rate in population (15-24 years)	
Year	SI	HU	SI	HU	SI	HU	SI	HU
1993	57.7	62.3	41.6	42.6	9.1	11.9	24.2	21.3
1995	58.7	58.9	41.7	38.4	7.4	10.2	18.8	18.6
1996	57.6	58.5	38.0	37.1	7.3	9.9	18.8	18.0
1998	60.0	58.4	45.3	40.8	7.9	7.8	18.2	13.5
1999	58.3	59.9	41.5	40.7	7.6	7.0	18.2	12.4
2002	56.5	59.8	36.7	34.4	6.4	5.8	15.0	12.3

Sources: For Slovenia: Statistical Office of the Republic of Slovenia (SORS), Labour Force Survey (LFS) data: 1993-98, 1999, 2003. For Hungary: Central Statistical Office, Budapest, LFS, Time Series, 1992-2001, and LFS for 2002

and to withdraw from the labour market). In Slovenia, female unemployment used to be lower than male unemployment in the first part of the 1990s (because the mass bankruptcies and lay-offs first hit the enterprises in heavy and metal industry, which mostly employed male labour), but, with signs of economic stabilisation in the second part of the 1990s, the situation changed, indicating a deterioration in the women's labour market situation. In 1997, unemployment rates for women in Slovenia exceeded those of men for the first time and since then that trend has continued and even increased – in 2003, according to the LFS, the male unemployment rate was 6.1%, while the female one was 7.1% (ESS, 2004). Gender differences are especially conspicuous in youth employment: the youth (15-24 years) unemployment rate in Slovenia in 2003 was 15.4%, but this involved an unemployment rate of 13.1% for young men and 18.7% for young women! Slovenian employers are often hesitant about employing young women, because of the possibility of them taking a long period of maternity leave (one year). Women represented 53% of all registered unemployed people aged up to 26 years and 56.2% of registered first-job seekers (ESS, 2004). Other empirical data show that young women have more problems than men in finding first employment, have a longer average duration of unemployment, and are employed for a temporary period more often than men (ESS, 2004).

The level of youth unemployment is lower in Hungary than in Slovenia, where it remains relatively high (see Table 6.1). In Hungary, the lower youth unemployment could partly be attributed to the tightening of eligibility conditions for unemployment benefit, which affected young people: unemployment benefit for school leavers was abolished in 1996, and an employment programme (subsidising first employment of young school leavers) was introduced instead. In Slovenia, young people without any employment record (first-job seekers) were never entitled to unemployment benefit. When in 1991 new employment was almost stopped, which largely affected the young school leavers, the government responded by introducing a measure of subsidising first employment. The measure was very popular, since it was at that time practically impossible for a young person to get a job without support from the employment office. However, the measure was first limited and, in the second part of the 1990s, gradually abandoned and replaced with other employment measures for young unemployed people, more oriented at improving their employability (training, education programmes, motivation programmes, improving job-searching skills and so on). In Slovenia, the policy of subsidising the first job of school leavers is currently only used in regions with the highest unemployment. Despite different employment measures, young people's labour market presence in both countries has diminished very recently, even when general performance has improved, and this is very much linked to an expansion of the education systems.

Flexibilisation of employment relations and the labour market in general became highlighted in both countries during the second part of the 1990s. In Hungary, employment protection legislation gradually declined. In Slovenia, however, employment security for permanently employed people remained relatively high. The policies of Slovenian government towards flexibilisation of labour market have been mixed: on one hand, the legal framework and the active employment policies were designed to make the labour market somewhat more flexible, while on the other hand, there are still policies in place focused at job preservation (Kanjuo-Mrčela and Ignjatović, 2004). Consequently, the flexibilisation of employment relations mostly affected newcomers, especially first–job seekers. Empirical evidence for Slovenia confirms that when young people manage to find their first employment, many of them have no choice but being engaged in casual, precarious jobs (Kanjuo-Mrčela and Ignjatović, 2004).

Recent developments in educational systems

The areas of education and training assumed great importance throughout the 1990s both in Hungary and Slovenia. This reflected various factors, such as labour market changes and increased demand for better educated and qualified labour (due to technological changes, changes in working location and so forth), demographic factors (high cohorts of young people born in the early 1970s), the increased educational aspirations of young people (realising the importance of education for a better position in the labour market), and the expansion of education on secondary and tertiary levels, which was enabled by the educational policy in both countries. The policy emphasis on integration of young people into education reflects the facts that at secondary education level all education is free[4] and that scholarships are offered to youngsters from poorer families. In Slovenia, the state also subsidises school meals for secondary school pupils and for students, whereas in Hungary this is true only for the children of large and poor families.

In Hungary, it has been a conscious policy of the governments since the beginning of transition to open wide the gates of higher education institutions (in order to avoid high youth unemployment) by increasing places which can be supported by the state, so tuition is free[5]. In addition, although admission requirements remained, it became possible for those who reached this level but performed rather poorly in the entrance exam to pay for their higher education. Moreover, new private colleges and universities have been established. Similar developments took place in Slovenia, where those youngsters who are not successful enough to be accepted on state-financed places in full-time tertiary education[6] have the possibility to enrol on part-time courses. Tuition fees have to be paid in Slovenia, and in most cases also in Hungary. In Slovenia, besides avoiding even higher youth unemployment, keeping young people in education for a longer period has also been a strategy aimed at improving the general educational structure of the labour force (an aim still strongly emphasised and lately associated with the notion of developing the 'knowledge-based' economy).

There are some distinctive features of the functioning of the educational systems in Hungary and Slovenia. Among the most important of these is the fact that the Hungarian educational system is considerably more decentralised than the Slovenian one, which has several consequences. Hungarian schools seem to have more autonomy in the educational process, and also in adopting the curricula to local and regional labour market needs, in finding local partners and in making connections to local and regional employers. The latest educational reform in Hungary (between 1996 and 1998) emphasised centralisation again, but in reality local governments remained the biggest providers of school services. The emphasis of the latest reform was especially on quality assurance. The educational tradition in Slovenia is somewhat different. In the late 1980s the previous 'career-oriented system', which had been the target of serious criticism for a longer period, was abolished. The two-stream system of general education on the one hand and vocational and professional education on the other was re-established. In general it can be said that the educational system in Slovenia has always been very centralised, the state being directly responsible for financing it, for school standards, the national curricula, the training of teachers and so forth. Local governments occasionally contribute in financing (but this depends on their financial situation). Practically all the reforms and changes in the Slovenian educational system have been organised and carried out through top-down approaches (including the modernisation of curricula), although in the designing of the changes and reforms many actors directly involved in education (teachers, school principals and school experts) participated through different committees and bodies. A more centralised school system in Slovenia and less autonomy of schools at the micro level are reflected in more traditional and less innovative teaching approaches and fewer experimental practices in schools.

The educational changes that occurred through the 1990s in Hungary and Slovenia are characterised by several common aims, such as adopting education to the new needs of the economy (therefore increasing the employability of school leavers), diversifying the educational system in order to enable all young people to achieve at least one qualification, and involving different partners in education (in implementation, in finance, in determining needs and so forth). In Slovenia, compulsory primary education was prolonged for one year (from eight to nine years, starting at the age of six instead of seven), with the last three years being slightly diversified for different groups of pupils, while in Hungary the compulsory schooling age has been raised from 16 to 18 years, which will apply first to those youngsters who entered the school system in 1998[7].

In Slovenia, a reform of the education system was carried out in the mid-1990s. It consisted of the modernisation of curricula at the primary and secondary levels, and the introduction of new forms of vocational and professional education, such as the dual system (apprenticeship) programmes (that only partially existed before) in secondary vocational education[8], and the new two-year, post-secondary (non-university) professional schools. The Slovenian education system since the reform has been based on two relatively separated educational streams, the general education stream and the vocational and professional stream[9]. The two streams are more separated than in the past, when transitions were possible and common at different levels. Since the reform, the transition options have been more structured but less frequently used. Developments in Hungary are similar (especially concerning the introduction of the two-year, post-secondary, non-university education). Changes in vocational education are also due to the fact that, with the collapse of state enterprises, apprenticeship places fell drastically, and many of the occupations and skills provided by the traditional vocational training system became obsolete. In addition, new labour market requirements emerged, demanding broader and higher skills. As an effort to meet these challenges, vocational training schools were entirely abolished as separate institutions in 2000, and their curricula were built into those of the other secondary schools. Also, as a result of introducing two-year, post-secondary professional education programmes, it became possible for students from the professional technical schools[10] to study two years longer than before. The aim of the newly introduced professional post-secondary education system in Hungary was obviously also to facilitate the adjustment to the changed labour market requirements and prevent youth unemployment. As a result of this measure, and of the expansion of the secondary school system in general, enrolment ratios among 15- to 19-year-olds have reached the average level of the developed countries.

Besides the similarities between Hungary and Slovenia in policy support for the expansion of secondary and tertiary education through the 1990s, the raised educational aspirations of young people and their parents are also a common factor. This is reflected in two features: in secondary education there is a shift of enrolments from vocational and professional programmes towards general secondary programmes that lead to studies at the tertiary level; and the numbers of students at the tertiary level have increased. Both can be illustrated with enrolment figures. In Hungary, the share of primary school leavers who entered secondary general education rose from about 47% to about 70% between 1989 and 2000. At the same time, enrolment into vocational schools was dropping both in absolute and relative terms (the share dropped by about 20%). In Slovenia, the same trend is visible, although the percentages are different: while in 1997/98 there were still 75% of youngsters in vocational/professional secondary schools and 25% in general secondary schools, four years later the share of pupils in general secondary schools exceeded 30%. The numbers of pupils in general secondary education in Slovenia would be even higher (according to the claimed intentions of young people), but the number of places in general secondary education is limited, making the competition for those places very severe. In both countries the numbers of students in post-secondary education increased notably during the 1990s, especially in university studies, but also in the newly introduced higher professional programmes (for which the interest is high among students and employers). In Hungary, the number of students in higher education more than doubled between 1989 and 2000 (from 72,000 to 171,000); in Slovenia, in the years between 1985 and 1998, it rose from 29,600 to 74,600 for the students of Ljubljana University alone[11]. In Slovenia, the proportion of young people aged up to 25 years in post-secondary education has now exceeded 40% (MLFSA, 2003). The numbers of part-time students are also quite high in both countries; in Hungary, their number increased fourfold during the 1990s.

However, despite rather generous educational policies in Hungary and Slovenia, the interest in studies at tertiary level surpasses the number of available places with free tuition. This has two consequences. First, the educational sphere has become a very competitive environment in which young people compete for better school success and higher grades that enable them to continue their studies. While in the past the school was still a somewhat sheltered environment for youth compared with the 'cruel adult world' of labour market and employment, similar mechanisms (competition) are at play in both systems now, and this is true not only for the secondary level, but also for the primary education. In this competitive school environment young people who can count on the extensive support of their parents (moral support and encouragement, and learning support, including paying for additional instruction in certain subjects and so on) are already in a more favourable position than their peers with less family support (see the discussion in the final chapter on parental cultural capital). Second, youngsters who are not successful enough in applying for available places in regular education at tertiary level can enrol for places where tuition fees have to be paid (in Hungary) or in part-time (adult) education, also with tuition fees (in Slovenia). The numbers of young part-time students in Slovenia are quite high and they are in an unequal position compared with their colleagues who study as non-fee-paying regular students[12].

With such an expansion of the secondary and tertiary education, today the main questions discussed both in Hungary and in Slovenia are connected to quality assurance, the employability of young people in changing economic circumstances, and the effectiveness of the system. In Slovenia, the latter question is connected to the relatively high drop-out level, both in secondary and tertiary education[13]. Until now most of the policy concern has focused on secondary school drop-outs; in a five-year observation period the drop-out rate was 13.7% (Trbanc, 2000). The highest drop-out rate is in vocational programmes (Trbanc, 2000), leaving these young people without a basic qualification and therefore hardly employable[14]. In fact, many of them return to education later, either by enrolling on another regular programme or through adult education schemes or employment policy measures. But some of them end up registered as unemployed with extremely low chances of getting a job. The young drop-outs who find themselves in the labour market without any qualifications are often deprived in other areas, have low family support and are therefore at risk of social exclusion. On top of that, it has to be emphasised that the drop-out rate of youngsters from school often reproduces the social marginality of certain population groups. Data show that the educational levels of parents of premature leavers are much lower than the average (Trbanc, 2000).

The effectiveness of tertiary education is less debated in Slovenia, although the figures show that it is very low. Only about half of the students enrolled in the first year of university studies continue into the second year (Mihevc, 2003). The students are studying on average one to two years longer than expected (four-year programmes take them five to six years). Eight years after initial enrolment, only 50% of students have successfully graduated, 6% are still studying and 44% have abandoned their studies (Bevc, 2002). It can be speculated that this situation is on the one hand a consequence of the conveniences connected to being a student and the possibility of part-time and temporary student work; on the other hand, it links with the trends that young people are staying at home longer than in the past, that the period of youth is prolonging well into the late 20s, and that parents (of broadly defined middle-class status) are prepared to support their children financially and emotionally for a very long period (cf Chapter Ten on Italy).

Employment possibilities for young people

The labour market position of young people is quite weak in both countries. In Slovenia this is reflected in high unemployment rates, in Hungary in their low labour market participation. The main contradiction for them is that although their educational attainment is higher than that of the preceding age cohorts, fewer job opportunities are available for them (Róbert, 2002). Due to the described expansion in education over the 1990s, this is especially marked in Hungary.

A special feature of the emergent youth labour market situation is the polarisation of job options, which is closely connected to individual educational attainment. While in Slovenia in the past, the youth labour market used to be more homogenous (regarding the type of jobs young people could get, employment conditions, pay and working conditions), during the 1990s it became more diversified. Young people with higher educational attainment have fewer problems in finding jobs (even first jobs) than less educated youngsters. They are significantly less likely to be unemployed, and the duration of their unemployment period is much shorter than that of poorly qualified young people (ESS, 2000). Many employers deliberately give priority to young professional graduates, because of the new knowledge and skills they bring and even more because they are considered to be more flexible and more adaptable to different work situations, to speak foreign languages and be prepared to work overtime. In certain fields (such as electronics, ICT and computer sciences) young graduates can find well-paid jobs and good working conditions. By contrast, young people with poorer educational attainment, or with qualifications in overcrowded occupations or in the declining traditional industrial occupations, have poor chances of getting jobs and stay unemployed for long periods. This is evident also from data on young registered unemployed people in Slovenia: as many as 41% of them have only completed primary school or short vocational training (ESS, 2000). Moreover, young poorly educated people often have high job expectations and are not always prepared to take jobs that are poorly paid, physically exhausting or performed in difficult conditions.

In Hungary polarisation of job options is evident in competition for good jobs in the foreign capital-owned companies (which increased in number from the mid-1990s). For graduates of certain universities this meant the start of a promising career, but nowadays demand is stagnating or even diminishing as some multinational companies leave the country.

Under these circumstances, flexible work arrangements, including so-called 'atypical' jobs (part-time work, self-employment and temporary contracts), could provide some kind of solution, facilitating the school-to-work transition for young people. Indeed, evidence shows that these forms of employment have become quite widespread among youngsters. In Slovenia, where the most common form of flexible employment is fixed-term (temporary), its share among all employees is 10.5%, while among young people (15-24 years) it stands at 42.9%; similarly, part-time employment, which is as low as 6.6% among all employees, stands at 15.8% for young people (Kanjuo-Mrčela and Ignjatović, 2004). Similar, although less pronounced trends, are seen in Hungary: among 18- to 24-year-olds a much higher percentage (18%) worked part-time than any other age group, and their share was also higher in the case of evening, night and weekend work (Sik and Nagy, 2002). It remains to be seen, however, to what extent flexibilisation is capable of facilitating the labour market integration of young people. It may indicate that young people's individual trajectories would take the form of what Plug and du Bois-Reymond call 'yo-yo' movements – failure to settle in one job and constant movement between various employment statuses. In addition, 'atypical' jobs could contribute to the further prolonging of transitions because they are insecure and unstable. However, in both countries evidence shows that youngsters who already have some work experience have more chance of finding a job after finishing their studies. Employers have more trust in people who are familiar with the most basic requirements of a workplace.

The boundaries between studying and working seem more blurred than in the past. In this respect the student labour market in Slovenia should be mentioned. Student work is not a new phenomenon in Slovenia, but was not so common in the past. In the 1990s the student labour market expanded for several reasons, but mostly because young people started to prolong the years of their study, thus needing additional finances. At the same time, employers started to look for relatively qualified and reliable labour that would be cheap and prepared to work on more flexible terms. Agencies for mediating student work proliferated (cf discussion of the UK in Chapter Five). Students typically occupy temporary and part-time jobs that need to be performed at unusual or changing hours, as well as physically difficult jobs. For instance, they work in retail and leisure; at weekends big shopping centres employ students as cashiers, sellers and entertainers, almost exclusively. Consequently, students already present competition to both unemployed people (especially the unqualified ones) and to school leavers looking for more permanent employment. This occurs particularly because under current legislation the taxation on student work is lower than taxation on any other type of work contract, making it cheaper for organisations to employ students than unemployed people. The legislation is expected to change shortly, which may decrease the amount of student work in the future, but the degree of decrease will depend on the further flexibilisation of employment.

Numerous active employment policy measures are in place to help young unemployed people in both countries[15]. They include such measures as job clubs (preparing youngsters for employment by teaching them job-search behaviour), career guidance, occupational counselling, skills acquisition (language, ICT and accountancy), on-the-job training and community work. Some of the measures, aimed at helping labour market entrants, are quite similar in the two countries – for example, a wage subsidy (for first jobs). In Slovenia, this is a partial subsidy for employing a young first-time job seeker in regions with above-average unemployment. In Hungary, there are two kinds of such programmes: one is called 'support for gaining work experience', the other one is a partial wage subsidy, aimed at creating job opportunities in the old apprenticeship places, where skilled youngsters used to attend on-the-job training. This subsidy can reach half the minimum wage and be claimed for a period of nine months, after which employers are obliged to provide a further 90 days of employment. Employers who undertake to hire skilled or unskilled youngsters for at least four hours per day are eligible for the work experience scheme. The subsidy could constitute 50-100% of the wage, and can be claimed for one year. In 2003, 16,000 youngsters were employed within this latter scheme, whereas only 500 participated in the former. Altogether, 40,000 school leavers benefited from one of the active programmes, the greatest proportion – almost 20,000 – receiving training support. In Slovenia, unemployed young people and first-time job seekers are most often included in motivation and orientation programmes, education and training programmes, and community work. As part of the education and training programmes, it is worth mentioning Slovenia's Programme 10,000 (started in 1998 as Programme 5,000), which is a 'second chance in education' programme for educational drop-outs, and is connected with a support programme of learning assistance (provided as community work). In 2003, there were 7,310 participants in this programme, of which 56.8% were aged up to 26 years (ESS, 2004).

An alarming tendency is that recently not only has the number of unemployed school leavers increased, but also that of jobless graduates. According to Hungarian registration data, their number peaked in July 2003, exceeding 15,000 people (about 4% of all those registered unemployed). It is estimated, however, that their number actually stands at a much higher level – 40-50,000 people. Similarly, in Slovenia in recent years there is evidence that the labour market situation has worsened for well-educated young people, although not as dramatically as in Hungary.

Conclusion

This chapter has shown that as a consequence of economic transformation, the majority of young people have become increasingly vulnerable. Ule (2002) claims that it is not the minority of youth that is socially vulnerable, but the majority (see Chapter Five). Although with the introduction of market relations, many new opportunities have emerged, youth has had to face increasing challenges at the same time. It seems that only a small number of young people can access the new opportunities successfully. Nowadays, although the level of educational attainment of labour market entrants has improved considerably, their prospects for finding jobs are quite poor. As a result, school-to-work transitions have become longer, similar to recent developments in Western Europe reported in other chapters. Thus the position of youth in Central and Eastern Europe has changed notably over the past two decades, and it can be assumed that this has caused even more frustration among young people in CEE countries than their West European peers would experience.

As regards their labour market performance, for a certain period of time the strategy of letting more people into higher education proved quite helpful from the point of view of avoiding high youth unemployment. In addition, graduates could be retrained more easily than people with lower educational attainment. The fact that more and more people go on to higher education, however, results in high pressure on certain segments of the labour market from the supply side when they finish their studies at times when demand is limited. As a consequence of declining opportunities on the labour market, more and more young people have to face uncertainty, insecurity and greater risks. Because of their inexperience and the shortage of permanent jobs, they are stuck in performing unstable and often low-paid jobs that provide neither economic independence nor social security. As a consequence, not only are young poorly qualified people in an extremely disadvantageous situation, but the number of frustrated highly qualified young people is increasing, and it remains to be seen to what extent membership of the European Union will alleviate this problem.

This period of labour market change has also witnessed broader changes in young people's social situations. In many CEE countries since the 1980s, the position of youth in society, previously perceived as a homogeneous social group defined by age, has changed. During the 1980s, youth played a prominent role in political changes by initiating and participating in emancipatory social movements and introducing new lifestyles. (This is especially true in Slovenia, where such emancipated, active and liberal youth contributed greatly to the events that enabled this part of the former Yugoslavia to gain its independence in 1991.) As a result, youth socially and culturally diversified and improved their position in society. This process has been labelled a 'deconstruction of youth'. Ule developed this concept further, describing the process as the first and positive phase of deconstruction (Ule and Rener, 1998, 2002).

However, as neo-conservatism and neo-liberalism flourished in the 1990s during the process of economic and political reform, young people's labour market position weakened again. This and the prolongation of education led to a deterioration in the overall social position of youth. The positive trend of 'deconstruction of youth' took the turn to a negative second phase. Once perceived heterogeneous and important, the young generation again appears to be undefined socially, culturally and in terms of lifestyle. The circle of social emancipation, started in the 1980s, ended in the 1990s where it began: at the point of private life and households of origin, which are providing refuge and a point of retreat in the face of pressures made by the increasingly ruthless world of adults.

Research on the response of young people to such challenges (for example, Ule 2002) points out some of the consequences of the increased social vulnerability of young people:

- Due to labour market limitations and high expenditure on prolonged education, the economic autonomy of young people becomes very limited and they are retreating to the safe haven of their original families, remaining economically dependent for a longer period of time. Family support and family social networks have become very important in the crucial transitions young people are facing.
- As a result of increasing challenges, some youth groups show greater political passivity. Their attention seems to have been shifted from political and general social problems to more particular and personal ones. A strong tendency towards individualisation can be observed among them. Instead of collective actions, young people increasingly seek individual solutions to their problems and lives (see also Chapter Eight).
- Worsening social status and the individualisation process adversely affect identity building, which is a prerequisite for managing risks in the modern world. In these circumstances, the influence of peer groups often decreases. Feelings of loneliness, isolation and competitiveness are gaining ground among young people.

As discussed earlier, social protection measures (in a broader sense, including active labour market programmes) are in place to support the most vulnerable groups of young people. Some data show, however, that they are not particularly efficient (especially in the case of social assistance) (at least in Hungary; see Fóti, 2003.). As regards general support for young people as a distinctive social group, it seems that although government institutions for youth problems exist, specific measures are lacking. As Kovatcheva put it, it becomes crucial to provide "general assistance and guidance for all young people in their life transitions in the increasing risky context of their transforming societies, based on monitoring youth careers and providing information and advice to protect them from making choices which lead to social exclusion" (Kovatcheva, 2000, p 62). These measures, however, should be introduced within the context of other social policy instruments.

Notes

[1] The difference between the LFS data on unemployment and registered unemployment (that is, administrative) is considerable in both countries, especially in Slovenia. It can be speculated that the difference between the estimate of the number of unemployed people according to the LFS and the number of registered unemployed people reveals the discrepancy between the real job seekers (not performing any paid work, actively seeking a job and being immediately available for work) and those who are registered with the employment offices, but are not actively seeking a job (passive, waiting for retirement, discouraged and so on) or are involved in hidden economy.

[2] Source: United Nations' Economic Commission for Europe (UNECE, see: Cazes and Nesporova, 2003).

[3] In Hungary, for example, in the wake of the emerging mass unemployment there was an urgent need for building up a network of employment offices, which had already existed before in Slovenia.

[4] Public schools at secondary level are still dominant both in Slovenia and Hungary, although quite a number of private institutions were set up during the 1990s. Curricula of all education programmes (including those provided by private institutions) have to be approved (verified) by the state and certificates are nationally recognised.

[5] Although the austerity measures of 1995 ('Bokros package') introduced tuition fees in higher education, the next government, which came into power in 1998, re-established free education for those who aimed at obtaining their first diploma.

[6] In Slovenia, the numbers of state-financed places in higher education increased substantially through the 1990s; however, they remain limited. The interest of youngsters in studies in certain fields, such as economy, law, social sciences and similar, surpasses the numbers of available places in regular (state-financed) studies, and the selection procedure for those places is based on secondary school success and the results of exams.

[7] However, the details of the extension have not been elaborated as yet. For example, important questions remain, such as whether whether it should be implemented exclusively within the system of public education, on a full-time basis.

[8] Participation of employers is essential for dual-system vocational programmes. In Slovenia, the Chamber of Crafts was an important actor in shaping them. However, the interest of youngsters in enrolment to these programmes remained relatively low for different reasons (ie raised educational aspirations, occupations not attractive to youngsters, parallel existence of similar school-based vocational programmes, poor possibilities for continuing education after completing such a programme).

[9] The general education stream consists of four-year general and professional secondary school programmes, leading to the external matriculation exam, and to four-year university studies that are concluded with a diploma. The vocational and professional education stream consists of three-year vocational programmes, completed with final exam and qualification, and four-year professional programmes, completed with an external professional final exam, enabling the youngsters to continue education in two-year post-secondary professional schools.

[10] There are two main types of secondary schools with final exams. Professional-technical schools, in addition to preparing students for higher education (through the obligation of taking the final exam), also provide them with some kind of vocational qualification.

[11] The University of Ljubljana is the oldest and biggest university in Slovenia. The other two are the University of Maribor and the newly established (2003) University of Primorska.

[12] Occasional discussions on introducing some form of tuition fees for regular tertiary education studies with the intention of making the situation of regular and part-time students more equal, and of stimulating them to study more efficiently, are as a rule met by the heavy resistance of regular students and broad middle-class public opinion.

[13] In Hungary, school drop-out is considered as mostly the problem of the Roma minority.

[14] The numbers of youngsters prematurely leaving secondary education actually decreased somewhat during the 1990s. Policy measures are already focused on both preventing premature exits from secondary education and helping youngsters who leave schooling without achieving any qualifications. In the former case, vocational guidance is emphasised as well as the awareness of teachers and the responsibility of schools in early detection of potential drop-out. The latter is reflected in employment policy measures intended

for young people without any qualifications (eg offering them second educational chances or training to prepare them for job search), and other alternative projects, initiated and carried out by non-profit organisations and associations (ie 'project learning for youngsters', 'street projects' for young people in some urban neighbourhoods, projects for immigrant children).

[15] However, empirical research in four CEE countries, commenting also on abolishing unemployment compensation for young people, concluded: "The withdrawal of unemployment benefit is not a 'big stick'. Nor are the Labour Offices' active programmes attractive 'carrots'" (Roberts et al, 1999, p 249).

SEVEN

Excluded youth or young citizens? Ethnicity, young people and the labour market in three EU countries

Gary Craig, Hans Dietrich and Jerome Gautié

Introduction

This chapter examines the process of entry into the labour market for young people of differing ethnicities in three countries – the UK, France and Germany – with differing traditions, legal frameworks and understandings of citizenship. Discrimination based on ethnic origin and skin colour is a common feature of national labour markets throughout Europe and this structures the opportunities that young people have as they leave school, the choices open to them in education, employment and training, qualifications and career prospects. Discrimination against minorities within labour market structures and institutions is only just beginning to be addressed in some European countries and the consequences for young non-indigenous people are serious. Minorities – and especially young minority group members – work in the most precarious and marginalised parts of the labour market, with insecure contracts, low pay and poor conditions. As a result they are subject to relatively high rates of unemployment and poverty, yet are sometimes blamed for unemployment and are not infrequently the victims of racist abuse and violence. Efforts of governments to address the issue effectively are hampered by the lack of adequate data. Increasing hostility to refugees and asylum seekers also undermines such legislation as exists to protect minorities.

Here, we look at ways in which young people's experience as they enter the labour market is shaped by their ethnicity. We do so in the context of three different national frameworks, those of England, France and Germany, chosen because they have differing conceptualisations of citizenship, reflected in national policy arrangements.

The first section establishes that discrimination against minorities is a widespread phenomenon throughout European national labour markets, and that most national governments are doing relatively little to address it. The next, consisting of three national case studies that draw on very recent research, shows how the issues of employability, ethnicity and citizenship for young people interact in these three countries. Finally, the chapter raises important research and policy questions for these countries in particular but for the European Union as a whole.

First, we examine the way in which the term citizenship is understood within these three countries. Britain has no written political constitution and the meaning of citizenship is therefore open to political and legal interpretation. Most commentators take Marshall's (1950) taxonomy of rights as sketching the outlines of what it means to be a British citizen. This covers civil rights (property rights, legal guarantees and freedoms), political rights (the right to vote and rights of association and constitutional participation) and social rights (entitlements to basic standards of education, health and social care, housing and income maintenance).

These rights do not, however, have equal weight and in the UK context access to all of them, and particularly social rights, are strongly associated with access to income and wealth (Dean and Melrose, 1999). Marshall's taxonomy in any case has been overtaken both by recognition of the need to assert the rights of women alongside men, the rights to reproduction and to participation (Lister, 2002) and, in the context of the increasing heterogeneity of national populations, the introduction of a category of cultural rights – that is, the right to be culturally different in a society where civil, political and social rights are open to all (Castles, 2000). The New Labour governments, elected in 1997 and 2001, associate citizenship most strongly with participation in the labour market, allegedly underpinned by a multicultural approach. However, as Lister and others argue (Lister, 2002; see also Lister, 2001; Craig, 2004), this emphasis on paid work effectively devalues care work, in terms of looking after children or dependants who are elderly or disabled, thus effectively constraining women's ability to achieve full citizenship, and limiting the citizenship rights of those not in the labour market. Recent restrictions placed on the social and economic rights of refugees and asylum seekers further constrain their ability to achieve citizenship rights equivalent to those of the majority population (Bloch and Schuster, 2002). Essentially, however, despite there being no constitutional basis for it, citizenship within the UK is ascribed by a legal process and has largely reflected *jus soli,* the right of residence, although for many migrants in the 1960s and 1970s it was ascribed through *jus sanguinis* (blood ties) – for example, near-family connections – as well as through historical connections (for former colonies).

In France, citizenship is based on the 'republican' conception, introduced by the 1789 French Revolution, reinforced by the republican regime since the 1880s. From a juridical perspective, 'rights' (civil, political, but also, to some extent, social) are linked to the nationality of citizens. The 1803 Napoleonic Civil Code (*Code Civil*) implemented *jus sanguinis* – the right based on blood – which, at that time, contrasted with the dominant conception elsewhere in Europe; this was abolished in 1889 and replaced by *jus soli* (the right based on place) because of low fertility rates, and in order to integrate into the army the sons of immigrants born in France (Weil, 2002)[1]. Beyond rights and entitlements, and in a more sociological (Durkheimian) perspective, the social dimension of citizenship also refers, in the French context, to social integration in the nation, defined – by Renan among others – as a common set of values shared by all citizens, regardless of ethnic, cultural and religious characteristics (Heckmann, 1999). The debate, which surfaced at the beginning of 2004, concerning the law intending to ban the use of religious symbols, including the Muslim *hijab* (head scarf), is a good example of this conception of an 'anti-communitarianist' conception of citizenship.

In Germany, the concept of citizenship remains strongly related to heritage and blood. German discussion on minorities remains concentrated on post-Second World War immigrants and does not refer to distinct minorities living in Germany for centuries and recognised as ethnic groups – such as the Danish minority in northern Germany or Sorbs in eastern Saxony – each possessing recognised rights as a cultural minority, but well integrated into German society. Discussion thus focuses on two distinct immigrant groups: those with cultural German backgrounds, the so-called *Aussiedler* (resettler), mainly from former USSR or Eastern European states, and foreign immigrants. The two discussions are only weakly connected.

Foreign immigrants are taken to include:

- war refugees; and
- asylum-seekers;
- labour migrants such as the so-called *Gastarbeiter* from the late 1950s onwards (after 1973 only family members were allowed to enter Germany, although from 1968 onwards labour market mobility of

employees from EEC member states was liberalised. For example, from 1991, it was easier for enterprises from Eastern Europe to dispatch employees [so-called *Werkvertragsarbeitnehmer*] to Germany and for seasonal workers to get temporary working allowances in Germany. Again, since 2000, the green card option has opened the border for new more highly qualified *Gastarbeiter*, albeit in a very selective way [Cyrus, nd]).

Effectively, in recent years, only a small subgroup of foreigners has acquired unlimited rights to residence combined with unlimited work permits. However, there are increasing numbers of foreigners with temporary work permissions. In terms of labour market access, foreign people who have no permanent permit to live in Germany may also have selective access to higher general qualifications, to vocational qualifications (the dual system), and to work.

In Germany, therefore, access to citizenship rights and nationality is complex, unequal and relies on specific preconditions and legal status. This situation is further complicated by the fact that immigrant children born in Germany remain legally foreign, a paradox that the 2000 citizenship law has only just begun to address (Green, 2002, p 2). At the time of writing (spring 2004), the new citizenship law has not become effective, although a decision was expected on the timing of its introduction early in 2004. Despite these differences, in any case, official statistics normally do not identify specific subgroups of non-German ethnic minorities, described collectively as *Ausländer*.

This continuing status of foreigner contrasts with the position of so-called *Aussiedler*. After two years in Germany, *Aussiedler* are registered as Germans and disappear as a distinct category from official statistics. Empirical findings, however, actually show increasing problems with integrating this group, especially with respect to recent young immigrants from Eastern European countries. In contrast to their recognised nationality as Germans, cultural and language differences are more marked and identify a new type of *Aussiedler*.

Discrimination in European labour markets[2]

Although the quality and comparability of current data on ethnicity from differing countries is highly variable – although universally poor – thus making international comparisons fragile, the evidence available shows that discrimination is highly significant in shaping the experience of minorities within national labour markets. This is true regardless of the particular nature of minority ethnic populations in different EU countries, which have developed as a result of a combination of differing factors. These factors include the existence of indigenous minorities, large-scale migration from countries formerly attached to European countries through ties of empire (particularly the UK, Spain, Portugal, France and Italy), immigration for the purposes of economic reconstruction after the Second World War and, more recently, flows of refugees and asylum seekers from countries affected by war, internal conflict or economic disintegration. The national responses to the totality of this immigration have been increasingly restrictive and it has been argued that immigration policy itself (increasingly characterised as Fortress Europe) has contributed to discrimination and racial violence against people of differing ethnicities on either an individual or a systematic basis (Craig, 2003b).

Local responses towards the civil, political and social citizenship rights of minority ethnic groups – and their specific rights within the labour market – are shaped by a combination of factors, most of all by the history of the establishment of these populations, their past connection with the host country, their size relative to the 'host' population and the manner of their arrival, as much as by any formal legal status they have. While formal civil and political rights for minorities – such as the right to vote – are relatively uniform across the EU, within labour market mechanisms discrimination is apparent, a result of the complex interplay of local factors. In a period of increasing globalisation of economic activity, of communication and of political responses, it is true also that local responses are increasingly shaped by global trends, of which increasing discrimination is the most dismal, as Wallace et al (2000) note in a study of their impact on young people.

Increasing – if uneven – labour market difficulties across the EU since the 1970s have led to increasing demands to limit immigration and for repatriation of existing 'foreigners', lending support to xenophobic campaigns in populist media and racialised violence against religious, ethnic and cultural minorities in countries as different in their culture and history of immigration as the UK (MacPherson, 1999), Finland (Virtanen, 1998), France, the Netherlands, Greece (ECRI, 2000), Hungary and Germany. These campaigns have driven the majority political view towards the right in almost every Western European country in the past few years. The growth of racialised violence makes the position of immigrants even more precarious both in relation to the labour market – where minority ethnic groups tend to occupy more physically exposed jobs within the service sector – and outside it, because of difficulties of accessing social protection systems. Popular discourse still continues to represent migrants as problematic and not as potentially national economic assets; studies are, however, emerging that reveal the economic contribution made by migrants to national economies. For example, the tax and social security contributions made by immigrants in Spain exceed their receipt of state benefits by almost 200 billion pesetas (IRR, 2000), while a study in the UK has estimated the net annual economic benefit of migrants to be of the order of £2 billion (Glover et al, 2001), and Gieseck et al (1994) suggest that recently arrived migrant workers in Germany paid almost twice, in tax and social insurance contributions, the DM18 billion received in benefits. Most European countries are now trying to balance political demands for restricting immigration (at least of racialised minorities) while responding to increasing demands for labour to fill growing gaps in their labour markets (Craig, 2002, 2003b). For example, Sweden most recently joined the growing list of Western European countries that have established quotas for immigration from countries from Western and Central Europe acceding to the EU in the next few years.

The continuing general 'colour-blindness' of many of labour market organisations is alarming when, on the one hand, most analyses of poverty and government responses to it, assert the importance of paid work as the most important route out of poverty, while the few available analyses of race and poverty show strong associations between poverty and membership of particular minority groups. For example, in the UK, Pakistani, Bangladeshi and African Caribbean groups – and particularly young men – feature disproportionately among the poorest in society (Modood et al, 1997; Craig, 1999; Platt, 2002). Similarly, research shows that 'foreign' immigrants (including recent flows of refugees and asylum seekers) – who constitute approximately 10% of Germany's population – are more vulnerable to poverty and marginalisation (Riphahn, 1999; see also EAPN, 1999), as measured by participation in social assistance programmes. A review of social protection in European countries notes that among the 5 million poor excluded people and the approximately 3 million unemployed in France, "several groups seem to be more vulnerable, especially young people ..." (Hirsch, 1997, p 33), among whom minority young people are disproportionately represented. Riphahn's findings are all the more striking since, for those with no permanent residence rights, "social assistance receipt is connected with a risk of expulsion" (1999, p 5). Numbers dependent on social assistance programmes are thus likely to understate the extent of poverty among minority ethnic groups.

Forms of discrimination against minorities that effectively designate 'foreigners' as responsible for the economic ills of countries (whether they are employed or not) have emerged on a national and transnational basis, leading, for example, to arson attacks and the murder of Turkish migrants in German streets and hostels, attacks in which UK white nationals were implicated. Even countries traditionally viewed as liberal and tolerant now witness the growth of influential racist political movements; one such is the Danish People's Party, with growing popularity ratings, which has argued for repatriation of immigrants.

The European Anti-Poverty Network (EAPN) lists a number of ways in which discrimination against minorities specifically affects the opportunities of minority ethnic groups in the labour market: these include having the least training, the least appropriate skills, poor pay, work without protection or security, higher rates of unemployment and work in the most unsocial sectors (EAPN, 1999, pp 18-19). The position of minority ethnic groups is also made more precarious by lack of language skills and knowledge of local welfare arrangements (ie a lack of social and cultural capital), impacting on health, social security, education and housing prospects. The EU has begun to acknowledge the difficulties faced by minority ethnic groups and "within the context of the European Employment Strategy ... explicitly set ... the target of intensifying efforts to deal with the employment problems of ethnic minorities" (Stille, 1999, p 5). Stille also argues that first-generation immigrants have greater difficulties than their children and grandchildren, that immigrant populations tend to have a younger demographic profile than the 'host' population and that minority groups generally have lower participation rates, lower employment rates than those of host nationals, and lower rates of self-employment (though with significant exceptions). Minority groups tend to have lower levels of qualification, though again this is not always the case: for example, there is a clear divide between the relatively better educational attainment and labour market experience of Indian and Chinese UK minorities on the one hand and the poor attainments of Pakistanis, Bangladeshis and African Caribbeans on the other.

With this context of discrimination against minorities and poverty, generally affecting minorities in all European countries, we now turn to examine the experience of minority ethnic young people within three national contexts.

Young people's experiences and policy responses

France

France has few scientific studies of immigrants and/or minority ethnic groups, compared with some European countries. Databases are particularly poor on the subject. The trauma of the wartime Vichy regime, which used files containing religious and ethnic information to persecute Jews, is still vivid[3]. The 'Republican' ideology, inherited from the French Revolution, is also very strong: every citizen is equal, and cannot be distinguished according to ethnic or religious characteristics. Nevertheless, there are estimated to be four million Muslims in France, 80% of them from Algeria or Morocco, and unemployment among second-generation Algerian immigrants is three to four times that among indigenous French people (*The Guardian*, 27 February 2004, p 9).

This kind of 'blind spot' is quite paradoxical, and mirrors the failure of many allegedly multicultural agencies in other countries to monitor ethnicity effectively. France was, as noted earlier, one of the first European countries to define precisely the 'nationality' of citizens. Another issue specific to France is that it has been a significant country of immigration since the 19th century, both for demographic and economic reasons, whereas at that time many other European countries were facing emigration (mainly to America). Since the Industrial Revolution, immigrants have played a crucial role in the emergence of the French working class (Noiriel, 1988)[4].

The lack of data is also important for youth policy. The great majority of youth from immigrant families were born in France (the so-called 'second generation'). Since *jus soli* now predominates, they are therefore French. Thus nationality cannot be a criterion to study them. However, no survey contains data on phenotypes – asking people if he/she is black, for example, is inconceivable in France. The only data that can be found in surveys is the country of birth of parents (usually the father). Empirical evidence here concerning 'ethnic youth' (EY) will thus mainly be based on youth (during the 1980s-90s) whose fathers were born outside France[5], one sixth of the 1.2 million 1998 school leavers at all levels (CEREQ, 2002). The following discussion will assess the empirical evidence of social integration and the consequences for the 'social citizenship' issue, as defined earlier.

Keeping these caveats in mind, one could summarise the French situation as follows. Controlling for their social origin – ie the occupation of the parents – EY perform at school globally as well as

Table 7.1: Family characteristics of ethnic youth (EY) and indigenous youth (%)

School leavers (all levels) in 1992	Father manual worker	Father unemployed	Mother without any diploma	Mother inactive	Number of children in the household
Father born in France (EY)	28	2	19	14	2
Father born in Maghreb (EYM)	45	6	59	48	4
Father born in Southern Europe (EYS)	54	3	56	25	2
All	30	2	24	18	2

Source: Frickey and Primon (2002): thus among the 1992 school leavers whose fathers were born in France, 28% had a father who was a manual worker, 2% had a father unemployed and so on

'indigenous people', defined here as those whose fathers were born in France. But at the same time, at any given educational level, EY face bigger problems in the labour market – especially if their parents come from North Africa. Eventually, gender differences must also be taken into account.

In absolute terms, the educational attainment of EY is lower than that of indigenous youth: in 1992, only 49% of school leavers whose fathers were born outside France had a high school diploma (or more), compared with 58% for indigenous youth. However, to assess the relative performance of EY at school, one must take into account social class background (Table 7.1). Not surprisingly, EY are more often children of manual workers, of a mother without any diploma, and have more brothers and/or sisters.

Taking these elements into account, it appears that EY perform at school as well as indigenous youth (Silberman and Fournier, 1999; Beaud, 2002). This is usually seen as a success for the assimilation process through the educational system, which has aimed, since the return of the republican regime at the end of the 19th century, to promote citizenship and meritocracy.

On reaching the labour market, however, it appears that meritocracy is but an illusion. At any given level of education, EY are more often unemployed, or hold insecure jobs. This is particularly true for those with Maghrebian origins (EYM). For instance in 1997, five years after leaving school, 13% of the college graduates and postgraduates (high-school diploma plus three years or more full-time study, whose fathers were born in North Africa) in literature, business and law, were unemployed compared with 6% for Southern European (EYS), and 5% for those with native parents (Frickey and Primon, 2002).

The striking difference between EYM and EYS is partially the consequence of different 'strategies' of the two groups. The fathers of EYS are more often manual workers in the construction sector, or self-employed craftsmen, whereas those of EYM are more often unskilled workers in traditional manufacturing sectors (automobile and steel) that have undergone substantial restructuring and downsizing during the two past decades. As a consequence, EYS tend to have a 'blue-collar' mobility strategy. They more often choose vocational training (in the educational system or via apprenticeship), and they can benefit from their 'social capital' (ie their family network) when entering the labour market (Silberman and Fournier, 1999) whereas for EYM the priority is to escape from manual work and the world of the factory. They therefore tend to reject vocational training and prefer general training. If they fail more at school (14% of EYM who left the educational system in 1992 had no diploma, compared with 8% for the EYS), they also are more likely to reach the highest levels (college and postgraduate) (15% for EYM, compared with 11% for EYS); but very often they fail at university – because of the lack of the required 'cultural capital' – or tend to choose dead-end curricula (Beaud, 2002). As a consequence, they leave university without credentials or with poorly marketable ones. Moreover, those disadvantages are not compensated for by labour market policy: EYM benefit less from schemes and, when they do, those schemes are more often temporary employment in the public sector than vocational training or employment subsidy in the private sector (Silberman and Fournier, 1999).

Gender differences matter, especially for EY from North and sub-Saharan Africa; usually their families accept the 'training' but not the cultural dimension of school, refusing the 'freedom' values of occidental society for their daughters. The latter tend to be more controlled, and are not allowed to leave school and their parents' home before marriage. Consequently, girls' school attainment is higher than that of boys (Timera, 1999). At the same time, they tend to develop a form of 'work asceticism' (Beaud, 2002) as a response to social control, and because they know investing in school is the only way to emancipate themselves.

Differences in strategy according to ethnic origin are not enough, however, to explain differences in labour market outcomes: despite difficulties with data collection and statistical assessment, it is clear that discrimination generates a self-reinforcing spiral leading to social exclusion. French researchers may argue, as have some British ones, that differences relating to gender or ethnicity may actually result from a 'hidden variable'. However, polls show that both immigrants and indigenous French think discrimination plays a role (Silberman and Fournier, 1999).'Testing' experiments held by anti-discrimination associations, and the very many testimonies of victims confirm this impression.Viprey (2002) argues that this 'invisible ceiling' has tended to strengthen during the past decade, especially for youth with African origins.

Both statistical surveys and field studies highlight growing frustration, especially among EYM males, who bear the brunt of unemployment and precarious jobs.They feel cheated by the educational system and discriminated against in the labour market (Beaud, 2002). This frustration has a negative feedback into their professional integration (Silberman and Fournier, 1999).As a result, the 'ethnicisation' of social relations and the increasing fragmentation into ethnic communities have increased in France during the past decade. Whereas during the 1980s EYM refused to be called 'youth with foreign origins' or 'youth from immigration', they now tend to assert their ethnic origin to confront the stigmatisation, and call themselves 'French Arab' for instance (Bertrand, 2002). This also mirrors a British trend.

At the same time social mobilisation (through associations such as *SOS Racisme*, created at the beginning of the 1980s) tends to be replaced by individual or collective deviancy.According to Lagrange (cited by Bertrand, 2000, p 6),"the breaking of the civil contract by delinquency is conceived [by the EY] as a response to the breaking of the 'social contract' by the rest of society, implying for them unemployment and discrimination". This parallels the sometimes violent responses of South Asian and black young men in UK northern cities during 2001 (Manawar, 2003). EYB often feel like 'second zone' citizens, relegated to ghettos ('les banlieue', the suburbs of the big cities:Viprey, 2002), rising up from time to time in guerrilla fights against police (burning cars has become a symbol), and feeding the fear of the rest of the population, as the results of the 2002 general election exemplify[6]. Social citizenship is at stake, and much has to be done to break this self-reinforcing spiral. Thus far, labour market and social policies – which have never specifically been targeted at EY – have had very few effective results. At the end of 2003, the Minister for Internal Affairs suggested (breaking with the long republican tradition of race relations in France) that an affirmative action policy should be introduced.This proposal outraged many people, President Chirac among them, because it does not fit the traditional French 'Republicanist' view. The High Council on integration, in a report published at the beginning of 2004, noted that adolescents of immigrant origin had been 'abandoned', but it is nevertheless opposed to affirmative action. Instead 'it favours positive mobilisation and promotion' based solely on merit (*The Guardian*, 27 January 2004, p 9).

Germany

Here, because again of the difficulties of collecting data, it is only possible to report some general patterns in educational, vocational and labour market integration. About 9% of permanent residents in Germany are foreigners, who are on average slightly younger (21% below 19 years old) than the German inhabitants (19% below 19 years old). Approximately 5% of the German inhabitants came into Germany as *Aussiedler*; again, this group is much younger than the German inhabitants (33% below 19).

However, German immigrants and foreign immigrants differ remarkably from the native Germans, according to general qualification patterns. Particularly in relation to the older ones, these findings could be explained by the duration of residence in Germany on the one hand, and the different cultural background of the home countries of foreigners on the other. Studies focusing on the second generation of young foreigners (born in Germany) show no evidence that their behaviour in terms of seeking qualifications converges with that of the majority. In fact, recent studies found evidence of increasing divergence. Arguments focus on the composition of the immigrant groups, which also causes second-generation effects (Riphahn and Serfling, 2002).

Even second-generation young foreigners perform more poorly than native Germans in the education system (at general and vocational qualification levels) and in the labour market. Particularly for second-generation young foreigners, this may not only be a question of mechanisms of inequality shaping participation in the qualification system and the labour market, but also a serious indicator of wastage of this specific group's capacities. In the following section, a short description of data regarding qualification and the labour market will be given, followed by some analytical results. These general findings will be placed alongside empirical findings concerning more disadvantaged young people.

Foreign young people's participation in the German school system differed markedly from that of young native Germans. While 32% of German school leavers reached low-level school certificates, 45% reached medium-level school certificates and 23% high-level certificates; 55% of young foreign school leavers, born in Germany

Table 7.2: Education and qualification (%)

Level of school-leaver's certificate	Germans	Foreigners[a]	Total
Low	31.7	54.8	31.9
Medium	44.9	28.2	44.8
High	23.4	17.0	23.3

Note: [a] Foreigners, born in Germany.

Sources: *Mikrozensus* (1997); Riphahn and Serfling (2002, Table 1)

(so-called 'second generation') only reached low-level certificates, 29% medium-level and 17% high-level general certificates (*Mikrozensus, 1997*; Riphahn and Serfling, 2002; see Table 7.2).

While, on average, 9% of all school leavers left school without even the lowest certificate, this proportion rises to 20% among all foreign pupils in Germany (Solga, 2002). Additionally, foreign pupils are remarkably over-represented at special schools for slow learners, a proportion increasing throughout the 1990s. This indicates that 'non-integrated' foreign pupils tend to be diverted from regular schools into special school institutions (Powel and Wagner, 2002, p 66).

German and foreign youth also differ with respect to vocational qualifications. While in 1998 only 11% of all 20- to 25-year-old Germans had not acquired a vocational degree, this is the case for 36% of all foreign people aged 20-25 years (Klemm, 2000, p 336, based on German census data 1998). In contrast, 66% of young Germans finished apprenticeship training in 2000, while only 38% of foreign young people did so that year (Beauftragte der Bundesregierung, 2002, p 45).

Focusing on the German labour market, empirical findings report strong ethnic background effects on inequality in acquired social status (Granato and Kalter, 2001). Three dimensions are relevant: who joins the labour force; what level of labour market status is achieved; and what level of income will be reached. The proportion of young people who have entered the labour force is correlated with age and nationality. Increasing labour market participation corresponds with education and training (including school-based and company-based vocational qualifications, eg apprenticeship training). From this point of view, labour market participation is based on the educational choice of young people, whereas higher educational attainment in this age group reduces labour force participation. Studies have also compared the experience of second-generation *Gastarbeiter* children with native-born Germans. According to this research, second-generation foreigners leave school and training earlier. However, as the unemployment risk is higher for

Table 7.3: Labour market status by nationality and age (%)

Labour market status	Germans			Foreigner (second-generation *Gastarbeiter*)		
	15-19	20-24	25-29	15-19	20-24	25-29
Education/training	88	33	9	82	23	5
Others out of labour force	2	11	9	3	12	18
Unemployed	2	6	6	4	14	13
Active labour force (employed)	1	50	75	10	51	64
Blue collar	54	37	32	71	64	58
White collar	37	51	55	22	32	34
Others employed	10	13	12	6	5	9

Source: German *Mikrozensus* (1998)

this group, the active labour market participation rate is similar to that of young Germans (Table 7.3).

In summary, young foreigners acquire lower levels of general and vocational qualifications, enter the labour force earlier and become established at a lower level of labour market status. Germans, by contrast, remain on average longer in the qualification system, reach a higher level of qualification, which then facilitates higher positions in the labour market. Given their labour market participation rate, Table 7.3 below shows strong differences and similarities in status. Thus, young foreigners show a higher proportion of blue-collar jobs than young Germans do. With increasing age groups, the share of white-collar jobs also increases.

According to Diefenbach (2002), however, young foreigners earn more in unqualified job positions than young Germans. Furthermore, net income differentials between unqualified, semi-qualified and qualified positions are much weaker for young foreigners than for young Germans. This could be resultant on selection processes within job positions, such that young foreigners reach better paid jobs but with more unstable and insecure working conditions in less recognised occupations, compared with those of young Germans. Furthermore, young foreigners join the workforce on average earlier, and accumulate more work experience, which affects their income.

The question arises as to whether qualification or discrimination underpins these results. According to Granato and Kalter (2001), discrimination, though significant, may be less influential than foreigners' under-investment in education. Even controlled for second-generation effects of young foreigners born in Germany or at least those who started primary schooling in Germany, this education effect explains most of the observed differences. Later on, Kalter and Granato

Table 7.4: Employment status after long-term unemployment (%)

Labour market status	Germans (without resettler)	Aussiedler (resettler)	Ausländer (foreigner)	Total
Still unemployed	14	12	21	15
Employment	43	43	53	45
Scheme participation	34	36	22	32
Out of labour force	9	8	4	8
Total	100	100	100	100

Source: Dietrich (2001a)

(2002) show that ongoing assimilation processes become weakened by demographic composition and educational behaviour. Following Diefenbach (2002), observable wage differences – themselves shaped by discrimination within the labour market – might be a strong argument for the educational decision making and observable under-investment in education even for second-generation foreigners.

In summary, the causal relation between educational attainment, educational choice, labour market expectation and job perspectives is still an ongoing question in Germany. Job orientation seems to be a more important factor for young foreigners than for young Germans or *Aussiedler*. Even young foreign unemployed people remain unemployed longer than others, waiting for a job opportunity. If and when they leave unemployment, a higher proportion becomes employed and a lower proportion enters a youth scheme or leaves the labour force (Dietrich, 2001a). Young *Aussiedler*, however, show the highest return rates to employment and to youth schemes (Table 7.4). Similar findings are shown for youth scheme participants (Dietrich, 2001b). Again foreign scheme participants are more strongly oriented to work and show a lower affinity to join another youth scheme or to leave the labour force (Dietrich, 2001b).

United Kingdom

Britain's minority ethnic population, about 8% of the total population, is dominated by those arriving since the 1950s, and originating from countries that were formerly British colonies. British minorities are concentrated in major urban centres, where older industrial sectors have borne the brunt of recession and the international restructuring of capital resulted in higher rates of unemployment. The evidence demonstrates, notwithstanding difficulties caused by the failure of most official agencies to engage in ethnic monitoring, that some minority ethnic groups are more likely, in some cases very much more likely, to be in poverty and on the margins of society, than the population at large. This evidence is drawn from qualitative studies, from 2001 census data that now offer a more appropriate ethnic classification, and from quantitative datasets such as the Labour Force Survey.

This ethnic marginalisation is the result of a combination of factors, including high unemployment (Pakistani and Bangladeshi rates for both men and women being three to five times as high as for white people throughout the 1990s), low levels of economic activity among women, low pay (Platt and Noble, 1999) and structural discrimination. Levels of competence in the English language are generally lower among Pakistani and Bangladeshi groups, and especially women (Modood et al, 1997), a result in part of cultural norms. Their disadvantage continues as they reach the age of labour market entry: Pakistanis and Bangladeshis with degrees are as likely to be in poverty as white people with no qualifications (Chahal, 2000). Discrimination affects the way in which people are selected for jobs or made redundant (Parekh, 2000); minorities are more likely to be working in low-paid jobs, partly as a result of more wide-ranging discrimination against minorities; and they have more limited access to adequate health and housing provision (PIU, 2002). Increasing restrictions on the ability of refugees and asylum seekers to access help from social assistance puts them particularly at risk. The social security system as a whole has failed to address the issue of the greater poverty of minority ethnic groups. Young black people represent a particularly problematic group since many of them have 'disappeared', due to structural racial discrimination, from official data (Chatrik et al, 2000).

Although most minority young people stay on in education post-16 (the earliest school-leaving age), African Caribbean young men take longer to achieve qualifications than white young people and fewer achieve qualifications at all levels. By the time young men reach the labour market, disadvantage is considerable: when the unemployment rate for young white men was one in eight, for young Africans, African Caribbeans, Pakistanis and Bangladeshis it was one in three. Young African Caribbean men were found to be twice as likely to be unemployed as white counterparts with the same level of educational attainment, and more vulnerable to unemployment during recession (Berthoud, 1999).

There are also significant differences among women in terms of labour market careers: "... while minority ethnic women in non-manual occupations have similar longitudinal occupational profiles to white women, those in manual occupations fare worse than their white counterparts, despite the fact that a larger proportion of minority ethnic women are in full-time employment" (Holdsworth and Dale, 1997, p 435).

Minority ethnic women are more likely to be in paid work because of poverty (although there are variations between groups because of, for example, the impact of religious customs and the lack of local childcare facilities) but are also more likely to be in poorly paid work and to lose their jobs because of employers' discriminatory practices.

Labour market opportunities for young people in the UK changed dramatically during the 1980s, a result of both economic restructuring and the requirements of employers, who sought more qualified and skilled workers. Young people themselves responded in part to these changes, to limitation of their access to social assistance benefit and to housing market changes, by staying on in further and higher education in greater numbers and by extending, in various ways, their transition from dependence to full social and economic independence (Craig, 1991; Jones, 2002). Jones suggests that staying on may be as much to do with the lack of attractive alternatives but in any case, as Pitcher notes (2002, p 474), "... despite the guarantee of a place in youth training, a significant proportion of young people leaving full-time education at the age of 16 have been without any job or place in education or government-sponsored training". Minorities, and other characteristically marginalised groups, tend to be over-represented among this excluded population. Attempts to rebrand such programmes and improve the quality of training have not been particularly successful. Jones suggests that, in these circumstances, the "youth labour market increasingly becomes a market for less-qualified labour" (2002, p 8) and, citing Bynner et al's (2002: especially Chapter Six) research, that "despite the longest sustained period of economic growth in the last 30 years and a massive decline in the numbers of young people available for work, a 'core' of unemployment among young people remains stubbornly present".

The 1997 New Labour government's major recent policy instrument for dealing with the social and economic exclusion of young people has been the Connexions strategy (www.connexions.gov.uk). This followed some years of political debate generated by research about the position of potentially marginal young people (see, for example, Istance et al, 1994; Istance and Williamson, 1996; Armstrong, 1997; Williamson, 1997). This research coined the phrase 'status zero' for those not in the identifiable statuses of education, employment or training. The 1997 government introduced a series of major policy changes to enable young people to be assisted into the mainstream of society including the New Deal for Young People (Chatrik and

Convery, 2000). This provided young people aged between 18 and 25 with four alternative routes into full labour market participation, through education and training, direct employment, voluntary sector activities, or through work on an environmental taskforce. An evaluation of the New Deal suggests that most young people in full-time education and training are "failing to win jobs or achieve qualifications at the end of it" (*The Guardian*, 31 July 2002, p 8), a criticism even more apposite in relation to minority ethnic young people.

One of the more general policy instruments of the Labour government in relation to issues of poverty and deprivation was the creation of the Social Exclusion Unit (SEU) in 1997. Given that the position of young people had not been the subject of much significant political debate during the early 1990s, and even where there had been political pressure, there had been little policy change, it was surprising that much of the SEU's early work focused on aspects of the welfare of young people (Coles, 2000b). The SEU's reports have acted, however, to focus attention effectively on this group and particularly on the position of 'status zero' young people or 'NEET' (not in education, employment or training), the government's own acronym for this group (SEU, 1999). The 1999 SEU report provided a long-term agenda for change in a number of policy areas, the most significant being the establishment of a new 'youth support service', Connexions. The SEU analysis raised familiar issues. Only about 20% of those within the NEET category became so immediately on leaving school, with substantial numbers 'dropping out' either from training or, more substantially, from employment or from further education. Young people who became NEET often did so on an intermittent basis, moving in and out of engagement over a period of years.

The SEU concluded that non-participation aged 16 was the single most powerful predictor of later unemployment, and for young women early motherhood often led to non-participation in the labour market. Excluded young people were again found to be concentrated in areas of substantial unemployment and deprivation and young people from minority ethnic communities particularly prone to poverty. Those from African Caribbean, Bangladeshi and Pakistani communities were over-represented in the NEET category.

The Connexions service was intended by government to provide "advice, guidance, support and personal development, differentiated according to need, to help them overcome barriers to participation in learning and work, and help them achieve a successful transition from their teenage years into adult life" (CYPU, 2001, p 3). The new service was intended to be a wide-ranging one for all young people, delivered not only through schools and further education colleges but by training providers and employers, Youth Offending Teams (established under criminal justice legislation), local authority social services departments, and community and voluntary sector projects. However, although Connexions was intended to be comprehensive (DfEE, 2000), it was simultaneously to give priority attention to the most vulnerable young people.

The Connexions approach is intended to be linked to much better systems of mapping and tracking young people (Craig et al, 1999; Green et al, 2000), felt to be necessary to enable all young people (and especially the vulnerable and at risk) to be identified, engaged at an early age, take an active part in career planning and have their progress monitored. Such a system would also, it was argued, begin to address the problems with data (where most data collected on young people tended to be static and short term). It would develop a system centrally dependent on the work of personal advisors, to one of whom each young person would be attached between the ages of 13 and 19. Personal Advisors would be the vehicle for young people to obtain all the forms of help necessary for their personal development. Other related provisions included the introduction of a Connexions ('smart') Card, which, it was hoped, would help young people access free public transport and discounts in some youth consumer markets. Educational Maintenance Allowances were introduced to give financial assistance to some 16- to 17-year-olds wishing to stay on at school who might otherwise be unable to do so, and government proposed subsidies to encourage young people to stay at school to study A-levels, following research that attempted to quantify the cost of their social exclusion (Godfrey et al, 2002).

As the Connexions scheme was being introduced, a study of the experience of black, white and Asian young people leaving school and entering the labour market focused on the experience of those likely to fall into the NEET category (Britton et al, 2002). This study estimated the size of the NEET population. In-depth interviews with young people were undertaken in two multi-ethnic fieldwork sites, two thirds of the interview respondents being non-white. The study found:

- there were significant numbers of 16- to 17-year-olds disengaged from education, employment and training – the numbers of these were substantially greater than government estimates;
- many of these young people were unknown to official agencies such as the Careers Service and a disproportionate number were

from minority ethnic groups: this reflected a failure of these agencies effectively to monitor take-up of their services by minorities or to engage in effective outreach work;

- young people who had been in public care institutions were greatly over-represented in the sample as a whole and, again, among these, young people from minorities were over-represented;
- nearly half the sample had been excluded from school and many had begun to drop out of education of their own accord at an early age: an earlier SEU report (SEU, 1998) had demonstrated the association between school exclusion and particular ethnic groups, notably African Caribbean young men;
- disengagement from school often coincided with incidents at home, including abuse, bereavement, threats of arranged marriages (for Muslim young women) and other traumatic events that appeared to have gone unnoticed by schools or professionals;
- minority ethnic young people had often experienced discrimination in school and/or in care. Again, official agencies appeared to have been unable to respond adequately to racial diversity; and
- local voluntary sector agencies were often the only agencies in effective contact with these young people. This was most true of those from minority ethnic groups.

These findings identify issues of discrimination affecting each key stage of the young people's movement from school into the labour market: in school, in care or within the family, during the process of leaving school, and in their attempts to access employment, further education or training. They provide a strong challenge to the Connexions policy goal of being accessible to the most vulnerable young people. In particular the researchers' conclusions were that better mapping and tracking systems were needed to locate and stay in touch with young people (emphasising one goal of Connexions) and much better ethnic monitoring would be required to keep in touch with minority young people. There would also need to be stronger emphasis on less formal voluntary and community sector agencies, especially those based in multi-ethnic areas, if outreach were to be effective (a suggestion which Connexions has yet to adopt wholeheartedly); that every agency continued to need to address issues of discrimination within its own policy, structures and programmes; and that there needed to be much better collaboration between the various agencies aiming to work with young people. In particular, formal agencies needed to learn from those agencies, often staffed by minorities, trusted by minority young people. The broader conclusion, that discrimination strongly affects the prospects of minorities entering and within the labour market has now been echoed by a wider analysis undertaken on behalf of the UK government (PIU, 2002).

Recent research (Coles, 2003) on the Connexions service suggests that it has yet to resolve the tensions between being a universal and a targeted service; and there are continuing difficulties in making partnership working an effective reality between a variety of differing (and sometimes competing) agencies on the ground. Most critically, in relation to the theme of this chapter, there is very limited evidence that the service is focusing effectively on the needs of black and minority ethnic young people or addressing the institutional racial discrimination that has limited their choices.

Conclusion

This evidence suggests that many minority ethnic young people within these three countries are disenfranchised from the benefits of citizenship – regardless of how it is defined – because of the failure of national policy and service frameworks to address discrimination against minorities within the institutions of the labour market. There is no reason to believe that the experience of minorities within other European countries will be any more encouraging (Craig, 2002). Research findings from the countries reviewed here show that ethnicity is clearly a key factor in shaping both individual choices and institutional responses – and the interplay between them – within the context of the labour market. The evidence paints a generally dismal picture of the inability of national governments to provide effective support for minority young people – in terms of educational opportunity at all levels, training and vocational support or access to the labour market. Perhaps of equal concern, despite some important studies, the level and overall quality of research is also generally low, often impeded by the way in which data can be collected and analysed, thus further disadvantaging minority young people.

There is clearly a range of important issues raised by this discussion that need further investigation both at national and European levels, especially as the EU itself is substantially enlarged. First, we have to recognise that, in the context of the increasing heterogeneity of national populations (facilitated by the free movement of labour within the EU), the social and economic trajectories of differing minorities may be increasingly divergent; some minorities may do considerably worse than others. Indeed, some minorities perform better than the 'host' population, such as the Chinese in the UK. Second, it is clear that the impact of culture is also increasingly apparent, both in terms of the choices made by different minorities as, for example, between work (however poorly rewarded) and education, and in terms of the differential opportunities available to, or limitations and expectations imposed upon, young men and young women. There is also a very important gender dimension to citizenship that has barely begun to be explored for minorities. Third, although there is some evidence to suggest that later generations of minority ethnic young people do better than their predecessors, the absolute position of minority young people appears in many cases to be deteriorating. This may not be surprising in the face of increasing levels of xenophobia (particularly since the events of 11 September 2001) and discrimination against minorities, especially Islamic groups, but it suggests that national governments and the EU cannot simply sit back and wait for time to take its course. The task of confronting discrimination against young minority people entering the labour market is now an even more urgent task than it has been previously. More research is needed but this task is hampered by the poor quality of data on ethnicity and the lack of preparedness of many governments to collect it effectively.

Finally, there remains a critical – and politically sensitive task – for all governments to review the meaning of citizenship in the context of increasing global movements of populations. Citizenship hitherto has been both an inclusive and exclusive term, offered by 'us' to those 'others' arriving within the boundaries of nation states, often in the context of assimilationist policies, where migrants would be expected to surrender their culture in return for the benefits of citizenship or would otherwise remain on the margins of the social, political and economic lives of nations. In the present context, of continuing but increasingly diverse migration patterns, of the weakening of the economic boundaries between nations within Europe, and of the justified refusal of migrants to surrender many important aspects of their own culture, neither approach is appropriate – if they ever were. The development of diverse multicultural societies requires a new political settlement with migrant populations, one that acknowledges a common core of human values and rights, respects difference and diversity, but includes a recognition that they have equal rights to effective and dignified participation in the labour market. This is needed both because of the importance of offering substantive common human rights to all, and also because of the enormous economic potential that is currently wasted among Europe's young minorities.

Notes

[1] It is interesting to note that the 'right of blood', which was adopted in Prussia 40 years later, and which is still predominant in Germany, was directly inspired by the French '*code civil*'.

[2] This section draws on a longer analysis (see Craig, 2002). The term discrimination is used here as common in all three countries studied, but the term racial discrimination would be as commonly used in the UK.

[3] In 1998, there was a controversial debate in newspapers about a new statistical survey held by two national institutes, which included more details on ethnic and national origins.

[4] In the 1920s, the immigration rate was higher in France than in the US. In 1930 there were 515 immigrants for every 10,000 inhabitants in France, compared with 492 in the US. After the Second World War, many immigrants came from southern Europe – eg Spain and Portugal – and from the former colonial empire – mainly from North Africa, eg Algeria.

[5] These are mainly the children – in some cases, the grandchildren – of immigrants arriving in France during the 1960s.

[6] The far right party Front National candidate reached the second round of the presidential election, eliminating the socialist candidate. The rise of delinquency – mainly attributed to EY – had become the main issue during the campaign, and has come to the top of the political agenda of the new right-wing government.

EIGHT

Activation or alienation: youth unemployment within different European welfare communities

Jan Carle and Torild Hammer

Introduction

What we would like to explore in this chapter is the possibility of discussing political behaviour among young unemployed people within the framework of theories of welfare, citizenship and trust. The argument for this discussion is based on four different explanatory perspectives often used within research on youth unemployment. One perspective explores unemployment as a *statistical phenomenon*. Within this context young people's political views, attitudes and actions are mainly understood on the basis of the numbers of unemployed and the duration of unemployment. The second sort of explanation focuses on *young people's life situation*, putting the emphasis on the influence gender, age and social class have on political attitudes and activity. Third, explanations dealing with *welfare states* put emphasis on the role different welfare arrangements have in shaping different life situations among unemployed people and how different possibilities within the welfare system then create different attitudes and political behaviour. Finally, the *risk agenda* deals with how people's awareness and feelings of distrust in political structures generate new political attitudes and new ways of expressing them.

The main questions we would like to discuss in relations to these different explanatory frameworks are:

• What type of political channels do young people use?
• Do young unemployed people have a feeling of trust in the political system?
• Do they trust the traditional political channels for exercising political influence or not?

Dataset and methods

To discuss these questions further, we will use a dataset from a study carried out in 10 different European countries. Marginalisation was the leading concept in the study, and the aim was to study the degree to which different labour market positions correlate with other social circumstances in the lives of young people (further details concerning the study can be found in Hammer, 2003b). The study was carried out in three major steps, in the Nordic countries in 1996, Scotland in 1997/98 (together with Ireland, which is not included in the discussion here) and in 1999/2000 in France, Germany, Italy and Spain. In all countries a representative sample was drawn from national unemployment registers. The study was based on young people who had experienced three months' continuous unemployment and explored what had happened to them six to 12 months thereafter. A number of questions dealt with political attitudes and behaviour. The differences in political attitudes are measured by a left–right scale. In the questionnaire the respondents were asked, "Where would you put your own political opinions?". They were then asked to tick in one of six different boxes 'definitely to the left', 'somewhat to the left', 'neither left nor right', 'somewhat to the right', 'definitely to the right' and, finally, 'I have no political opinion'. This type of scale has been widely used in different comparative studies within Europe.

We also asked questions about participation in political actions and willingness or reluctance to participate. Respondents were asked about their involvement in several pre-specified political actions on three illustrative levels: whether they had engaged in a stated political action; could imagine carrying out a stated action; or absolutely could not imagine carrying out a stated action. This type of technique has also been used in international as well as national studies (for example, Eurobarometer). The following actions were covered in our study:

- signing a petition;
- taking part in boycotts;
- taking part in legal demonstrations;
- taking part in wildcat/illegal strikes;
- occupying buildings or factories;
- wearing a pin to show support for a cause;
- voting;
- attending meetings organised by a political party;
- attending meetings organised by a union organisation;
- attending meetings organised by other organisations.

Along with the questions about political attitudes and political participation, the questionnaire contained questions on social support, work experience and education, unemployment experiences, financial situation, health situation and experiences of labour market schemes. It is also important to know that at the time of the questionnaire some of the young people were still unemployed, whereas others were in employment, some in education or on schemes, with a few engaged in other activities, such as military service or childcare.

Theoretical perspectives and previous research

The concepts of political action and political participation refer to a wide range of different social and cultural aspects and historical changes. One can refer to the most obvious aspects within western democracies: collective bodies organised as political parties and individual actions to take a stand and vote in elections. However, one can also refer to other forms of collective bodies and actions often referred to as 'new social movements', such as the green movement, feminist movement or branches of youth movement in the 1960s. It is not that clear if these movements, either in a theoretical or empirical sense, should or could be seen as political movements, because the intentions of the actors in these movements are not in the first place to exercise political power, but to develop new ways of expressing social and cultural expectations. However, these new forms of social action enforced society to think about influence and power in new and different paths. The aim of this article, though, is not to discuss these concepts in general and in such a broad sense, but to discuss them in relation to youth in general and youth unemployment in particular. However, as a point of departure we would like to use Lukes' (1976) concept of power to draw some lines in our discussion.

In our opinion it is possible to discuss aspects of political actions by using his theory about the three faces of power (Lukes, 1976). The first face of power concerns taking part in situations where formal choices and actual decisions are made. This is the feature of exercising power that is articulated in political and democratic assemblies and contexts. The second face of power deals with how citizens bring issues to the political agenda, and with what opportunities exist to do so. The third aspect describes how, behind opinions about important social issues, there are interests that are rooted in social and cultural conditions. In this context power deals with the extent to which an interest − for example, in environmental action within the green movement − can be traced to the conflicts of interest that arise from people's social origin, gender, age, generational affiliation and occupational situation. If we follow the line of environmental support as an illustrative example, it is about the possibility of showing how a social or economic question is linked to people becoming interested in such a question as a political matter (to use different power channels in order to make specific changes possible). It can also be linked to different structures of political participation (using different channels to exercise power) that vary according to different social, cultural and welfare structures. This discussion returns to debates on new social movements, and a widespread view that, compared to adults, young people in general are more interested in and active within social and political activities focused on the problems of late modernity (such as environmental questions); and that young people are more active in these new social movements because they can offer a new set of political actions and structures (Furlong and Cartmel, 1997). One interesting question is whether there is a general trend involving all young people, or if the power of the old social structures means that political activity even within new social movements is structured by the expressions of the old social structures, social class and gender inequalities within the economy and labour market.

We draw on a Swedish study to explore this further (Carle, 2000a). The clearest differences of opinion towards environmental issues are in regard to social background and differences that have to do with welfare and economy. Young people with higher education, from higher social groups, and who have established themselves in society with work and their own homes, are generally also more interested in and committed to social issues – and the same is true for environmental issues. Young people who have lower levels of education and are in paid work display a positive attitude toward the welfare state, whereas the young with higher education who are studying have positive opinions about diverse issues of solidarity, internationalism and the environment. This difference between the two groups also emerges in their political conduct regarding the environment: the former are more inclined toward actions and collective participation, and the latter toward facts and forming opinions, working through organisations and practising what one preaches.

Opinions about the environment are chiefly influenced by gender but, to a certain extent, also by class affiliation. This applies to opinions about environmental issues, to the performance of environmental actions, and to acting politically in the environmental area. Again, it applies to which knowledge one thinks one has, and seeks to obtain, concerning the environment. While young people's class affiliation may not determine their opinion on any specific question, behind their opinions on diverse environmental problems lie different perceptions of how rapidly they want to pursue environmental work, which types of measures they consider best, and how they think they have acquired knowledge about the environmental issue – all of which vary with their class affiliation.

The environmental issue is thus a class issue, and in that sense clearly linked to unemployment and welfare. It is possible to find at least two different types of views and practices on environmental issues. Among the *knowledge-oriented reformists*, we find those with higher education, in social groups one and two, and who are active in politics and associations, with an interest in solidarity and welfare, leaning slightly toward the political left. They see themselves as possessing knowledge in environmental matters, and they actively seek ways of increasing this knowledge for their own sakes as well as society's. They are young people who use many types of channels for influence, but who also consider personal responsibility, individual action and opinion building to be the best means of influence in environmental issues.

The *action-oriented radicals* comprise groups of young people with partially distinct social circumstances as a background. They are a mixture from social groups two and (especially) three, with lower levels of education or still in the educational system. They are not active in politics or associations except for environmental purposes. They lean clearly toward the left and advocate more laws, rules and bans, believing that environmental work must be pursued more rapidly and radically than is currently the case. Thus, we can expect that conflicts in the future will centre upon political forms of action, since opinions about various environmental problems are basically rather similar between these two groups.

A line of this discussion has to do with the idea that young people are more active in new social movements because they offer new ways of expressing political matters and exercising power and influence. But our data show that the picture is somewhat more complicated. Opinions about the environmental issue as a social issue are weakly related to gender, age, educational level, social group and employment. This is in sharp contrast to opinions about welfare issues, which are strongly related to social circumstances – especially social group, education and employment. If we compare young people and adults, or compare internally within youth groups, a pattern is visible throughout: the environmental issue is evaluated more positively by women, the young, the better educated, social groups one and two, and young people who are undergoing education.

But the pictures change when it comes to actions. Adults, elderly people, women, and older generations perform environmental actions more often than young people, men and younger generations. Among the young, women claim to perform such actions more frequently, and we find connections with social circumstances that indicate that the will to perform environmental actions is related to social circumstances.

Women are more active than men in trying to exert political influence in environmental matters. Women are especially more active as regards participation in networks and taking indirect measures, while men are more active in politics and organisations. Less than 10% of the young men and women have participated in any of the political actions on environmental issues that are defined as more demanding, and the difference between genders is smaller there. Analysis also shows that both the better educated and the higher social groups prove to be somewhat more active in exerting influence, while the less educated and unemployed are more active in opinion building and demonstrating.

If we put these results within the context of unemployment, we would expect that according to Marshall's argument (1973), social rights should be a strong condition for active political participation. However, those who criticise Marshall's argument believe that the opposite may be true. Generous welfare provision may create welfare dependency, which may be associated with political passivity and alienation. Third, as shown above, there might be some new as well as old links between opinions, actions and social structures that can qualify the discussions on the links between unemployment and the sphere of power and political actions.

In accordance with previous research, we would expect lower political participation in all kinds of activity among long-term unemployed youth in all countries. The next question is whether such political marginalisation expresses alienation or opposition. Alienation would indicate mistrust towards political authorities and could be expressed by active objections to participating in regular political activities such as voting in elections, and probably less interest in politics. On the other hand, political opposition could be expressed through participation in 'irregular' political activities and objections to 'regular' political participation (further discussion later). If young unemployed people are more politically marginalised compared with young people in education or work, another interesting question is whether there is a basis for political mobilisation among those unemployed. What kind of attitudes do unemployed youth have towards different types of political activities? It is important to stress that we cannot draw any conclusions about whether or not political marginalisation or alienation is caused by unemployment. However, we will argue that it is interesting in itself to explore the relationship between, for example, political activity and financial deprivation and social exclusion among unemployed young people. To participate in politics may be a social phenomenon, indicating that those who experience social isolation will have a lower level of activity. It is reasonable to assume that irregular political activity will depend upon participation in specific youth cultures. Low levels of activity among long-term unemployed youth may therefore be explained by social marginalisation. Employment has important integrative functions and long-term unemployed youth may experience social isolation as well as financial marginalisation. It is also well documented that unemployed youth report more mental health problems than those in employment. Such problems may be related to withdrawal and political passivity.

On the macro level and when it comes to policy matters, different countries within Europe have handled the unemployment problem in different ways, with regard to both labour market measures and welfare policy. An interesting question is what kind of consequences different welfare arrangements have for unemployed young people and their citizenship. Unemployment benefits have been withdrawn from young people under 18 years of age in Britain. This is important since about 30% of the cohort end their formal education at the age of 16. Moreover, the New Deal programme (see Chapter Two) implies that all young people must be in training or studying in order to receive benefits. British researchers have questioned whether the withdrawal of benefits for young unemployed people is a withdrawal of citizenship rights (MacDonald, 1997). However, in a previous paper based on comparative analyses of countries in northern Europe, Hammer (2002) found that public support based on different regimes of social protection of unemployed youth could not explain differences in political participation. Those who were entitled to unemployment benefits did not have a higher level of political activity than those dependent on the less generous social assistance or other means-tested benefits.

It is reasonable to assume that the affected group of young unemployed people might respond to unemployment with mistrust towards the political system. However, the important question is whether there is a basis for political mobilisation of this group. Research seems to indicate that this is not the case. In areas with very high youth unemployment, such as southern Europe, interest in politics among young people, both unemployed and employed, was no greater than it was in countries with a lower youth unemployment rate (Bay and Blekesaune, 2002). However, unemployed youth in Europe have a stronger left-wing orientation than employed youth (Bay and Blekesaune, 2002). These results are in accordance with our survey from northern Europe (Carle, 2000b). According to some researchers, though, there is no clear evidence that unemployment produces alienation from politics (de Witte, 1992; Griffin, 1993; Furlong and Cartmel, 1997; Rantakeisu et al, 1996; Wallace and Kovatcheva, 1998). It is not really clear if experience or duration of unemployment engenders higher sympathies with the left or right on the political scale. Both trends are reported in research (Furlong and Cartmel, 1997; Wallace and Kovatcheva, 1998). In some studies there is evidence suggesting that unemployment does not influence young people's political behaviour at all. Instead, it seems that other factors besides unemployment play an important role and interplay with people's political activity – for example, gender, family background, social class, origin of birth within and outside the country (Furlong and Cartmel, 1997; Wallace and Kovatcheva, 1998). Different aspects of active and passive labour market policies in combination with family support, friends and acquaintances also play an important role (Lazaridis and Koumandraki, 2001).

Participation in different political actions

Table 8.1 shows the percentage of the young people in the study who reported participating in different types of political activity[1].

The table shows that 82% have participated in an election but only 5% have occupied buildings. Participation in elections is lower in Scotland and Germany. Behind these figures, we can also witness a well-known pattern: the percentage voting in elections increases with age. Our data show the effect of the low participation rate among first voters (73% among 18- to 19-year-olds and 85% among 20- to 24-year-olds). If we look at employment status, we find the lowest voting rate among the unemployed (77%) and the highest among those in education (88%), and this pattern persists even if we take age into consideration. Participation in elections is slightly lower in relation to experience of unemployment, but the differences are not great: 85% among those with one to six months of unemployment experience participated in elections compared with 80% among those unemployed for more than three years. This poses an important challenge to any

Table 8.1: Participation in political action, by country (%)

	All	Italy	Spain	Iceland	Sweden	Denmark	Norway	Scotland	Finland	Germany
Voted in elections	82	87	86	86	85	89	83	68	80	70
Signed a petition	55	30	63	61	74	59	63	60	46	38
Attended organisations' meetings	18	30	22	26	18	19	18	18	11	4
Carried badge	19	10	24	34	15	21	26	43	9	6
Taken part in official strike	12	36	31	12	15	14	15	11	6	5
Taken part in boycott or strike	14	10	7	19	26	22	16	14	11	5
Attended political meetings	14	20	21	19	12	13	14	11	4	14
Taken part in demonstration	15	47	39	2	2	2	3	2	1	21
Attended union meetings	12	6	10	15	17	27	16	8	5	9
Occupied factories, etc	5	36	3	1	1	1	2	4	1	1
Mean of action	2.5	3.1	2.9	2.7	2.6	2.6	2.5	2.3	1.7	1.7

Note: The figures on Italy are somewhat obscure and this has to do with the way some of the questions were asked. They should be regarded with caution.

idea that duration of unemployment has significant effects on political behaviour.

Besides voting, the young people have in ranked order 'signed a petition', 'worn a badge', 'attended other organisations' meetings', 'taken part in demonstrations', 'taken part in boycotts or strikes', 'attended political meetings', 'attended union meetings' and finally 'occupied factories, etc'. In all cases but signing petitions the overall participation rates are low, with less than one fifth of respondents participating. There are some major and interesting national variations. The figures for taking part in official strikes and in demonstrations are considerably higher in Italy and Spain compared with all the other countries, perhaps reflecting the volatile nature of Mediterranean politics.

The general impression is that participating is higher in Mediterranean and Scandinavian countries with the notable exception of Finland; participation is lowest in Scotland, Germany and Finland. To check out this impression, we made an index that was a total mean of all the different actions (index value from minimum 1 to maximum 10). The countries divide into three groups: Finland and Germany clearly below overall mean, Italy and Spain above overall mean and the rest of the countries close to the overall mean.

So what about the question of types of activities favoured by unemployed youth? As indicated earlier, it is possible to split these different actions in two groups:

Regular political activities:

- voting in elections (82%);
- attending meetings organised by a political party (14%);
- attending meetings organised by a trade union (12%);
- attending meetings organised by other organisations (18%).

Irregular political activities:

- signing a petition (55%);
- taking part in boycotts or strike (14%);
- taking part in legal demonstrations (15%);
- occupying buildings or factories (5%);
- wearing a badge to show support for a cause (19%).

This typology is based on theoretical arguments that suggest that disadvantaged and disaffected people are more likely to become distrustful of regular political processes and take to more militant types of activity. On the basis of this, one would expect a very low participation rate among unemployed young people within regular activities and a high participation rate within irregular activities. However, that does not prove to be the case among our respondents. It is important to stress that young unemployed people are in fact active within regular political activities. Within each category there is one main activity, voting in elections (regular) and signing a petition (irregular). Perhaps these types of activities might be viewed as representing a current political action 'habitus'. Further exploration (based on factor analysis) does not, however, support this type of reasoning. Instead, taking part in demonstrations, occupying factories and taking part in strikes fall within one cluster while all the other action types fall into a second category.

However, our data do not support the idea that unemployment forces young people to be more militant in order to be heard on the political scene, even if it is possible to find indications of higher activity within militant actions among those who have faced long-term unemployment. Nonetheless, the data also show lower activity among the long-term unemployed; passivity then seems to be more accurate as a characterisation of the political behaviour of this group than militancy.

Economic and social hardship

According to Marshall's argument, social rights should be a condition for active political participation. As the Scandinavian countries have the most generous welfare arrangements, we should expect higher political activity among unemployed youth in these countries than in countries with more residual welfare arrangements such as Britain. In Britain, unemployed youth receive the Jobseeker's Allowance, which is a flat-rate benefit and rather low compared with the Scandinavian countries. They are not entitled to any other support, except housing benefits in the case of those young people who are not living with their parents.

In contrast, young unemployed people in Scandinavia who have previous work experience receive unemployment benefits, which typically cover 60-90% of their previous income. Those among unemployed youth who do not have any work experience are only entitled to social assistance, which is much lower. Social assistance is means tested and not related to previous income.

The question is how financial marginalisation is related to political marginalisation, both theoretically as well as empirically. Financial deprivation may mobilise young people politically, in order to get access to different social rights and benefits – for example, housing. However, research has revealed that the long-term unemployed participate less in politics than the short-term unemployed (Carle, 2003), and this group also experiences greater economic hardship (Hammer and Julkunen, 2003). Whether long-term unemployment is related to financial problems will be dependent on young peoples' citizenship rights in different welfare regimes in Europe. As discussed in earlier chapters, Gallie and Paugam (2000) have developed a typology of welfare regimes based on various protection systems for the unemployed in Europe. The sub-protective model is dominant in the south of Europe and entails very incomplete coverage and a low level of support. The liberal model, as is found in the UK, has incomplete coverage and a low level of support. The employment-centred model dominant in France and Germany provides a higher level of support than the liberal model, but exclusively for those who are already established in the labour market. Dominant in Scandinavia is the universalistic model with a high level of support, a high degree of coverage and a very active labour market policy.

In our study it is possible to find some correlations between hardship and political activity and attitudes. Comparing unemployed youth in Spain, Italy, Germany, France, Finland, Scotland, Sweden, Denmark and Norway, we found that Scottish and Finnish youth have the highest level of deprivation and are also among the countries with the lowest level of political activity (Hammer and Carle, 2004). However, Scottish and Finnish young unemployed people were more willing to participate in politics in the future than young people in the other countries. The results may indicate that these young people can be mobilised politically. Moreover, it is interesting that there were no differences between participation in regular and irregular activities. In other words, irregular political activities do not mobilise young unemployed people any more than regular activities. Those who vote or attend political meetings also have a higher probability of participating in demonstrations, signing petitions and so on.

It is important to underline that the level of deprivation and the unemployment career explained some of the variance in political activity. The excluded group of long-term unemployed had a lower probability of participating, when controlled for political attitudes, deprivation and social marginalisation in all countries. Their lack of interest in politics could also be explained as an active objection to participating in politics, although the effect was rather weak.

The argument that welfare dependency may be related to political withdrawal and passivity had some support in the data. Social assistance clients in all the Nordic countries, as well as those receiving housing benefits in Scotland, reported less interest in politics, less political participation through regular political channels and a higher reluctance to participate. However, social assistance recipients had a higher participation in irregular political activity, if they had a left-wing political orientation, compared with other unemployed youth across countries. Generally, social assistance clients reported a stronger left-wing orientation than other unemployed youth. These results are indeed interesting, because some research indicates otherwise, that unemployment is associated with right-wing activity (Björgö 1997). Moreover, it does provide some evidence of deprivation increasing militancy.

Previous research has documented that both irregular and regular political activity is higher among young people with higher education and shorter duration of unemployment (Carle, 2003). Since social assistance clients in all the countries have lower levels of education, a higher rate of school drop-out and longer duration of unemployment than other unemployed youth, we would have expected different results. However, social assistance clients also reported a higher degree of financial hardship than other unemployed youth. It is probably this factor that mobilises this group politically. Those who reported financial problems had a significantly higher participation in irregular political activities than other unemployed youth. The lower participation in regular political activity among social assistance recipients, combined with a higher participation through irregular political channels, may also indicate political opposition and distrust in the formal political system. In other words, the results do not support any simple relationship between political and financial marginalisation. We would have expected that those who received benefits in countries with a very generous compensation level would have a higher level of political participation, but this is not the case.

It is difficult to draw any conclusions about the relationship between welfare regimes and political participation. However, it seems clear that the generous welfare model found in Scandinavia does not increase political participation to such a degree as one might expect. The sub-protective model in the south of Europe is actually more protective when it comes to unemployed young people (which might be explained by a higher degree of family support) and they had a higher level of activity compared with other unemployed young people. A reasonable conclusion seems to be that a high level of deprivation, such as in Finland and Scotland, increases political passivity, and so does long-term unemployment, which in these countries is strongly related to deprivation (Hammer and Julkunen, 2003), although, as we have seen, there is also a slight tendency to favour irregular political responses.

The results do not seem to support the notion that generous welfare benefits create political passivity or alienation. Deprivation seems to increase the probability of political participation in countries with more generous protection of unemployed young people. In Scotland, which represents a liberal model of support, or in Finland, with a very low level of support, political disinterest and passivity are more dominant.

In conclusion, different welfare models and protection systems in different countries were not clearly related to the level of political participation among unemployed youth. However, we find some evidence of a relationship between welfare dependency and political disinterest and passivity. Contrary to expectations, we found higher political activity in people dependent on welfare who had a left-wing political orientation, but such activity was outside the formal political system (Hammer, 2002). However, the evidence from our data and that of other researchers is not as clearcut as it is often expressed in the public debate (which suggests either that the unemployed will take to the streets or that they are totally disaffiliated from all political activity). For example, Bay and Blekesaune's study (2002) using 1990 Eurobarometer data suggests that the development of the welfare state does not appear to be that crucial for political confidence and political activity among young unemployed people. On the other hand, these results seem to be in contrast with the general theoretical discussion on the importance of a welfare state.

The relationship between long-term unemployment and political marginalisation may have different explanations. It is possible that less involvement in politics can be explained by the consequences of unemployment, such as withdrawal from society or social exclusion. However, other factors like stigmatisation or financial marginalisation may also reinforce such processes. On the other hand, political activity may be explained primarily by political orientation and attitudes. European surveys have shown that unemployed youth have a stronger left-wing orientation than young employed people, but it is hard to see how this would indicate a lower level of activity (Hammer and Carle, 2004). One explanation falls back on the concept of trust.

Trust

A well-known argument in western societies is that today we are witnessing a decline in trust among people towards the traditional political system. This arises from the belief that actors within the traditional political system are unwilling to listen to and to follow the will and the voice of the people. Across Europe, such distrust is seen to lead to political upheavals (for example, the rise of some right-wing politicians such as Jean-Marie Le Pen in France or Pim Forteyn in the Netherlands, the success of some outsiders to the political system such as Silvio Berlusconi in Italy or Robert Kilroy-Silk in the UK, or the protest votes against leaders who ignored mass demonstrations to lead their nations into the Iraq war): "These attitudes imply that policies which respond to economic globalisation and demographic and social changes likely to increase costs by means of retrenchment and a hollowing out of the state will encounter substantial opposition" (Taylor-Gooby, 1999, p 11).

It has been shown, on the basis of Eurobarometer data, that young unemployed people throughout Europe show more distrust towards the political system than young employed people (Bay and Blekesaune, 2002). According to Goul Andersen (1999), it is generally possible to find different attitudes among the unemployed and employed related to the concept of trust:

> We find a high level of political distrust among the publically supported and among those who are affected by unemployment in this age group (the young) – ie political trust is also more polarised. To a certain extent, this seems to hold even for extreme voting, but not for socialist voting; there is a movement to the right among the younger generation that affects all groups, regardless of labour market position.... At least on some dimensions, this pattern could conform with the idea that labour market position is increasingly important whereas class is becoming less important. (Goul Andersen, 1999, p 27)

This has been confirmed by studies in the UK. Bynner and Ashford (1994) found that unemployed youth were less interested in politics and less likely to vote in elections than employed youth. Banks and Ullah (1987) found in a study of 1,294 17- to 18-year-olds that unemployed youth were clearly more politically disaffected than those who were employed. However, these studies are restricted to the UK and, in a comparative study based on all EU countries, Bay and

Blekesaune (2002) found that such differences between unemployed and employed youth were much more marked in the UK than in other European countries. This distrust is especially high among unemployed youth in Britain, and is lower in Scandinavia. A reasonable explanation could be the different welfare policies the various countries implement to deal with unemployed young people (Hammer and Carle, 2004).

The problem has been discussed as the emergence of different political trust structures among citizens, related to different social and cultural structures in a given national and local context. It has been related to the size of a given municipality or political structure: a localised and small municipality means more activity compared with a centralised and large municipality (Denters, 2002). We are more likely to find greater trust and activity within states and municipalities that provide people with jobs, social security and safe surroundings with low criminal rates. We are also more likely to find trust and activity among states and municipalities that offer young people good educational and employment opportunities since they will grow up as citizens who are willing to take responsibility in society (Levi and Stoker, 2000; Bay and Blekesaune, 2002; Denters, 2002). Schweer and Erlemeyer (2001) argue, however, that empirical research on the relation between political actions, political commitment and trust in relation to different life situations is rare.

It is possible to find research showing that a growth in materialistic values (which goes hand in hand with the growth in wealth and social capital) actually undermines the level of social trust, which might in the end undermine political activity at least in its traditional forms (Rahn and Transue, 1998). The role of education in relation to political and social activity is normally thought of as positive, but the additional effect is not as great as normally assumed in research (Egerton, 2002). McLeod (2000) discusses the role of the media in relation to family, peers, teachers, school and so on. McLeod argues for a more differentiated perspective on young people as active citizens rather than mere passive respondents to a changing social environment. The old top-down thesis is less relevant in modern society. McLeod argues that young people today are much more active citizens, using their indirect cognitive skills learned from school, media and interpersonal relation and networks. Young people combine their formal and informal knowledge to play a part in an active participation in everyday life as well as in political activity. This line of discussion actually emphasises the life situation in modern society, which sees citizenship as a more complex concept compared with a more legal and static one.

Young people are involved in exploring their identity, their place in their local society, within their families of origin and destination and within the state. This means negotiating a place and a space, which involves an active citizenship within different social spaces (Hall et al, 1999). This links to the discussion of risk society developed by Thomas Ziehe, Ulrich Beck and Anthony Giddens. They argue that modern society redefines citizenship as an act of market choices and risks, rather than a situation of being a legal member with rights. In a situation of declining economy and unemployment the state ends up using actual and possible risks of social exclusion as a way of managing social control (France and Wiles, 1997).

Conclusion

The results presented here indicate that political passivity among young unemployed people is not easily characterised as either alienation or opposition. Many of them, especially young women, have positive attitudes to political participation in the future. Among young people receiving less generous support such as social assistance, political participation is lower. The results indicate a positive relationship between social and political citizenship. However, low political participation among Finnish and Scottish young people cannot be explained exclusively by a higher level of deprivation. British youth report more distrust towards formal politics than other young people in Europe (Bay and Blekesaune, 2002), and a lower level of participation may be expected. Moreover, previous research has shown that the level of irregular political activities is lower in Finland among young people than in the other Nordic countries (Togeby, 1989).

However, the results presented here indicate that even those who are unemployed can probably be mobilised to participate in politics. Social integration in a youth culture where unemployment is not stigmatised is an important presumption for political participation. These findings do not come as a surprise. First, political actions are social phenomena, often engaged in together with friends. Second, it is reasonable to assume that political knowledge, attitudes and practice are created through political socialisation where in this age group friends may be more important than parents.

In our study we have also tested different arguments on political participation among unemployed youth. We have looked at different welfare arrangements in these countries, analysing the political participation where young people are entitled to rather generous unemployment benefits in Scandinavia compared with the flat-rate

Jobseeker's Allowance in Scotland. The results showed that, in Scandinavia with generous benefits, unemployed youth only had a slightly higher level of political participation than in Scotland with a much lower level of support (means of 2.6 and 2.3 respectively) and that political activity was highest in the Mediterranean countries where state support was less than that of families.

To sum up then, what are the answers to the three main questions stated at the beginning of the chapter?

• What type of political channels do young people use?
• Do young unemployed people have a feeling of trust in the political system?
• Do they trust the traditional political channels for political influence or not?

The short answers would be:

• Young people mainly use traditional political channels (voting and so on) instead of irregular activities (wildcat strikes and street actions) but we find that experience of long-term unemployment on the individual level leads to a switch to irregular activities as well as passivity.
• It seems as if the unemployed young people do have a feeling of trust in the political system, but that there is some negative influence from experience of long-term unemployment and deprivation that may induce passivity. It is likely that some effects, like the lower levels of trust shown in Scotland (low voting in elections) and the rest of the UK, or militant activities in Spain and Italy, may relate to differences in national political cultures.
• High levels of voting indicate that a majority have trust in traditional political channels, even if there also seems to be an influence from long-term unemployment on the willingness to participate in irregular activities.

As we indicated at the start of the chapter, there are a number of possible explanations for political involvement among those young people who are unemployed and those who have experienced long-term unemployment. One explanation has to do with unemployment as a statistical phenomenon. This line of explanation falls back on a simple statement: long-term unemployment comes together with lower political activity in general and different patterns of political activity. In one sense this is true; there is a clear and strong correlation between different activity, attitudes and *unemployment as a statistical phenomenon*. However, this explanation only makes sense if you take into account a specific statistical correlation. The problem is that this type of conclusion fails to take into account the effects of the process of selection on the individual level. The young people facing long-term unemployment are in fact a selection from those hit by unemployment in the first place. Second, there is a selection that takes place within the subcultures of youth unemployment as a social and cultural context. Long-term unemployment is simply not a statistical tool that can be used in a simple way. The effects of long-term unemployment are also affected by the strategies that young people adopt to navigate their lives within a given welfare structure.

The concept of *welfare regimes* suggests that the way a given welfare system is structured makes different individual strategies more likely to happen than others. The concept of welfare regimes therefore does give possible reasons for some of the similarities and differences in political attitudes and actions between different countries. On the other hand, however, there does not appear to be such a strong and simple correlation between different welfare systems and political activities.

Aspects of young people's life situations as a whole are an interesting line of explanation that is often forgotten in the discussions on youth unemployment. Jones and Wallace (1992), dealing with the life situations of young people in modern societies, put their analysis in the perspective of Marshall's theory of citizenship:

> citizenship offers a more useful framework than adulthood for understanding the 'end product' of youth: it allows us to consider process, but at the same time allows us to consider inequality – while citizenship rights are gradually acquired during youth, access to these rights, including to full participation in society, is still determined by social structures of inequality such as social class, race, disability and so on. (Jones and Wallace, 1992, p 18)

As a young person you have to watch out, be strong and try not to get into trouble. As an economic phenomenon it is clear that unemployment is a structural problem, but as a social and cultural phenomenon it is still viewed in terms of individual deficiencies, as Reiter and Craig argue in Chapter One. This is why unemployment is such a tricky situation to deal with within a society, and this is why it is so easy to end up 'blaming the victim', as Ryan put it (1976). What are the political strategies of a victim, in the real sense or in the rhetorical one? Research (at least in Sweden) indicates that when the pressure on the system gets higher, the labour market authorities are forced to use more (lower) economic benefits rather than active labour market schemes. This is of course, paradoxically, in opposition to the official doctrines. This will change the way in which young people devise strategies to cope with and politically respond to unemployment. It will also enhance their dependence on their families. In this type of situation gender, social class, family relations and ethnicity play important roles in shaping the structure of unemployment. This highlights the contribution of the family, as discussed by Jones in Chapter Two, and the different roles families play in different welfare contexts (Hammer and Julkunen, 2003). In the Nordic countries there seems to be a tendency to underestimate the importance of the family within young people's everyday life (Carle, 2002).

Finally, *individualisation and risk*. It is quite unproblematic to state that in a modern society people have to be aware of different aspects of risk, and people are also forced to deal with these risks in an individualistic way. Unemployment is a very obvious risk for young people, and unemployment is also a risk that is treated as a very problematic situation for young people as a group. Young people as individuals very quickly learn that unemployment is associated with drop-out, misfit and marginalisation. Anthony Giddens (1991) focuses on the necessity to understand that the reflexive individual is a result and reflection of a society in late modernity. In this society people have to adjust to a constant risk of being unemployed, divorced or forced to move. People are therefore forced to adjust and reconstruct their work relations and family lives into new patterns and relations. The importance of work has not vanished: it remains a powerful force, but one under reconstruction; and young people of today are in the middle of this era of reshaping and pioneering new forms of working relations. The ways in which unemployed young people actually navigate within society and act as citizens are perhaps a very good seismograph of the shaping process of futures in societies to come.

Methodological notes

Sampling: the sample sizes and response rates were: Denmark, 76% of $n = 1,540$; Finland, 73% of $n = 2,386$; France, 51% of $n = 4,000$; Germany, 65% of $n = 3,000$; Iceland, 63% of $n = 2,280$; Italy net sample, $n = 1,421$, 89% of $n = 1,590$; Norway, 56% of $n = 1,997$; Scotland, 56% of $n = 1,500$; Spain, 52% of $n = 5,000$; Sweden, 63% of $n = 3,998$.

Measures and indices: we have constructed one additive index of irregular activities and one index for regular political activities, both range 0 to 1. Index of irregular activities, mean = 0.23, sd = 0.23, Chronbach Alpha = 0.63.

However, in most analyses we have used three different measures including items of both irregular and regular activities.

Participation in political activities, mean = 0.27, sd = 0.20, Chronbach Alpha = 0.70 (range 0.60 to 0.77).

Potential political activities, mean = 0.3, sd = 0.24, Chronbach Alpha = 0.71 (range 0.52 to 0.62).

Objections to political activities, mean = 0.42, sd = 0.27, Chronbach Alpha = 0.78 (range 0.76 to 0.84).

- Political interest was measured by dummy variable yes/no.
- Political orientation was measured by a five-point scale from left-wing to right-wing sympathy.
- Political attitudes were measured by seven statements (items) on a five-point scale from 'strongly agree' (1) to 'strongly disagree' (5):

   "What kind of society do you think we should be working towards?"
   − a society with more private enterprise and a market economy;
   − a society that protects the environment even if this results in lower economic growth;
   − a society that utilises advanced technology like computers and robots;
   − a society of law and order;
   − a society of equality with small income differentials;
   − a society of equality between men and women;
   − a society of equality between ethnic groups.

Note

[1] Table 8.1 and small parts of the text above and below this table have been published in Hammer (2003b).

Part Three: Policy options

This third part of the book moves on to study aspects of the policies developed in various countries to deal with youth unemployment, focusing especially on the notions of dualisation and activation. In most European countries a policy debate is going on about a much-deplored mismatch between the world of education and the world of work. This is seen both as a barrier to economic innovation and as a major source of problems for young people making the transition from school to work. Therefore a revitalisation of vocational education and training that combines in one way or another theoretical instruction and work experience training (dualisation) is generally viewed as an important strategy for preventing youth unemployment and a sound foundation for lifelong learning. In Chapters Nine and Ten, van Hoof and Bianchi discuss aspects of training and education in the Netherlands and Italy respectively. In both countries there is a trend towards strengthened vocational pathways into the labour market; while there is approval of this as a broad strategy, the papers highlight some of the limitations of using training and education as a solution to the problems of the youth labour market. Bianchi in particular exposes the problem of lengthened dependency on families, as discussed in Part One. Skills training is also an important element of many activation programmes that are targeted at unemployed young people. In Chapter Eleven Malmberg-Heimonen and Julkunen, drawing on the findings of the nine-country youth survey, explore the effectiveness of active youth programmes in getting young people back into work, and highlight the dangers of getting trapped in an endless cycle of scheme participation.

NINE

Vocational education and the integration of young people in the labour market: the case of the Netherlands

Jacques van Hoof

In the eyes of many European governments, vocational education and training (VET) has become a strategic policy domain. It is seen as a central element in a strategy to enhance the competitiveness of the economy. A general upgrading of skills should be the answer to the competition from low-wage countries in a globalising economy (Crouch et al, 1999). At the same time VET is considered the best way to integrate young people into the labour market. In this way it has also become an important element of policy to prevent marginalisation and guarantee citizenship for young people. Ideologically this policy is often supported by arguments from human capital theory, which has become quite popular in most European centres of government. In this way the lack of appropriate skills is held responsible for many of the problems young people encounter when entering the labour market. This fits in well with the individualising tendencies in European youth policy described by Reiter and Craig in Chapter One that make young people themselves accountable for successful integration into the labour market and citizenship conditional upon their own efforts.

One such European country that has spent much effort in improving its VET system is the Netherlands. Two decades of debate and experiments led in the mid-1990s to a new law on vocational education. This introduced a new regime by integrating public vocational education with apprenticeship training, and by giving employers' associations and trade unions a formal role in determining the standards of competence and vocational profiles. This chapter, which is intended as a kind of exemplary case study, will describe this reform of vocational education and assess its consequences for the position of young people in the labour market. It will do so from a comparative perspective, by making use of some recent comparative studies of different VET systems in Europe and of the transition from school to work in different European countries.

In the first instance these studies will be discussed with an emphasis on institutional differences in the way VET systems are organised. The next part introduces the debate on vocational education in the Netherlands. The changes will then be described, before we turn to an analysis of the consequences of the new system, as far as they are made visible in some recent Dutch studies. The last part summarises the results from the comparative perspective introduced at the beginning of the chapter.

VET systems and the transition from school to work

In their study, *Are skills the answer?*, Crouch et al compare the VET systems of five Western European countries (Britain, France, Germany, Italy and Sweden), Japan and the US. Contrary to many recent studies on the importance of education and skills for the labour market, they follow a neo-institutionalist approach. I will take this approach as a point of departure, because in this chapter I want to highlight the role of institutional arrangements for the transition from school to work. According to them, a high general level of occupational skills represents a collective good that makes collective action necessary to produce it. However, collective action is made difficult by conflicting interests of the actors whose cooperation is needed to make it successful. A theoretical reason for this is that occupational skills are an *impure* collective good: they are non-excludable (no firm can be excluded from access to them), but they are usually scarce so firms have to compete for them. As a result, if left to the market, problems of under-investment may arise, because firms tend to limit their training from fear of losing skilled workers to their competitors (Crouch et al, 1999, pp 25-6).

Employers, therefore, face a dilemma: "while they unambiguously share a general interest in higher skills, they are reluctant to do anything about it" (Crouch et al, 1999, p 18). Trade unions face a dilemma too. They also have a long-term interest in a general upgrading of workers' skills, in order to prevent the development of a large segment of unskilled workers. However, in the short run they tend to look after the interests of their members first, by ensuring that they get a fair share of in-company training. In this way, the division between insiders and outsiders on the labour market (which was discussed in Chapters Three and Five) can become more pronounced.

Under these conditions, collective action to bring about higher skills becomes primarily a task for the government. However, here we meet another dilemma that influences VET policy to no small degree: it may be acknowledged that state intervention in the VET area is necessary, but in the prevailing neo-liberal climate it is also viewed with suspicion and/or criticised, because state-provided vocational education is supposed to lag permanently behind the needs of industry.

From this point of view, Crouch et al (1999) analyse different institutional arrangements (or regimes as I would like to call them) for providing VET and discuss the problems associated with each of them. In doing so, they examine both vocational education preceding entry into the labour market (initial VET) and vocational training during careers (further VET, an important part of lifelong learning). In this chapter I will limit myself to initial VET.

In some countries initial vocational education remains firmly the domain of the state. Crouch et al (1999) use the examples of France and Sweden to illustrate the problems associated with state-provided VET. The main problem of a public VET system is how to keep up with the new demands of industry. In countries like France, Sweden and Italy (see the next chapter for recent developments in Italy), the gulf between the schools and the world of work is often deplored. An important background for these complaints is the transition in many Western countries from a Fordist to a more flexible type of organisation that attaches more value to polyvalent and social skills. To adapt vocational education to this development, a closer contact between schools and firms than is usually found in state-provided VET seems to be necessary. Moreover, in the countries mentioned, the vocational tracks often suffer from low prestige in comparison with the academic tracks in secondary education. As a consequence, they mainly attract those students considered unfit for the academic tracks. This further reduces the reputation of vocational education with employers (Crouch et al, 1999, Chapter Four).

Another type of regime is found in Germany (and in other countries such as Austria and Switzerland). Here initial VET is regulated and administered by corporatist associations including both employers' organisations and trade unions. In these countries the traditional apprenticeship systems evolved into a dual system: a system in which students, having the formal status of apprentices, receive vocational training in companies according to an officially recognised programme with complementary theoretical education provided by schools.

According to Crouch et al (1999), this type of institutional arrangement seems better able to combine public goals and a sensitivity to business needs than a state-led VET system. But here, too, typical problems present themselves (Crouch et al, 1999, Chapter Five).

First, although this model has a kind of built-in flexibility, it is also a model based on extensive consultation and negotiation. Therefore, adaptation to major changes in skill requirements that imply a thorough revision of the curriculum can become a time-consuming process. This rigidity is reinforced by the central role of a traditional concept of occupation, which is associated with specialisation and a strong sense of identity. Second, corporatist arrangements are generally prone to insider–outsider conflicts of interests. Although the German system is inclusive (that means accessible to all who finish lower secondary education), access to the system is contingent upon a sufficient supply of training posts. A shortage of training posts leads to the exclusion of a smaller or bigger group of young people. Because in Germany there are few alternatives outside the dual system, this category may become subject to processes of marginalisation. Third, participation of firms in the system is still voluntary and rests more on trust in the advantages of the system and informal pressures than on formal obligations. Therefore, individual companies may opt out of the system and they will probably be more inclined to do so when the economic climate encourages opportunistic behaviour.

Crouch et al (1999) discuss still another regime, one that can be found in the US and Britain. In these countries the provision of initial VET is left much more than elsewhere to the market. The role of the educational authorities is restricted to creating an institutional framework that defines uniform standards of competence (the National Vocational Qualifications in Britain) and examination requirements. Moreover a system of incentives is set up to encourage voluntary, non-corporatist participation of firms. The main problem associated with this type of regime is that it emphasises a short-term flexibility at the expense of a long-term effort to raise the level of skills throughout the economy. The risks of under-investment and marginalisation seem particularly high in this type of regime.

As argued earlier, most governments expect that VET systems will contribute to a better integration of young people into the labour market. Therefore we now turn to two comparative studies of the transition from school to work. Van der Velden and Wolbers (2001) studied the factors influencing the integration of young people into the labour market (as measured by unemployment among those who finished school less than a year ago) in the EU member countries during the period 1992-97. They conclude that, after controlling for the overall employment situation and human capital variables, three institutional factors explain the remaining differences: the statutory protection of insiders (those with regular jobs) against dismissal, the structure of wage negotiations (centrally coordinated negotiations being more conducive to integration of new entrants) and the presence of a dual system. In particular in those countries where youth unemployment was very low at the time (Austria, Denmark, Germany and the Netherlands), young people seemed to profit from the presence of an apprenticeship system.

That specific institutional traits of VET systems make a difference can also be concluded from a study by Shavit and Müller (2000). This study includes 11 advanced industrial societies, among them six EU countries (Britain, France, Germany, Italy, the Netherlands and Sweden). They conclude that in general VET systems protect young people better from the risks of unemployment and under-employment (entry into unskilled jobs). This is more pronounced when vocational education is more occupationally specific, when it is more stratified (more differentiated into separate tracks with little mobility between them, tracking starting at an earlier age), and when more linkages between schools and firms exist. Not surprisingly, these three characteristics are strongly interrelated, countries with a dual system scoring higher on any of them. However, Shavit and Müller also found that it is in those countries that the separation between vocational and higher education is most pronounced. Apparently, vocational tracks not only make the transition from school to work run more smoothly, but also 'divert' students following them from reaching the most prestigious occupations.

Therefore we may conclude that, by moving from a state-provided VET system to a system with a stronger dual and corporatist character, a country may improve the correspondence between vocational education and the needs of industry and the transition from school to work. However, this may come at the price of more institutional rigidity and fewer chances for upward mobility within the education system.

The debate on vocational education in the Netherlands

In the past three decades the Netherlands, like many other countries, has fallen under the spell of the concept of 'learning'. A fully developed system of vocational education institutions and training facilities that meets the needs of companies and forms the basis for lifelong learning is deemed to be of vital importance for the functioning of the labour market and innovation within the economy. After a period during which vocational education in Dutch education policy had been pushed into the background in favour of the discussion of structural reforms in general secondary education (in particular regarding the introduction of comprehensive education), the sharp rise of unemployment at the end of the 1970s and the criticism of employers about the quality of vocational education led to a debate on the lack of correspondence between education and labour market requirements (Hövels, 1994; van Hoof, 1997, pp 115ff). Gradually, a basic level of vocational skills came to be seen as the best guarantee for young people to enter the labour market successfully.

In this debate three issues played a prominent role. The first concerned the relationship between mainstream vocational education at the lower and intermediate levels, which is a part of the public educational system[1], and apprenticeship training, which up till the early 1990s was governed by trade and industry (including the trade unions). In many industrial trades apprenticeship training had a long tradition and coexisted as a separate training system alongside school-based vocational education. At the beginning of the 1980s, though, apprenticeship training was severely damaged by the economic crisis. Stimulated by an increasing interest in the dual model as a way to bridge the gap between education and work, government, employers and trade unions joined forces to revitalise apprenticeship training. However, this made it all the more necessary to define the place of apprenticeship training within the system of public vocational education.

A second issue concerns the formal responsibility for vocational education. Formerly educational policy (including the policy on vocational education) used to be the sole responsibility of the educational authorities and educational interest groups mostly organised on a denominational basis. However, employers and trade unions together now claimed a role of their own in determining vocational policy and vocational programmes. This became known as the principle of 'shared responsibility' and occurred against the resistance of the educationalists increasingly supported by the government. Since the mid-1980s, new procedures allowing for the participation of employers and trade unions have been developed for the programming of vocational training, and new forms of consultation between the representatives of the educational community and trade and industry, organised both by sector and by region, were created.

A last issue in the debate is the scope of initial vocational training. Due to the increasing popularity of such concepts as 'learning to learn', 'lifelong learning' and (recently) 'employability', vocational education came to be viewed in a much more dynamic perspective, emphasising the preparation for a professional career that will be increasingly characterised by change and mobility (see, for an early statement, van Hoof and Dronkers, 1980). This led to a broader view on the goals of vocational education. The question raised here is whether initial vocational training should prepare for a number of clearly defined starting positions for school leavers or be directed to broader qualifications that enhance employability during the career. In the latter case, vocational programmes should have a broader scope than the rather narrow, occupation-specific programmes in traditional vocational education.

The reform of vocational education

Taken together, the elements mentioned earlier constitute a new way of thinking about vocational education and training, which set in motion a transformation of VET policy. This transformation has not been limited to *initial* VET. A remarkable development in *further* vocational training has been the joint efforts of trade unions and employers to develop a sectoral approach to further training and retraining based on collective agreements and jointly administered Training Funds in the different trades of industry. This process, which clearly illustrates the role corporatist arrangements can play in lifelong learning, has been dealt with elsewhere (van Hoof, 1997, 2000).

In this part we focus on the reform of initial vocational education. This took shape with the introduction of the 1995 Adult and Vocational Educational Act (WEB), which can be seen as the conclusion of 15 years of discussion and lays down a new institutional framework for the further development of vocational education. For the purposes of this chapter its two most important parts are, first, the introduction of a standard national system of qualifications (NSQ) covering both daytime vocational education and apprenticeship training and, second, a new division of roles between the various actors involved. These two issues will now be taken up.

A national system of qualifications

The national system of qualifications consists of the systematisation and standardisation of all occupational qualifications which can be reached by following vocational education. Qualifications are seen as skill profiles with a 'broad and stable' character, which means that they should be relevant to a broad range of jobs and have some permanency in relation to the frequent changes in job contents[2]. These qualifications do not only include professional skills, but should also include skills that enable students to continue their education at a higher level, and incorporate elements of social and cultural skills that are necessary to function as a competent member of the enterprise and society in general (a kind of training for industrial citizenship).

The NSQ serves as a link between job profiles and job requirements on the one hand, and vocational programmes and educational goals on the other. In this respect it is explicitly intended as a way to bridge the much-deplored gap between vocational education and the world of work. Qualifications are graded on four levels: assistant, basic skilled worker, fully skilled worker and middle manager or specialist. These have been elaborated into sets of educational goals specifying in detail, for each qualification, the skill requirements to be mastered by the trainees in the course of the programmes. The second level (basic skilled worker) plays an important role in Dutch policy, because it is this level that is seen as basic for an occupational career. Therefore it is a generally accepted goal that all young people should have the opportunity to reach at least this level before entering the labour market.

Within vocational education two separate *educational routes* are distinguished, differing from one another in the emphasis given to the theoretical or the practical component of the programme. The apprenticeship training route is dominated by the practical component (which must form at least 60% of the duration of the course), while the vocational training route places greater emphasis on the theoretical aspects. These educational routes are basically equal; in other words, it should be possible to gain each qualification via either route.

In this way an attempt has been made to solve the problem of the relationship between school-based vocational education and the apprenticeship system. They are no longer considered as two autonomous and competing types of vocational training, but as two different educational tracks (one of them with a more extensive practical component than the other) leading to the same qualification. Craft training and vocational education have therefore been integrated into a single system. This, at least in theory, amounts to an upgrading of the apprenticeship system, as it opens up a broader range of higher-level qualifications for those students who do not feel attracted to school-based vocational education.

A new division of roles

From the administrative point of view, the key element in the new set-up is the process of determining qualifications and educational goals. This can serve to illustrate the new relationship between the parties involved (the state, the education sector, and trade and industry) that has taken shape in the field of vocational education in recent years. The 'shared responsibility' which was previously advocated is expressed in the new set-up in the construction of a system of consultative and collaborative bodies (per sector) within which representatives of education and industry meet, the National Boards for Vocational Education. The national system of qualifications has been determined by the authorities on the basis of the structures of qualifications worked out by these national bodies for their own sector. They also play a major role in drawing up the educational goals. The task of trade and industry is to indicate (for example, in the form of occupation profiles) what requirements future employees need to meet. On the basis of this information, a catalogue of educational goals is drawn up by representatives of education and industry. After an independent advisory committee has checked whether the educational goals satisfy a number of principles and guidelines, they are then adopted by the authorities. The education institutions, finally, translate the goals into training programmes that (assuming the goals have been approved) are provided with public financing.

To complete the picture, something has to be added about the role of the public vocational schools. Due to a process of concentration initiated by the government, these have grown into large-scale regional institutions including colleges for daytime and part-time vocational training and schools for adult education. Within the framework of the new law, these institutions have been given a much greater degree of administrative and financial autonomy. It is expected that because of this they will be better able to take account of the wishes of regional trade and industry and participate successfully in the expanding market of training courses for employees. The law also introduces, therefore, elements of regional decentralisation that were formerly unknown.

We conclude that trade and industry (represented by the employers' associations and the unions) have been given a great deal of influence on vocational training. In this way, Dutch corporatism gained a strong foothold in the system of vocational education. At the same time, the dual element in the system has been strengthened, not only by giving apprenticeship training an equal status with school-based vocational education, but also by strengthening the work experience component in the school-based track. On the basis of the studies discussed earlier, we might expect therefore that the reform of Dutch VET must have a positive influence on the correspondence of vocational education with labour market demands.

Consequences for the labour market position of youth

We now turn to the effects of the changes in the VET system on the labour market position of young people. We will discuss three topics in particular:

• the development of the NSQ as the main link between vocational education and the occupational system;
• the transition from school to work for those who completed vocational education;
• the transition from lower secondary education to vocational education as an indication of the openness of vocational education for those youngsters with only elementary education.

This part is based mainly on the results of some recent studies that were part of an official evaluation of the 1995 law on adult and vocational education (the evaluation being prescribed in the law itself). They cover the period 1995-2000. Considering that the law took effect in 1997 and that most programmes on levels 3 and 4 take four years to complete, this five-year time span is evidently too short to allow definitive conclusions. So we have to be careful in drawing conclusions.

First we present some information on the general development of the system of vocational education in the past decade. At present the total number of students enrolled in vocational education is only slightly higher than 10 years ago: 469,000 in 1990 against 473,000 in 2002. The number declined in the period 1992-97, but started growing again from 1999 onwards. However, as the total number of people aged between 15 and 24 years declined considerably during the same period, the proportion of students in vocational education increased from 20% in 1990 to 25% in 2002.

Moreover, within vocational education as a whole, a shift has taken place between the vocational (school-based) track and the dual track (the former apprenticeship programmes). Although the former has still been by far the most numerous in the past decade, the proportion of dual-track students has risen continuously (from 29% in 1990 to

35% in 2002).The recent growth of vocational education can almost entirely be attributed to the growth of the dual track.

Therefore we may conclude that vocational education managed to improve its 'market share' after the introduction of the new system, but that the dual track profits most from this development.This fits in neatly with the fact that, according to a recent survey, employers generally have a more positive opinion both of the dual track itself and of the skills and direct employability of the employees who complete it (Heijke, 2001, p 91). Later in this part we will find other indications that the dual track is doing well at present.

The development of the NSQ

As said before, the introduction of the NSQ was intended not only as a means for the standardisation of skill requirements for the whole of vocational education, but also as a way of developing *broad and stable* qualifications. This goal is clearly related to the new vocational philosophy discussed earlier, which connects initial vocational education with lifelong learning and employability and advocates a broadening of vocational programmes. The question as to whether the NSQ fulfills these expectations was a central theme of the evaluation of the law.

The official report is highly critical of the present state of the NSQ. It concludes that the mechanism linking the principal actors "leads to a greater degree of differentiation than is necessary and to vocational programmes which qualify in an insufficiently broad and permanent way for occupational practice and citizenship" (Stuurgroep Evaluatie WEB, 2001, p 57, translation by the author).This indictment comes as no surprise (see van Hoof,1997, 2000). The present NSQ is in fact not much more than the sum of the occupational structures that formerly existed in different sectors of industry and were transplanted by the National Boards (which still have strong links with sectoral organisations) within the new qualification structure. The NSQ therefore 'fixed' the relationships that have grown up between different occupational sectors and between existing vocational programmes, rather than regrouping them into a limited number of broad and stable qualifications. Instead, the National Boards directed their efforts to the detailed translation of qualifications into educational goals.

In this way an intricate and rather rigid structure has been created consisting of more than 700 qualifications, each of them elaborated into hundreds of educational goals. It will surprise no one that this has made the NSQ rather unresponsive to new skill requirements – for example, those connected with the diffusion of ICT. A characteristic of ICT is that it cuts through occupational boundaries and creates overlap between occupational sectors. The development of new ICT-related qualifications therefore asks for the combined efforts of several National Boards, but until recently they were slow to rise to this challenge. More generally, because of the new corporatist and often bureaucratic set-up of the National Boards, changing occupational profiles and educational goals tends to become a rather slow process[3].

We conclude that, although the NSQ was intended to lead to broad and stable qualifications, many forces relating to the new regime of vocational education work in the opposite direction. By enlarging the influence of trade and industry on the processes of determining qualifications and the profiles of vocational programmes, sectoral interests have become firmly entrenched in the relations between the educational and the occupational system. Often they express the opinion of employers of small and medium-sized companies that vocational programmes should fit closely to the specific skill demands of employers. Even the way of financing vocational education favours further specialisation, because it makes the creation of new qualifications financially more attractive than combining two or more qualifications into a new one (Heijke, 2001, p 57). Therefore it looks as if the short-term perspective of moulding vocational education to the immediate requirements of industry gains the upper hand above the long-term perspective of learning to learn and promoting employability.

The transition from school to work

We turn now to the transition from school to work in order to answer the question whether the labour market position of those who finish vocational education with a proper qualification has been improved since the reform of Dutch vocational education in the mid-1990s. To put the results into perspective, we first need to say something about the development of youth unemployment in the Netherlands.

Dutch youth unemployment reached peak levels in the early 1980s and since then has decreased substantially. In 1992 the youth unemployment rate (among 15- to 24-year-olds) was already down to 8%. During the period 1993-95 youth unemployment rose again to 12.8%, although not as sharply as in the EU as a whole (20.8% in 1995). Afterwards the decline was resumed. In 2000 the youth unemployment rate reached the 6% level, one of the lowest rates within the EU. At present, however, the labour market situation is rapidly deteriorating and youth unemployment is rising again (10% in 2004).

The question, therefore, as to whether the improvement of vocational education may make young people less vulnerable to the fluctuations of the labour market remains as relevant as ever[4].

As was argued before, Dutch youth social policy is firmly based on the belief that a minimum level of vocational education is the best guarantee of a successful start on the labour market and that therefore all youth should have the opportunity to obtain such a basic qualification. The first thing we need to know, therefore, is whether the proportion of young people who enter the labour market without a vocational qualification at level 2 has decreased since 1995. According to a recent study that covers the period 1995-99, there has indeed been a slight decline (Hövels, 2004). However, at present almost one fifth of all young people aged 15-24 still do not have an adequate qualification.

Among ethnic minorities this proportion is much higher: about one third (30% in 1999) do not qualify in this sense for entering the labour market. This shows clearly that the position of youth from ethnic minorities still lags considerably behind that of others, despite the favourable labour market conditions of the past few years. In this respect, the situation of Dutch minority youth clearly resembles the situation of minorities in Germany, France and the UK, as discussed by Craig et al in Chapter Seven. However, their position seems to have become slightly better since 1995, as is shown by a modest increase of the proportion who have at least obtained a level 2 qualification.

It must be added that overall drop-out rates within vocational education remain high (about 30% of each cohort do not finish vocational education), higher than in any other type of secondary education. If there is at present only a slight increase in the proportion of young people with at least a basic vocational qualification, this must be blamed mainly on these high drop-out rates. This is related to push and pull factors, the tight labour market of the 1990s without doubt being a strong pull factor.

Before discussing the transition from school to work itself, we have to emphasise that an ever increasing proportion of those who complete vocational education do not enter the labour market, but move on to higher education. This was stimulated by the new law that holds that vocational education should also qualify students for entering higher education. As a result, in 2000 40% of those who finished vocational education at the highest level (level 4) moved on to higher professional education, as against 25% in 1990 (van Asselt and Visser, 1999). Clearly the upwards pull that is a familiar phenomenon in any strongly stratified system of education (see the first part of this chapter) is operating here too, notwithstanding the effort to make vocational education a more attractive alternative for young people. This might have important long-term consequences for the status and market value of vocational qualifications.

However, there can be no doubt that the labour market position of those leaving vocational education with a full qualification has improved considerably in the second half of the 1990s. The results of the yearly surveys among school leavers show that:

- unemployment among those leaving vocational education has almost completely disappeared during this period[5];
- the proportion of those having flexible jobs one year after leaving school has been reduced considerably;
- the average hourly wage for those who start working has risen continuously since 1995;
- the proportion of school leavers who found jobs corresponding to their level of qualification has also increased considerably (ROA, 2002).

We should remember that the late 1990s were exceptional because of the very strong growth in employment. This might explain most of these results. More significant seem to me the differences between the two tracks that appear in these surveys. Most remarkably, it seems that the dual track is in some respects more successful than the school-based vocational track. Those who complete the former more often find themselves in possession of a permanent job and earn higher wages than those who finish the latter. This seems particularly valid for those who took programmes at levels 3 and 4. Overall, the level 1 and 2 programmes of the vocational track have the least favourable position. This might be seen as another indication of the upgrading of the dual track. There is one notable exception, however: those who followed vocational programmes at levels 3 and 4 more often ended up in jobs corresponding to their level of qualification than those who finished dual programmes (54% as against 71% in 2000). This indicates that their career prospects might be better.

We conclude that, in the second half of the 1990s, for those who completed vocational education the risks of unemployment, precarious employment and underemployment have been reduced. Moreover, at first sight the dual track seems to contribute most to this development. It must be added immediately, however, that this is probably mainly the result of the exceptionally favourable labour market conditions of the late 1990s. With the available data it is difficult to tell whether the reform of vocational education had any independent effect. As the labour market is now declining and youth unemployment is on the rise again, the next few years will become a demanding test for the new system.

The accessibility of vocational education

The last point to be discussed is the accessibility of the new system of vocational education. As we explained earlier, Dutch vocational policy follows a kind of bottom-line approach by defining a level 2 qualification as a necessary basis for entering the labour market. Such an approach risks creating a bigger or smaller group of youngsters who fail to meet this requirement and may therefore reinforce already existing marginalisation tendencies. In the Netherlands this applies most to those youngsters who leave lower-level general secondary education (MAVO) or the preparatory vocational schools (VBO) without certificates. However, those who after completing the one or the other enter the labour market directly without any kind of further training also have a vulnerable position.

The parties who were involved in the design of the new system were conscious of these risks and sought means to reduce them. In particular, the introduction of the assistant level (level 1) into the NSQ was intended as a way to bridge the gap between the new system of vocational education and those youngsters with only a minimum of preparatory education. Accordingly, most vocational colleges tried hard to develop level 1 programmes and tailor-made courses for those who entered vocational education with specific educational deficits.

Have these efforts been successful? Again, the figures produced by recent studies conducted as part of the evaluation of the law on vocational education are not completely conclusive. Generally, however, these studies lead to a cautious optimism. It was found, for example, that after the introduction of the law fewer youngsters completing lower secondary education entered the labour market directly and a higher proportion of them started vocational training. This did not lead to higher drop-out rates in the first year of vocational education (de Jong and Berkenbosch, 2001, pp 113-14). The differences are small, however.

More important seems to be that the proportion of ethnic youth moving on from lower secondary education to vocational education (in particular to level 3 programmes in the vocational track) rose considerably (from 65% in 1995 to 85% in 1999). In this respect, the position of youth from ethnic minorities seems to have profited from the introduction of the new system. For them vocational training has become increasingly the most important road to integration into the labour market[6].

These figures, however, only present part of the picture. First, they exclude school drop-outs. It is this group that most faces the danger of disappearing into the margins of the labour market and therefore represents the biggest challenge for the bottom-line approach mentioned before. Recently the two tracks of lower secondary education (MAVO and VBO) were brought together into a new type of lower secondary education (VMBO), in an effort to upgrade lower secondary education generally and to improve the link up with vocational education in particular. First experiences show that this new type of school is rather less successful in preventing drop-out, because the programme is much more general than vocational and tends to demotivate those youngsters with practical skills and an interest in practical subjects. Therefore, in the near future the number of drop-outs may even grow, further complicating the tasks of vocational education.

Second, the assistant-level programmes – considered to be the most important way to integrate those with a low level of preparatory education into the system of vocational education – appear to have a dubious labour market value. In a survey nine out of 10 employers indicated that they did not have any use at all for those who follow this type of programme (Heijke, 2001, p 49). Therefore, this level does not seem a very promising starting point for improving the position of youngsters with only a low level of preparatory education.

We may conclude that although a modest improvement of the flow of students to the VET system has taken place (more marked for youth from ethnic minorities), it remains difficult to reach those youngsters with only a minimum of general education. As yet, the efforts to link up lower secondary education with the VET system have not been very successful. Evidently, the improvement of vocational education in itself is not sufficient to prevent the marginalisation (in labour market terms) of a still quite substantial group of youngsters with only an elementary form of general education.

Conclusion: dilemmas of vocational education

This chapter has dealt with vocational education as an important element of a policy to prevent youth unemployment and guarantee social citizenship for young people. Traditionally, Dutch initial vocational education is state-provided and school-based, but in the past 10 years both corporatist and dual elements have become more prominent and have been institutionalised with the introduction of a new law on vocational education and training in the mid-1990s. Following the comparative studies discussed briefly in the first part of the chapter, we might expect these changes to bring about a better correspondence between vocational education and the demands of the occupational system, and therefore fewer difficulties in the transition from school to work. This is certainly what many policy makers in Europe hope for when they advocate vocational training and dualisation. However, they might also lead to more institutional rigidity and – by introducing insider–outsider problems – strengthen the risks of exclusion for those youngsters who only have an elementary level of general education. Does the analysis confirm any of these expectations?

In my opinion three conclusions stand out:

- Generally, the position of vocational education as a gateway to the labour market has become stronger and a greater proportion of young people are now following vocational education, but it is the dual track – which seems to enjoy an increasing popularity both among students and employers – that contributes most to this development.
- The NSQ, which links vocational education with the occupational structure and is a product of a corporatist consultation framework, has not yet developed into a system of *broad and stable* qualifications as was intended, but remains a highly differentiated and rather inflexible structure of specialised vocational profiles.
- Although the flow of students from the lower-level secondary schools into vocational education has slightly increased (more marked for youth from ethnic minorities), it remains difficult to reach the group that is most threatened by marginalisation (the school drop-outs).

As the new law has only been operational since 1997, as yet no definitive conclusions can be drawn about its effect on the transition from school to work. Generally, for those finishing vocational education with a proper qualification, the risks of unemployment and under-employment decreased considerably, but this will mainly be the consequence of the exceptionally good labour market situation of the late 1990s. However, it is worth mentioning that again the dual track stands out favourably in this respect. If the correspondence between vocational education and the occupational system has become better, this is probably due to the expansion and upgrading of the dual track.

At the same time this Dutch case illustrates very clearly some of the dilemmas associated with vocational education as an instrument for upgrading skill levels in the economy as a whole and improving the labour market position of young people. The first dilemma has to do with the difference between a short-term and a long-term perspective on the skill needs of industry. Generally, as is argued by Crouch et al (2001, p 17), in assessing the potential of VET for improving the employment situation in advanced economies the distinction between the short-term and the long-term is vital. By bringing employers (and trade unions) into the VET regime, as was done in the Netherlands, at the same time the tensions between a short- and a long-term view on skill development become more apparent. Should vocational education primarily be directed to the immediate skill demands in the various branches of industry by focusing on the direct employability of school leavers? Or should it pay more attention to future changes by focusing on skills that improve the trainability of young workers and employability in a broader sense? Trade and industry often speak with different voices in this respect, small and medium-sized companies and their spokesmen being more in favour of the short-term approach leading to rather narrow vocational training. In the Netherlands the short-term view seems to dominate at present and it may become even more dominant when the economic situation of industry becomes worse and companies start to cut on training budgets.

The second dilemma is related to the position of vocational education within the educational system as a whole. Dutch education is (to borrow a concept from Shavit and Müller, 2000) highly stratified. It is characterised by a strong separation of academic and vocational tracks, both in secondary and higher education. Also, the distinction between lower and higher secondary education is well marked. Tracking, moreover, still starts right after the completion of primary education. In such a system higher education exerts a strong upward pull throughout the system as a whole, with the consequence that youngsters try to pursue academic tracks as far as possible. As a consequence, vocational education – and in particular its lowest level – often ends up as a kind of residual education, taken up only by those who are deemed unfit for any other form of education.

In view of this, state policy in the VET domain has to combine somewhat contradictory aims. On the one hand, it should try to upgrade vocational education, in order to meet the demand for higher skills and make vocational education more attractive. On the other hand, it has to pay special attention to those with only a low level of general education, and to ensure that by upgrading vocational education this group does not miss the boat. The Dutch reform of vocational education evidently does not escape this dilemma. At the upper end of the system, upgrading opens up new opportunities for students to move on to higher vocational education, which has led to a much increased outflow to higher education. At the bottom end, proclaiming a basic vocational qualification as a condition for entering the labour market successfully means that many efforts have to be directed at making special provisions for the sizeable group of youth with only a low level of preparatory education: efforts that up till now have not been very successful.

In the end, this leads to the fundamental question as to whether the ambitions of VET policy may not be too high. Crouch et al (1999) argue, rightly in my opinion, that raising skill levels is not a cure-all for all the problems of employment that most advanced industrial countries face. I believe the same should be said for VET as an instrument to strengthen the position of youth in the labour market. As the Dutch case shows, it certainly has limits in this respect. And of course, as is argued elsewhere (see, for example, Chapter Four, in which Alvaro and Garrido discuss the job-seeking efforts of unemployed young people), a lack of appropriate skills can never be the only factor explaining youth unemployment. Therefore other forms of active labour market policy as discussed in this volume (see in particular Chapter Eleven) remain necessary to reduce youth unemployment and prevent marginalisation. We will return to this issue in the concluding chapter.

Notes

[1] In the Netherlands a distinction used to be made between lower vocational education (LBO), intermediate vocational education (MBO) and higher vocational education (HBO). The latter is part of higher education and will not be dealt with here. Lower vocational education, which had a poor reputation, was some years ago renamed preparatory vocational education (VBO) to emphasise that it must no longer be considered a fully fledged form of vocational training. School leavers who finish this type of education should continue their training either within the apprenticeship system or in the MBO to reach a full vocational qualification.

[2] This concept of qualification is comparable to the German concept of '*Ausbildungsberuf*'.

[3] As a response to the criticism expressed in the evaluation study, the National Boards – which were renamed Knowledge Centers for Vocational Development – now try to substitute a limited number of core competencies for the long catalogues of educational goals in order to create more flexibility in the vocational programmes. The number of qualifications was reduced in 2004 to about 320.

[4] An interesting analysis of the Dutch youth labour market can be found in Salverda (2000).

[5] Unemployment among those who finished vocational education in 2000 is even lower than among those who finished higher education.

[6] The transition rates of young females have also become better. Moreover, their distribution among different training sectors has become somewhat more equal.

TEN

Young people's transitions between education and the labour market: the Italian case

Francesca Bianchi

Introduction

There is now widespread consensus that in a globalised society knowledge has become the most important commodity of exchange. Indeed, along with technological growth, the valorisation of information has marked every sector. Policy makers also recognise the value of this collective good, acknowledging that the quality of a nation's human resources is at least as important for national growth as the quantitative level of income it produces.

The nature and development of the professional skills needed in today's labour market have also changed. From an individual perspective these new skills particularly concern the capacity to handle progressive autonomy in terms of self-motivation, responsibility, and the work process itself. In addition, rather than accumulating skills in a linear fashion over time, workers are instead expected to increase and diversify their capabilities transversally through experiences in various contexts. These transformations have been noted and incorporated into numerous European Union documents, where policy makers aim at guaranteeing citizens not only the professional skills necessary for entering the labour market, but also those that allow for shifting from one type of job to another. Training, then, becomes a crucial phase in the acquisition of the skills necessary for autonomous and positive insertion into everyday working life: the thick web of opportunities and constraints from where most citizenship rights are derived (Sen, 1986, 1994; Dahrendorf 1995). This development has two important implications. First of all, training constitutes a factor of social identity, membership and progression. It is a priority for the personal development of citizens within cognitive society. Second, it becomes a necessary condition for avoiding marginalisation and subsequent under-employment in an ever more competitive international labour market.

In this scenario, schools and the education system in general are responsible for encouraging the acquisition and development of fundamental skills that individuals can subsequently use to adapt to changes in their existential situations (Colombo, 2001). These requirements have motivated a number of the important changes recently seen in professional training and education programmes in Europe. Regardless of the diversity of education policies, states have reached a common diagnosis of what is afflicting the labour market, and educational reforms reflect a fair amount of convergence. The most serious problem, with some variation across countries, appears to be unemployment and joblessness among young, first-time job seekers.

The lack of correspondence between the world of school and the world of work has compounded the traditional problem of access to the labour market. Young people in search of their first job suffer the most from this mismatch. In fact, the transformations in social relations and systems of action that this demographic group encounters (from school to work; from adolescence to adulthood; and from dependency to autonomy) make young people more vulnerable to fluctuations than other age groups, and they are the first to feel the effects of the contradictions between training and the labour market (La Rosa et al, 1996; see also Chapters Three and Five). Indeed, it is well known that many young people have trouble finding work after they complete schooling because employers do not consider them 'employable', or fit for employment. Luciano Gallino defines employability as the capacity to "carry out a specific task": employability is considered a "personal characteristic comprising the sum total of one's formal skills, practical know-how, the capacity to work with others, and experience in the field" (Gallino, 1998, p 242).

There are a number of reasons for this presumed inadequacy. First of all, jobs themselves have become more specialised because of technological innovations and organisational transformations. Next, the dynamics of firms have changed the qualifications they look for in the labour force. Finally, as a result of overall higher levels of education, employers can be more choosy in terms of their material, social and symbolic requirements. Once more, the mismatch between school and work, one reason for joblessness, is evident here.

Along these lines, the most serious problem influencing the transition from school to work is the gap between education and the world of production. It should be emphasised that upon the successful completion of training or other course of study, most youths should be employable. Up to now, however, in Italy the school system has done little to guarantee such employability. It is therefore necessary to act in advance so that employability manifests itself earlier and resists decline until much later in one's employment career. Of course, while most youth do leave the school system with a good set of basic skills, they often have no real conception of the world of work. Employers, in turn, are unfamiliar with the skills that young people have already acquired. There is a solution to this problem, however.

A better correspondence between education and employment could be produced if a bigger work element were included in training programmes, and more training activity were included in work. There are a variety of techniques to realise this, but all tend to emphasise alternation between training and work via one of two basic approaches. The first entails practical training sequences or internships that count towards the requirements of a degree or diploma, completed while the young person is still a student. The second approach is managed by employers, and participants earn their qualifications following the completion of a period of work experience and theoretical education (Giovine, 1994). While the former school/internship approach is still the most widely diffused method in Italy, the frequency of 'mixed objective' work contracts between employers and young people is increasing.

Italy is a singular case: the national specificity depends on the particular combination of individual and institutional factors (education and labour market). In some countries like Germany, Austria, Denmark and the Netherlands there is a lot of emphasis on the importance of vocational training and the link between the education system and the labour market is strong: vocational training is well organised because it is considered crucial for the productive system. In Italy the links between education and the labour market are very poor and vocational training is often addressed at improving the general knowledge of 'weak' students rather than providing 'marketable' skills. Vocational education should have the function for which it is created – that is, to offer a more specialised and qualifying education for those who do not want to go to university. This means recognising the fundamental role that vocational education has for the improvement of the economy and changing the idea that it is an education of lower importance and prestige, mainly addressed to students not able enough to succeed in academic schools. The Italian educational system has traditionally privileged general education over vocational specific training even in vocational and technical schools, thus reducing the ability of educational qualifications to attest to the capacities of potential employees. Nevertheless, by the 1990s the new educational system emerging from various projects of reform presented new and positive aspects, such as the introduction of a larger range of educational alternatives and a stronger connection between schools and the labour market. According to this, we can point out that the Italian situation is an interesting and peculiar case, different from the other countries, but nevertheless illustrating the turn towards vocationalism that is taking place in many European countries with a strong tradition of general, state-provided education and the obstacles that have to be overcome to make it more responsive to the world of work.

Following some background information on the characteristics of the Italian labour market, this chapter will focus on the employment experiences of young people. The difficulties young people encounter when attempting to first enter the labour market bring the mismatch between training and employment into high relief. These difficulties in turn highlight a series of complicating phenomena that can only partially be attributed to the structure of the labour market, and that instead are strongly associated, in terms of both explanations and responsibility, with the education and training systems. In the third section I develop an overall sketch of recent employment and education policies in Italy, elaborating on the reforms that seem to have had the most impact on the Italian context during the past decade.

Youth in the Italian labour market: the risk of unemployment

Discrimination against young people is a disturbing characteristic of the Italian labour market. Indeed, the higher than average level of unemployment among young people alone warrants in-depth reflection. For this group, the unemployment rate is nearly as high as that found in Greece, and young Italians are more likely to experience unemployment than older people. This generational problem is most acute in terms of access to the labour market.

An update of Reyneri's age-differentiated models of unemployment (1997) with 2002 data reveals that Italy and Greece together constitute a first model of unemployment where the unemployment rate is extremely high for young people but rapidly declines until it reaches levels comparable to the European average for adult men. A second model, in which youth are not the most at risk for unemployment, seems most applicable to the German case. There, unemployment rates for young people and adults are nearly identical up to the age of 54. Many unemployed people between the ages of 55 and 59 are actually awaiting early pensions. Not only was Germany one of the countries least affected by youth unemployment until the explosion of the phenomenon in the mid-1970s, but it has since managed to keep imbalances in check to the level that they are almost non-existent. It should, however, be noted that in some European countries the disadvantage of young people with respect to adults in the labour market is hardly less than that found in Italy and Greece. As was reported in the Introduction, Spain, France, Belgium and Finland also demonstrate high rates of youth unemployment. The poor performance of the Mediterranean countries is thus not unique, appearing also in parts of continental Europe (one new development in these patterns is the reduction of youth unemployment in Spain from an absolute high of 40% in 1997 to 22.2% today, a level not far from those reported by Finland and France).

This brief analysis of unemployment rates demonstrates the important age differences that emerge in European countries. These aspects cannot be ignored, and from them one can trace a more general picture of the most problematic issues in the Italian labour market structure.

In Italy the educational system is based on four cycles:

1. pre-school education for children aged from three to five, not compulsory but attended by a large number of children;
2. compulsory schooling (lasting eight years up to 14). This consists of elementary school lasting five years and lower secondary school lasting three years;
3. upper secondary school lasting five years divided into the academic courses (*licei*), technical training (*istituti tecnici*), vocational tracks (*istituti professionali*), teacher training (*istituti magistrali*) and arts courses (*istituti artistici*);
4. university (from three to six years) and training courses or PhD degrees after university.

Youth in general have been seeking higher levels of education. There has been a significant improvement in overall education levels. More than 80% of eligible teenagers, for example, attend high school (cycle 3). We can observe a great increase in educational attainment, particularly among younger generations of women. In the past 20 years, young women have caught up with and actually overtaken their male peers in terms of education levels. The current cohort of 20-year-old women is more educated than their male counterparts, and the gap seems likely to increase in the future. This influences their activity rates.

The following data illustrate the direct relationship between educational attainment and female activity rates. In 2001, among 30-year-olds, 80% of women with a college degree, two thirds of women with a high-school degree, and 64% of women with some other professional qualification were active participants in the labour market. The completion of at least obligatory schooling seems critical: only 43% of women with a middle-school education are active, and less than 20% of women with an elementary education or less are active (ISTAT, 2001). While the impact of higher educational attainment is clearly important, it should also be noted that female labour force activity has increased for all levels of education. In 2001 the level of activity among women with high-school diplomas was higher than it was in 1993, and the same was true for women with a middle-school education. Only women with little or no education remain excluded from these across-the-board increases. In other words, the increase of the female labour force seems part of a larger process that involves almost all women, regardless of their level of education.

High-school completion rates, however, show a somewhat less positive trend. While 72.1% of students received the final diploma in the 1997/98 academic year, only 70.2% graduated in 1999/2000[1]. As a consequence, dropping out before the final diploma examination leaves pupils without any formal recognition of the time spent at school, or any kind of qualification.

Following graduation from high school, fewer young people go to university. In 1999/2000, the enrolment rates at universities were nearly the same as those of the previous year, while the matriculation rate per 100 university-aged students declined by 0.4% (this amounts to about 20,000 fewer matriculations). In fact, increases in general enrolment numbers relate to a technical distortion, and do not reflect a real increase in the number of new students.

Participation in the Italian education and training systems remains lower than in other European countries, and constitutes a major reason for low levels of educational attainment for individuals between the ages of 25 and 64. From a comparative perspective, Italy demonstrates especially low educational attainment among older age cohorts. For example, in 1999, 53% of the active population in Italy had either a secondary, post-secondary or tertiary certificate of education, compared with 80% in Austria and Germany, 66% in Belgium, 67% in France, 78% in England and 90% in the US. Active populations with lower educational status are found only in Portugal and Spain: only 77% and

57% of active workers in these countries, respectively, had a degree that would be considered a middle-school degree in Italy (ISFOL, 2001; OECD, 2001a). It seems that the great waste of human resources that characterised the Italian university system prior to its reform left Italy behind with respect to the general European context: only 10% of active Italians between the ages of 25 and 34 have obtained a university degree, compared with the OCSE average of 16.5% (CENSIS, 2001).

Furthermore, youth unemployment appears most marked in the countries (Italy included) where the increase in educational attainment was most rapid, and where the symbolic importance of higher degrees is greatest. The education system seems to have created very high expectations for employment among students and their families, and many take for granted that certain good jobs in their field will be available to them upon completion of their degrees. The problem is that the rapid increases in the educational attainment of the new generation, no longer restricted to a small elite, are not accompanied by an equally rapid growth in the number of jobs located at higher levels in the occupational hierarchy (Reyneri, 1997; Teichler, 2000). Consequently, highly educated young people who expect to obtain the types of jobs that have been considered in keeping with their level of education remain frustrated. Enjoying the support of their families, however, these prospective workers do not feel compelled to accept jobs they consider below their educational status. They instead wait, often for quite some time, until they obtain the type of job they think is due to them, or until they revise their idea of what is suitable. This is why graduate unemployment seems to be so widespread in Italy, especially in the south, where the level of schooling is higher than in the central and northern parts (Barbagli, 1974; Iannelli, 1999).

The initial transition into work appears to be the most difficult hurdle to overcome for young people seeking employment. For example, we can observe a difficult situation for young people looking for employment (31.2% of the total population between 15 and 24 years is looking for a job) but it is among those having only a primary-school certificate or no degree that the situation is worse (37.1% is looking for employment) (see Table 10.1). This lack of training puts them at significant risk of social marginalisation (ISFOL, 2001; ECB, 2002).

In absolute numbers, however, it should be noted that unemployment is at present most concentrated among 20- to 30-year-olds, the effect of increased time spent in schooling, and demographic changes. The size of younger cohorts is expected to continue to decline: according

Table 10.1: Population looking for a job (% of labour force) by qualification and age (2000)

Qualification	15-24	25-29	30 and beyond	Total
University degree	27.8	23.6	3.4	6.3
School-leaving certificate	34.1	17.3	5.0	11.2
Professional qualification/secondary-school diploma	22.7	10.2	4.8	8.1
Middle-school certificate	29.9	16.6	7.8	11.8
Primary-school certificate or no degree	37.1	30.2	9,3	10.9
Total	**31.2**	**17.5**	**6.4**	**10.6**

Source: ISFOL data processing ISTAT data

to ISTAT predictions, the cohort of young people between the ages of 15 and 24, currently 7,817,000, will probably be about 6,000,000 in 2005, and 5,600,000 in 2010 (ISFOL, 2001). This phenomenon, however, seemingly banal, is often overlooked in examinations of decreased youth employment activity. The increase in time spent in school has led to overall higher educational attainment. Diminished activity rates among this age category are at least in part the effect of an increased investment in human capital. In all European countries, the first entry of youth into the labour market has been delayed by their participation in the scholastic and training systems, not to mention the various forms of employment that can now be combined with training.

The mismatch between supply and demand also seems to be partly driven by the extended periods of time young Italian workers spend seeking out the 'right' kind of job. As in other countries, the transition period from school to working life is much longer than in the past. Contemporary careers follow a less linear path than those in the past: the trajectories do not always lead to secure positions, and instead can often be characterised as a journey of socialisation and confrontation with the complexity of the world of work (La Rosa et al, 1996; Anastasia and Corò, 1999, see also Chapter Three). Young people go through an exploratory phase in which they are often left to themselves to find a position. Obviously, the level of education represents a competitive advantage (Colombo, 2001). Data on the duration of job search until first employment indicate that the average waiting time for a young person's first job grew to 45 months in 2000, an increase of two months with respect to 1999 (in the south, young people had to wait 49 months!) (see Table 10.2).

The value of academic qualifications deserves mention: the labour market still prefers academic degrees, and waiting times are certainly inversely related to the level of education achieved. The Italian youth

Table 10.2: Average duration (months) before finding first employment, by qualification and region (2000)

Qualification	North	Centre	South	Italy
PhD/university degree	14	26	38	31
Post-secondary-school diploma	14	29	41	32
School-leaving certificate	19	38	47	42
Professional qualification/secondary-school diploma	23	41	47	41
Middle-school certificate	33	45	52	50
Primary-school certificate or no degree	36	56	60	58
Total	**23**	**39**	**49**	**45**

Source: ISTAT data

labour market thus presents a genuine gap: while the rate of employment has gone down, the average amount of time a young person must wait for his/her first job has increased. Those who cannot place themselves in the world of work by virtue of their educational qualifications thus face a longer period of unemployment than they might have in the past. For this reason, in light of shifts in unemployment rates that affect every age group, the efforts and policies to integrate training more aptly with the needs of the labour market appear particularly appropriate for the Italian context. The most promising seem to be those that incorporate experiences aimed at promoting and facilitating the transition process from school to work. In fact, employment prospects for young Italians have improved in the past few years, thanks to increased hiring flexibility introduced in 1997, as well as some other well-timed legislative reforms[2].

Some important explanations

There have been two main explanations for the high rates of youth unemployment in Italy. First of all is the traditional high level of protection enjoyed by workers in the middle age categories, especially heads of families. This has meant that employers' recent needs for more flexibility mainly affect younger workers now entering the workplace. In fact, the generation gap between young people and adults seems to correspond to the traditional dualism between *insiders* (employees who are never dismissed because of legislative or trade union protection) and *outsiders* (the young generations) created by the strong rigidity of the labour market (Ichino, 1996; Crouch et al, 1999; Esping-Andersen, 1999b).

The second explanation focuses on the mismatch between what employers need and what new workers can provide, given their preparation. Many non-economic institutions, including schools, vocational training programmes and the family, have been identified as having had a misdirected influence on the skills, preferences and ambitions of young people. The family, the first and most immediate socioeconomic context experienced by individuals, appears strongly to influence the behaviours and individual decisions of young people. Indeed, the physical and psychological well-being of individuals is highly dependent on the quality of support received or requested by other members of the family (ISTAT, 2001). In general, younger generations appear to be afflicted by a sort of 'Peter Pan syndrome'. The age at which they acquire all the necessary qualities and skills to become autonomous adults seems to be ever more delayed. This becomes especially evident in the Italian context. Why is this the case?

For one thing, young people need more time than they did in the past to complete a series of essential transitions (Livi Bacci, 1999). Not only do young people spend more time in the education system but, once in the world of work, they also take longer to form their professional identity. They delay their exit from the family household, and their decisions to marry and start families of their own. Because these stages usually pass in succession, the entire arc of time necessary to complete the cycle, or its significant sections, greatly increases. It is still a widely debated question whether this belated transition to adulthood is a physiological adaptation to the structural changes of society, or if it instead is a pathological phenomenon. It is certain, however, that we should give it some consideration in relation to the different dynamics found in labour markets throughout Europe. Though the signs of this phenomenon are extremely evident in Italy and other Mediterranean countries, it is also surfacing elsewhere and seems to have augmented over the 1990s. According to ISTAT, the proportion of men and women residing with their families of origin increased from 52% in 1990 to 59% in 1996. The growth was particularly notable among 25- to 30-year-olds, increasing from 39% to 54% (ISTAT, 1996).

The model of transition to adult life in Italy thus seems particularly interesting. Students who take seven or eight years to complete a university degree that, on paper, only requires four, are one manifestation of this Italian peculiarity. Another is the willingness to wait for a convenient job that is, ideally, close to home (Livi Bacci, 1999). This behavioral phenomenon, known as 'Italian familialism', deserves close attention (see Chapter Two). Though the expression now carries mainly negative connotations, behind it is concealed an important and complex mechanism. The family institution has long served to absorb generational tensions, attenuate economic difficulties and, above all, make up for deficiencies in other social institutions and protect against the kind of marginalisation that is found in highly segmented labour markets (Accornero and Carmignani, 1986; Saraceno, 1998).

In Italy, the family has become the social, cultural and, of course, economic substitute for an inadequate welfare system that other and more fortunate European countries are only now beginning to know on an institutional level (Crouch, 2001). While in central and northern European countries the costs of unemployment are absorbed by society in general (because nearly everyone receives some form of public subsidy), in Italy, when the unemployed person happens to be young and still in residence with his/her parents, the cost of unemployment is paid by the family. From this point of view, parallels can be drawn between Italian behaviour and that found in countries such as Greece and Spain. Indeed, many sociologists have proposed the existence of a 'Mediterranean model'. Esping-Andersen's observations are especially enlightening: "In the familiaristic political economies of Mediterranean countries, the well-being of almost everyone is tied to the career of the head of the family. This means that the advantages associated with life-time job security become very high" (p 189).

In contrast, in the Scandinavian countries:

> Ever since the 1960s, dual-income families have become the rule. Scandinavia's triple emphasis on wide income guarantees, active labour market policies, and a notable growth in employment tied to the welfare state should minimize individual insecurity and maximize, at the same time, employment flexibility. (Esping-Andersen, 1999b, p 189)

Of course, the demographic behaviour of Italian young people has begun to differentiate itself from the past. Some habits, however, have remained relatively unchanged. Young Italians still tend not to form independent households, for example. On average, Italian 30-year-olds have spent less than four months living either alone or with friends, while their Swedish and French peers average two, and one-and-a-half years, of such experience, respectively. A second constant is the persistent tendency to bear children only within marriage. Though cohabitation has become widely accepted, as many opinion polls confirm, in 1997 85% of Italians still agreed that marriage is the ideal (IRP, 1998).

The important role played by the family has only recently become the object of research (Barbagli and Saraceno, 1997; Saraceno, 1998;

Livi Bacci, 1999). We have been rather late in recognising the hand the family institution has had in feeding and sustaining the 'Peter Pan syndrome' – a set of behaviours that appears to have shaped not only demographic trends, but also imbalances in the labour market. Consequently, the planning and implementation of significant reforms aimed at inverting these typically Italian/Mediterranean tendencies have also been late in coming. As we will see later, these reforms, mostly the product of the past decade, are aimed at increasing the training investment in young people, removing obstacles blocking entry into the labour market, encouraging mobility and providing housing incentives and, finally, rewarding initiative and entrepreneurship (Livi Bacci, 1999).

Turning now to the educational system, it is important to underline that vocational training and apprenticeship systems had become deeply inefficient and unattractive to young people because of their complete isolation from the regular educational system. The general impression is that they were second-rate training programmes for students who failed in the regular school system. It is important to keep in mind that the Italian education system has until now been highly segmented: it was characterised by a strong separation of academic and vocational tracks. As a consequence, vocational education came to be seen as a kind of residual education.

The productive system, dominated by small and medium-sized firms, is also to blame, however. First of all, these firms have not demonstrated a capacity to take advantage of the up-to-date technological innovations and knowledge that newly trained young people can bring to an enterprise (Moscati and Rostan, 2000). In effect, young people are often 'over-educated' for the work that is available to them, and thus frequently fall into the category of 'under-employed.' Furthermore, young workers are also highly disadvantaged because employers still privilege experience in making hiring decisions, precisely the asset that young people most obviously lack. The qualifications these types of firms require are most relevant to static production systems characterised by minimal organisational and technological innovation, and in which training is based on learning by doing. They are not the types of skills that easily accommodate change. Indeed, workplace-based studies indicate that firms anticipate new workers entering with only a basic preparation, on which they can then build the necessary skills through on-the-job training. The resulting skills tend to be job-specific and probably are not easy tranferable to other jobs outside or even within the firms.

What appears most crucial for young people entering the labour market is the capacity to learn combined with a set of basic skills and knowledge on which the various specialisations can be grafted. The need to re-evaluate education and training policies thus comes into high relief. Policies should provide more effective investments in education and in continuous and ongoing training, and should be in close coordination with the resources and needs of the regions to cultivate a culture of employability among both workers and employers (Bianchi and Giovannini, 2000). Policies should also be directed at improving the communication between young people and the market, starting with the opportunity to try original initiatives that provide training similar to apprenticeships (Anastasia and Corò, 1999). It is also important to set down clear guidelines for how and when young people should alternate their work and school periods, and how that might be reflected in their final qualifications. There might also be an investment in counselling that would allow for the tracking of each young person, with individual input on his/her work/training choices, as in the UK Connexions programme described in Chapters One and Two. Internships should become commonplace, and there should be concrete support for territorial mobility so that individuals have access to the widest possible range of opportunities. Finally, there is a need for basic, universal protection for all workers, whether employed or unemployed, in precarious or short-term contracts, furnishing, on a case-by-case basis, services to support and promote entry into the professions, and so on.

Recent changes in the education and professional training systems

The evolution of employment policies

As in other European countries (see Chapter Eleven), the diffusion of passive labour market policies preceded the development of active labour market policies in Italy, and the system was consolidated in a particularly dense context of laws and guarantees protecting the rights of (male) workers.

Passive policies are those that attempt to counteract the most immediate disadvantages associated with unemployment, and tend to be of a temporary and assistance nature. They are used to sustain the income of workers who are excluded from productive activity. This support is usually either insurance-based or solidarity-based, and comes in the form of workers' compensation, unemployment subsidies, unemployment insurance and so on. By contrast, active policies are all those aimed at supporting or redistributing employment, facilitating the mechanisms of supply and demand, stimulating job creation, and providing incentives for the creation of jobs and new businesses. The prevalence of passive policies in the past can without a doubt be traced to income support measures for unemployed workers, and the highly bureaucratised and inefficient public placement system (Negri and Saraceno, 1996).

The 1990s marked a significant turn in Italian labour market policy. There was progressive deregulation of the workplace and an advancement in the debates on labour market reforms. We can assume that the increase of labour market flexibilisation has reduced the protection of *insider* workers and has facilitated the access to the labour market of young people, who previously were considered *outsiders*. For the first time, both public decision makers and social partners explicitly called for a general reform of labour market policy on issues such as job training and job placement, the legal working day, employers' incentives and social shock absorbers.

The parallel interests of the social partners were consolidated in the 1996 Employment Agreement, which was incorporated into law no 196 of 1997. This law provided for a substantial revision of all the main active and passive labour market policies constituting Italy's system of institutional protection against the risk of unemployment (Gualmini, 1998). With regard to these programmes, the employment agreement raised the compulsory school age to 15, and reformed vocational school programmes by linking them to the academic system and to programmes on innovation technology and research. The apprenticeship system and work/training contracts were also significantly revised, and scholarships and merit-based loans were introduced to promote lifelong education. The Employment Agreement attempted to redevelop the conception of vocational training as an active labour market policy and, therefore, an instrument to promote new employment. With this end in mind, the resources and objectives of the programme were shifted from basic skills training, the traditional focus of the Italian system, to continuing education and lifelong learning. Though the agreement did not propose a precise model, the development of continuing education programmes has been facilitated by the development of a formal system of recognition for training credits. Lifelong learning has likewise been encouraged by new provisions for leave, sabbaticals, and training fellowships opportunities that have been available to workers in other European countries for quite some time (Gualmini, 1998).

In conclusion, we cannot avoid mentioning the recent law no 30/

2003. This new law (also called Biagi law), concerning employment and the labour market, has assumed particular importance for labour market policy. The law addresses a range of themes related to labour market regulation and employment policy, including the Public Employment Services (SPI), financial incentives to stimulate employment, social shock absorbers, part-time work and the working day. and the introduction of new forms of atypical work (job sharing, job on call, staff leasing and so on)[3] (Ministero del Lavoro e delle Politiche Sociali, 2001b, 2002).

The evolution of training: towards an integrated system of training

In recent years, new demands from the world of work and new community-level strategies have stimulated reforms in the Italian education and training systems. The legislation putting these reforms into practice was supposed to transform the contours of these systems. Law no 30/2000[4] designed a new system of education and training with some interesting elements. Vocational training was placed within the general education system, while on the other hand it has also been recognised as a pathway to adult training that merits the same amount of dignity and respect as the traditional educational system:

> There is a need both to integrate general and vocational programmes
> and to enable young people to move easily between different kinds
> of education, training and work experience during this period of
> their lives rather than being channeled into narrow pathways.
> (Iannelli, 1999, p 187)

Vocational education was intended to offer a more specialised and qualifying education for those who did not want to go to university.

The most important innovation in post-secondary education has been the reform of the university system. This reform introduced a three-year university degree, in place of the traditional course of study, which places the Italian system in harmony with other universities throughout Europe. The new degree programmes were designed with the specific intention of bringing university preparation closer to the needs of the world of work, and providing a more professionalising course of study. Unlike the old system, these new programmes require attendance, and students have more interaction with teachers. Students are also given more direction, and strongly encouraged to complete the exams of the various disciplines in sequential order. It is hoped that these changes will reduce drop-out rates, and diminish the time students take to complete their degree.

The current model of vocational training is clearly more articulated and differentiated than before, offering a variety of experiences and a range of training options throughout a worker's lifetime. Segmented trajectories, composed of isolated periods of training and work that, though being internally coherent, did not particularly overlap, seem to have been left by the wayside. The new training system should provide the option of alternating training periods with work, or even mixing the two (Besozzi, 1998). Two conditions are necessary for realising a fully integrated system. The first entails the dissolution of the rigid boundaries that separate the various realms of training and working experience, and the associated encouragement of different approaches to acquiring knowledge and skills. The second is equal recognition and respect for paths of vocational training that have been outside the academic system and that have up to now been considered marginal or inferior to the imaginary hierarchy of excellence in titles and qualifications. With these considerations in mind, apprenticeships deserve special mention.

The apprenticeship system constitutes the heart of the employment policies recently proposed in Italy. It is a significant support measure for youth employment both in terms of the number of individuals involved, and in the amount of expenditure dedicated to it. Apprenticeships, together with work/training contracts (Cfl)[5] represent important institutions of training and insertion into work, and data confirm that they provide special access to the labour market (see Table 10.3). While the large widespread adoption of work/training contracts in Italy was largely disapproved by the EU, apprenticeships contracts, which are encouraged by social partners, have been rising in number in recent years.

Table 10.3: Job creation tools (1998-2001)

	1998	1999	2000	2001
	Number of beneficiaries			
Apprenticeships	311,270	394,391	446,025	430,068
Cfl	406,960	384,779	328,387	277,343
	Costs (thousands of euros)			
Apprenticeships	1,953,443	2,745,672	2,819,364	1,624,700
Cfl	2,065,442	2,066,080	2,120,831	896,246

Source: Data processing CENSIS and Ministero del Lavoro data (2002)

Other European countries also appear to be rediscovering the value of the apprenticeship system (Ni Cheallaigh, 1995; Crouch et al, 1999) and have made recent attempts to relaunch this important pathway to employment (see Chapter Nine). In France, efforts to revive the apprenticeship system are restricted to the artisan sector. Germany has increased the amount of training, and raised salaries for apprentices. In addition, the most recent reforms have encouraged more flexible preparation to provide what are called 'polyvalent' skills (Crouch et al, 1999). There is a positive development in the sense that apprenticeship appears to increase the employment content of early working life: compared with full-time vocational education, its effects on pay and promotion prospects are less clear, possibly negative, but, compared with labour market alternatives, positive. If the case for apprenticeship is therefore less than dramatic, it is increased in the European context by the importance of reducing youth joblessness. European countries with larger apprenticeship systems show superior youth employment patterns, particularly employment shares in skilled occupations and in high-wage sectors, to those with little or no apprenticeship (Ryan, 2000).

Between training and work: apprentices in the Italian context

Apprenticeship is an important form of on-the-job training. It effectively combats unfocused training both during and after the compulsory schooling period, and represents a moment of genuine fusion between what is effectively an employment situation (employers pay apprentices wages) and an experience of education, cultural growth and professional specialisation.

In Italy, apprenticeship contracts (largely in the crafts trades, though there were some examples of industrial apprenticeships) were first regulated by law no 55/1955 and later amendments. The contracts were called mixed contracts, *contratti a causa mista*, because they provided a sort of combination of work and training at the same time. Unfortunately, by the 1970s training was eliminated by the contracts. This was for many reasons: because of the increase in schooling between the primary- and secondary-school diploma, but also because of the failure of the training courses. Finally, apprenticeship was radically reformed with the laws no 196 of 1997 and no 144 of 1999, and was widely relaunched as an employment strategy. With the main reforms introduced by article 16 of law no 196, the use of apprenticeship contracts was extended across all sectors of activity; the minimum and maximum age limit for participants was set at 16 years and 24 or 26 years (depending on the regions), with an extended provision for handicapped workers; and the length of apprenticeship contracts was set at a minimum of 18 months and a maximum of four years. The innovations concerned the training obligation (external to the firm) and the conditions for taking advantage of contribution-based benefits. Article 68 of law no 144 made school attendance compulsory up to age 18, starting from 1999; it defined the training curricula that exempt individuals from the same obligation (education, professional training); and it provided for the recognition of credits across systems. The new contractual framework was better tailored to the needs of the market, and it has already demonstrated itself to be a key factor for gaining access to jobs and making the transition from school to work.

Importantly, the apprenticeship programme benefits not only low- to medium-skilled workers, but also those with higher qualifications (de Maio, 2000). In the new typology of apprenticeships, training represents the key strategy for responding to young people's need for professional growth, and the organisational necessities of artisan workshops. The training dimension assumed greater weight, and the programme is now open to older apprentices and those with education beyond compulsory schooling. From the employers' perspective, the skills of the 'master', fundamental for the apprentice, are valorised, and the artisans, in return, are given discounts on social contributions. The aim of the programmes is not only to develop a concrete connection between training activity and work experience, but also to facilitate the transmission of professional skills from artisans and specialists to new workers. Finally, it is meant to furnish apprentices not only with the specific skills necessary for carrying out a trade, but also the know-how required for running a business, managing work relationships, and becoming effective problem solvers and decision makers.

Conclusion

Reforms in employment and training policies have introduced significant improvements in the functioning of the Italian labour market. New initiatives to increase labour market flexibility, combined with an extensive reorganisation of the instruments involved in the transition from school to work, have improved the patterns and strategies of young people, the weakest segment of the labour market. These new measures could have a positive effect on both employment in general, and the specific employability of young people. It is only through targeted, internally coherent employment policies, keyed to the needs of individual territories, that we can hope to favour young people's access to the labour market, and reinforce their permanence there. In this way, young people can gain social leverage and be recognised as contributing members of society.

Policies, however, are not enough, and these programmes need to be monitored and regulated. Indeed, in the coming years, the priority assigned to these initiatives will be making sure that institutional actors are capable of evaluating them and adjusting to their outcomes. Policy makers should look for best practices, sustaining those programmes that obtain good results and quickly abandoning problematic or inefficient measures. The new connections forged between education, training and work call for practitioners in each of these domains to take a role in registering the strengths and weaknesses of the model. The real struggle will then be to address the unintended effects produced by the policies, which in turn requires not only a strong capacity for experimentation, but also a keen understanding of the needs of those individuals who are most disadvantaged in the labour market: young people.

For example, experiments with the apprentice programmes, conducted first at the regional and then at the national level, demonstrated the strategic importance that the initiative can have in terms of professional training. It also revealed, however, the logistical, didactical and organisational difficulties associated with the activation of a complicated policy. In this case, the training requirement for the apprentices to follow a fixed amount of training hours has been found to be an especially tricky dimension to manage. On the other hand, the apprenticeship programmes represent an invaluable opportunity to protect a population of young people who would otherwise be excluded from training programmes. It is a concrete effort to support a particular segment of the population and the organisations that hire them (Vergani, 2000).

Regions and social partners play a critical role, for example, in determining the degree and quality to which these programmes are developed. In fact, we have to consider that in Italy (like the Netherlands, as was argued in the previous chapter) an important role is played by collective bargaining and the social partners, which have been primarily involved in reviving and spreading the adoption of apprenticeship contracts. It is thus important that the objectives expressed in the provisions are accompanied by clear references to the financial resources that will be available to support them (Forlani, 1999). It is also necessary to encourage firms to take advantage of the full range of work-training provisions. *Job sharing*, for example, entails fewer hours on the job and more time spent in *off-the-job* training and might be more attractive to some employers and job seekers, while a *multi-firm* apprenticeship would be the better solution for others. All are worth trying out in the Italian context.

Another problem concerns the institutions charged with carrying out the training dimension of the programmes. As one might guess, the educational and professional requirements of apprentices vary, and should be fairly ad hoc. There should therefore be provisions for continuous training for instructors. While there have been new initiatives in this area, up to now they appear much too expensive and time-consuming, and poorly supported by the local pedagogical culture. However, it is important to point to the work of a particular Committee (*Commissione di lavoro*) established in 1999 and composed in 2001 of representatives of the following organisations: the Ministry of Work, the Ministry of Education, the Regions, employers and trade unions. The Committee has started to identify the qualifications needed for successful external training courses: in that way, for the first time, professional skills are clearly defined for every qualification.

There is an additional, more significant aspect to these changes. It would be difficult to believe that these transformations have not had some effect on the individuals at whom they are aimed. Considering the apprentice, the identity of this figure has changed, and will continue to change with respect to the traditional image that we have inherited from the past. First of all, it must now be considered in a context of advanced and accelerated technological changes. Next, while in the past apprenticeships were the main strategy for placing undereducated young people directly in the labour market, they now have assumed a strong education/training element of their own.

So we may conclude that the apprenticeship system seems to be partially remaking itself in the model adopted by many European countries. However, a new educational reform raises some doubts about the course the government wants to follow. Recently, a new law promoted by Minister Letizia Moratti (no 53) has been approved by the Parliament on 28 March 2003. With this law the compulsory school age has been reduced to 14: young people now have to choose at the age of 13 between going to the secondary school or entering the vocational training system. This suggests that general education and vocational training pathways might again become two separate systems. This could appear to be a return to the educational system of the past, despite all the reforms of the 1990s.

It is important to consider also that the apprenticeship system is being touched by the new law. It identifies three different types of apprenticeship contracts: the first is a contract that provides a possibility of reaching the compulsory school or training age; the second provides the attainment, by training on the job, of a qualification, and the third is a contract for a degree attainment (*alta formazione*). The law no longer establishes a fixed amount of training hours (despite Law no 196/1997) except for the second type of apprenticeship contract (120 hours). At present in Italy, there is a strong political discussion about the effects of this law, but it is not so easy to grasp what it will bring for the future of the new apprenticeship system. However, all this flurry of legislation suggests that there is likely to be continued policy debate about vocational and academic options, and about the way to provide young Italian people with proper routes into labour market success.

Notes

[1] It is difficult to reach a clear conclusion on this phenomenon, however, because the data are based on estimates. It is not clear if the decline is due to actual technical or social factors, or if it is simply a product of poor data (ISFOL, 2001).

[2] Consider, for example, ISTAT estimates that nearly 60% of the new jobs created in the past eight years are temporary jobs. It appears that temporary work allows students to develop work experience that they can later draw upon when they decide to look for full-time work. Temporary work, introduced by Italian law no 196 in 1997, is an innovation that recognises the importance of appropriate training for improving the relationship between supply and demand. In fact, there is an employer's tax to encourage businesses to make new initiatives and take advantage of the proposals put forward by training agencies. Training programmes are presented as an individual right associated with temporary work, and constitute, for the worker, a strategy and guarantee at entry into a system that acknowledges additional qualifications and employment opportunities in other contexts (Lozzi, 2000). Compared with other European countries, however, there are still relatively fewer students who engage in part-time, temporary work. For example in the Netherlands, the significant increase in part-time work is due not only to the female component, but also to the diffusion of these types of contracts (less than 12 hours a week) among students (Ministero del Lavoro e delle Politiche Sociali, 2001a).

[3] The law was approved by the Chamber of Deputies on 30 October 2002 and by the Senate on 5 February 2003, after extremely heated debates and an impasse between trade unions and the government. Recently, one of the

most important trade unions, CGIL, came into conflict with the government on the law that regulates the possibility of firing workers. This is considered by the right-wing parties an excessive regulation of the labour market that inhibits genuine flexibilisation of the labour market.

[4] The law *"Riordino dei Cicli dell'Istruzione"* (the Reorganisation of the Education Cycles), elaborated the stages in the curricula of early childhood education, the first cycle of education, subsequently called primary school, and the second cycle, now known as secondary school. The years of compulsory school age were stabilised as six years of age to 15 years of age. The law also determined the duration and objectives of nursery schools, primary schools and secondary schools. Complementary training activities and initiatives, also in cooperation with other institutions (agencies and professional training centres), were provided for from the second year of secondary school. Students who regularly attended any segment of secondary school, whether annually or in modules, earned training credits that could be used in the transition to professional training. Analogously, individuals who participated in professional training courses earned credits that could have been used for access to the educational system (Ambrosini, 2000).

[5] The Cfl is a work/training programme designed to promote the hiring and training of young people. It offers two important advantages. First of all, it is a temporary programme that meets employers' needs for flexibility. Second, as an incentive, employers pay lower social contributions on the associated workers. Some laws (law no 451/1994 and law no 608/1996) have expanded the categories of employers and unemployed workers who can qualify for Cfl – the age limit, for example, was extended to 32 years. Law no 451 provided for two types of contracts, one aimed at providing medium- to high-level skills, and a shorter one aimed at favoring entry into jobs that require only practical skills. Law no 196/1997 brought other changes (Alacevich, 1998). The scope of Cfls has already been altered with the changes to the apprenticeship system, and in relation to studies made by the EU, and at present it is under revision (by laws no 30/2003 and no 53/2003).

ELEVEN

Integration into work through active labour market policies in different welfare state regimes

Ira Malmberg-Heimonen and Ilse Julkunen

Introduction

In the great majority of the EU countries, the principal emphasis in social policy has been on tackling the risk of social exclusion after people have become unemployed (Gallie, 2002). Increasing youth unemployment levels have resulted in training and labour market schemes becoming significant policy instruments across Europe (Dietrich, 2003).

Generally, labour market schemes aim at preventing labour market marginality through maintaining and strengthening the individual's working capacity by improving his or her chances of finding employment. There is continuing debate on whether these activating programmes do, in fact, have these effects and whether they have an impact on more vulnerable groups of people, such as immigrants and long-term unemployed young people (Craig, 2002; van Oorschot, 2002). The schemes are frequently criticised for having less ambitious functions, such as cleaning up the statistics and just storing the workforce (cf Hyyppä, 1999), or temporarily parking young people in transitional labour market measures, as Reiter and Craig put it in Chapter One. An important issue is, therefore, whether these policies are adequate for ensuring longer-term employability.

When analysing the role of labour market policies, employment is usually seen as a necessary precondition for social integration. There are still other aspects that need to be taken into account, such as the quality of jobs, the role of return to education and motivation. First of all, the extent to which employment offers opportunities for social integration depends crucially on the quality of jobs. As Gallie (2002) has argued, for work to provide social integration it should offer meaningful work tasks that allow permanent employability. The quality of jobs is important while temporary work contracts have been demonstrated to increase the risk of labour market marginality of young people (Harsløf, 2003). Furthermore, measures promoting the (re)enrolment in post-compulsory education may also in themselves lead to integration. For young unemployed people, increased educational motivation and return to education is an important precondition to integration (Hammer, 2003a). An important issue is also the subjective impact of scheme experiences, since results from previous studies have demonstrated that motivational factors are important for increasing the positive outcomes of the schemes (Caplan et al, 1989). Hence, the essential question of integration is for whom and to what.

The general aim of this chapter is to analyse different occupational outcomes of labour market measures among young unemployed people in Finland, Sweden, France and Germany. These countries represent different welfare regimes, the Nordic universalistic regime and the employment-centred regime as exemplified by France and Germany. As noted in previous chapters, Gallie and Paugam (2000) define a universalistic regime as being the only type that provides comprehensive benefit coverage, an entitlement which is based on mere citizenship, and a relatively high level of financial compensation. In employment-centred regimes benefit eligibility depends more on previous labour market involvement. Although there are differences between these two regimes, employment is still considered to be the major policy aim in both. From a comparative perspective, it is thus interesting to analyse how effective labour market programmes are in different national contexts.

Unemployment and labour market policies in Europe

Unemployment is a fairly new phenomenon in the Nordic countries compared with the rest of Europe, but there are also differences between the Nordic countries. Unemployment increased dramatically after the recession in the 1990s in Finland, while Sweden was hit by the crisis somewhat later. Compared with the rest of Europe, the Nordic countries have much lower rates of long-term unemployment. However, Finland deviates from this pattern and the rate is similar to that of the rest of Europe. The unemployment situation in Europe can be differentiated by using two dimensions: unemployment history and unemployment level. Unemployment history can be divided into short- and long-term experience. Short-term experience refers to the increased

Figure 11.1: Unemployment dimensions in Sweden, Finland, Germany and France

	LOW unemployment level	HIGH unemployment level
SHORT **unemployment history**	Sweden	Finland
LONG **unemployment history**	Germany	France

unemployment level mainly after the recession of the 1990s, whereas long-term experience refers to the increase since the second oil crisis. Current national unemployment levels can be categorised as high or low by comparing them with the EU average of 9%. Combining these two dimensions produces the groups shown above in Figure 11.1.

The development of youth unemployment level in the studied countries is displayed in Figure 11.2. In 1990 the youth unemployment rate was lowest in Sweden and Germany, but also relatively low in Finland. In France, on the other hand, the unemployment rate among young people was close to 20%. In all the studied countries there was a sharp increase in the unemployment figures in the mid-1990s. This increase in unemployment was sharpest in Finland and smallest in Germany. Since 1995 the youth unemployment level has been

Figure 11.2: Unemployment rates for the age group 15-24

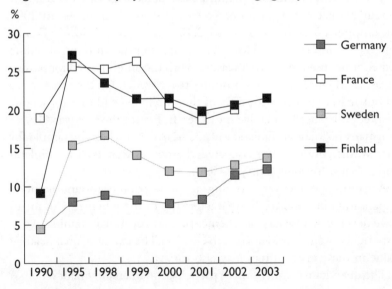

Source: OECD statistics (2004)

decreasing in all countries, except for Germany. Currently, unemployment rates for young people are above 20% in Finland and France, 14% in Sweden and 11% in Germany. From a European perspective, the rate of youth unemployment within Europe was 18% in 2003, which is twice the unemployment rate experienced by adults (9%) (OECD, 2004). The high rate of youth unemployment has occurred despite a demographic decrease in youth cohorts. The changing nature of the labour market seems to play an important role. As Reiter and Craig point out in Chapter One, the macroeconomic changes in the globalised economies affect youth labour markets more negatively than adult labour markets.

Abrahamson (1999a) has argued that social policies in late modern societies are changing radically from a reactive to a proactive approach to risks and social problems. Welfare policies are being broadened in scope and are changing status, with growing emphasis on active labour market schemes. In several countries there has been a growing trend from passive income transfers to active measures and also a tendency to strengthen both incentives and duties by tightening social security (cf Chapter Two). These trends have had a particular impact on unemployed young people and social assistance recipients for whom several European countries have introduced welfare-to-work programmes, to enhance re-employment in the regular labour market (Hanesh et al, 2001; Lødemel and Trickey, 2001).

The amount of public expenditure as a percentage of GDP used for labour market policy varies between the studied countries. In 2002 the amount was 3.07% in Finland, 2.45% in Sweden, 3.06% in France and 3.31% in Germany. However, comparing the amount of public expenditure used for active measures with the amount used for passive measures (Figure 11.3) demonstrates that Sweden has the most active labour market policy with 57% of the public expenditure for labour market policy used for active measures. In France the rate was 41%, in Germany 36% and in Finland only 33%. In 1995 when the sample for the Nordic countries was collected, the figures were 29% for Finland and 53% for Sweden (OECD, 1996).

Activation policies vary not only according to the amount of public expenditure but also to the characteristics of the schemes. Countries have developed a variety of schemes such as vocational training, work experience, wage subsidies and job creation. The extent of qualificatory value in these programmes may also vary.

The quantitative dimension of participation in employment schemes is, however, quite high in all the countries. During the year 2002 the participant inflows to active labour market programmes as a percentage

Figure 11.3: Active and passive measures in public expenditure programmes

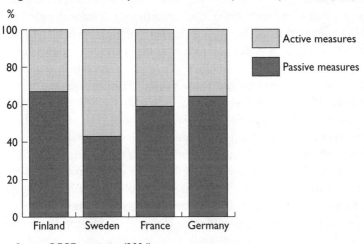

Source: OECD statistics (2004)

of the total labour force were 7.6% in Finland, 6.0% in Sweden, 8.0% in France (2001) and 3.6% in Germany (OECD, 2004). Comparing these figures to the overall unemployment rate in each country during that year (9.1% in Finland, 4.9% in Sweden, 8.8% in France and 8.6% in Germany) gives us a picture of the quantitative dimension of scheme participation in each country.

Although there is a tendency towards more proactive approaches in social policy, there is also a tendency towards dualisation of the welfare state. This means that the labour market takes care of the 'well-to-do' workers through various corporate arrangements, and leaves the less privileged groups in society to local institutions, in the shape of the municipalities or private charity (Abrahamson, 1999b). This process of dualisation is to be found in Europe in the division of active labour market policies within the social insurance system in terms of rights to secure employment or upskilling, and within the social assistance programmes that emphasise the obligations of claimants. The French RMI (revenue minimum d'insertion, a basic income system) and changes in the Social Assistance Act in Denmark may be the best known examples of more compulsory activation where the right to social assistance is linked to the obligation to take part in training or employment activities on the basis of an integration contract (Bouget, 2002; Goul Andersen, 2002). According to Walther et al (2002), European integration policies utilised two approaches to explain the lack of social integration. These are the structural perspective – in other words, the system is seen as the reason for unemployment – and the individual perspective, where the individuals themselves are blamed for their unemployment. Nevertheless, different selection processes may also exist within active labour market policies. Spies (1996), for instance, argues that in general all public institutions select their clients, to a certain extent, on the basis of the degree of cooperation. An effect may be that certain groups are marginalised. This can be seen in the case of the UK, where research has indicated that there are many young people who fall out of the system. They are not in education, employment or training, as Jones points out in Chapter Two.

Esping-Andersen (2001) argues that as a welfare regime the Nordic model has been famous for its emphasis on employment and the removal of family responsibility for providing welfare. Recently, though, it has been argued that the ability of individuals to shelter themselves from market risks is in decline. This trend to recommodification (greater exposure to the market) follows from a weakening of social institutions in the labour market, the welfare state and also the family (Julkunen, 2002; Hammer, 2003a). Regarding youth, increased market-based risks can be seen through the implementation of different workfare models in social policy (Lødemel and Trickey, 2001). Abrahamson (1999b), on the other hand, claims that there has not been much evidence pointing to re-commodification or to support the argument that the Nordic welfare states show a dual character, with good levels of payment and services for the labour market active population, and less generous levels for marginalised groups.

The effect of employment measures?

Overall, increased activation of unemployed workers has emerged from an idea that the reasons for a high and persistent level of unemployment are traditional cash benefits, which increase passivity among the unemployed (Heikkilä, 1999). As a consequence, the rights and responsibilities of the unemployed have been made more visible and more integrated with the unemployment benefits. Refusals of job offers as well as offers of education or active labour market measures lead to economic sanctions. There is a strong emphasis on monitoring the whole job-search process by means of individual plans, follow-up interviews and intensive job-search training (Julkunen, 2000; Hanesh et al, 2001; Lødemel and Trickey, 2001; Goul Andersen, 2002).

Hence, the ideology of employability seems to have changed. As is also argued by Reiter and Craig in Chapter One, the unemployed are held more accountable for their employability and the responsibility to deal with the unemployment situation is to a higher degree seen as an individual matter than a welfare matter. These changes can be explained by neo-liberal ideologies gaining ground in the welfare debate (Jessop, 2002). According to this reasoning, the welfare state is not defined as a source of protection of risks, but as a generator of risks by increasing welfare dependency and passivity among individuals (Dean and Taylor-Gooby, 1992; Williams, 1999).

Nevertheless, it is uncertain whether the tightening of social security and activation of unemployed job seekers have positive effects. For instance, the study by Bergmark and Palme (2003) demonstrated that the tightening of social security during the welfare crisis in Sweden negatively affected the labour market situation of the most disadvantaged groups, such as young people and immigrants. Due to stricter eligibility criteria regarding income-related benefits, these groups were not as newcomers qualified for insurance benefits but were left on social assistance, which weakened their relative position on the labour market.

Looking at previous studies of the effect of employment measures, it can be claimed that the results in general are highly controversial and difficult to compare. Choices of control groups, surveys, research design, methods and measurements vary. One might say that there is some unity in that it is difficult to prove beyond reasonable doubt the positive and negative effects of labour market policies. The outcomes of the programmes may also vary for specific subgroups. An evaluation of the Dutch activation policy by van Oorschot (2002) showed also, for instance, that on the aggregate level activation measures have facilitated labour market participation of the resourceful unemployed, whereas it has failed to improve the situation of vulnerable groups of unemployed people. Activation policy has rather weakened the level of social protection for the more vulnerable groups of unemployed by stricter eligibility criteria and lowered duration of benefits, and making it more difficult to requalify for benefits and sanctioning (Johansson, 2001; van Oorschot 2002). A Danish study by Weise and Broogaard (1997) demonstrated similar results in showing that labour market programmes targeted at unemployed people with social and health problems produce less positive re-employment outcomes than when the same measures are targeted at the more resourceful unemployed.

Hence, there are strong links between socioeconomic structures and labour market outcomes (Furlong and Cartmel, 1997, 2003). It is the more disadvantaged youth lacking the needed material and symbolic resources who have fewer prospects of gaining inclusive employment and lifestyle options in an individualised society (Raffo and Reeves, 2000; MacDonald and Marsh, 2001). Previous studies have generally shown that immigrants are less integrated into the labour market, compared with non-immigrants. If they are working, they are working more often in low-skilled and low-quality jobs (OECD, 2001b). In Chapter Seven Craig et al documented this in more detail for France, Germany and the UK. Furthermore, the level of income among immigrants is lower and they have poorer health compared with non-immigrants (Chandola, 2001; Hammerstedt, 2001; Iglesias et al, 2003; Newbold and Danforth, 2003) and the welfare policies aimed at increasing immigrants' integration into the labour market seems to have failed (Gowricharn, 2002). Besides immigrants, longer-term unemployed youth and youth without work experience are also in a vulnerable position on the labour market while welfare policies do not seem to be sufficient to improve their labour market situation (Bergmark and Palme, 2003).

The evaluation of different schemes for unemployed youth has mainly been undertaken in a national context and there is an insufficient body of knowledge about how schemes function in different contexts with regard to different unemployment levels. There are, however, some recent findings that have demonstrated positive effects of scheme participation in Sweden, weak effects in Spain and non-existent effects on employment in Germany (Caroleo and Pastore, 2003). Another study (Dietrich, 2003), which used the same data, did not find any positive effects of former scheme participation on the income level of young people. Whereas the study by Dietrich analysed outcomes of former scheme experience on employment and income, Caroleo and Pastore (2003) analysed outcomes of former scheme participation on unemployment, employment, training, education and inactivity in the labour market.

This chapter analyses the outcomes of past scheme experience among unemployed youth in different countries. While other studies have paid attention to different outcomes, this study focuses on recurrent scheme participation as well as the outcome of subjective scheme experiences. Furthermore, this study places emphasis on analysing the outcomes of scheme participation for various groups of unemployed. For instance, some studies (Bergmark and Palme, 2003) have found that in particular immigrants, long-term unemployed youth and unemployed youth without work experience have a more vulnerable position in the labour market, as is also discussed by Álvaro and Garrido in Chapter Four. Moreover, a study by Harsløf (2003) demonstrated that young people in temporary work demonstrated a high perceived risk of future unemployment, compared with young people who were employed in a stable job, especially in countries with higher levels of unemployment. For policy implications it is therefore important to acknowledge for what groups the outcomes are favourable as well as the groups for whom the outcomes are more negative.

Data collection and method

This research is based on a European survey on youth unemployment that was conducted in 10 countries (Carle and Hammer, 2003). The study was completed in 1996 in the Nordic countries, in 1997 in Scotland and in 2000 in France, Germany, Italy and Spain. The study was cross-sectional. Representative data were collected on unemployed young people who had been continuously unemployed at least three months during the first half of the year. Postal questionnaires were completed six to 12 months after the sampling, at which time some young people had found jobs, entered schemes or returned to education, while others remained unemployed. The response rate in the survey varied from 79% in Denmark to 58% in Scotland.

Representative data have been collected in all countries studied and the analyses enable us to measure the outcomes of labour market programmes in comparative settings. The results demonstrate how labour market schemes generally function in different countries. Including five different outcomes (unemployment, temporary employment, permanent employment, re-entering education and participation in labour market schemes), we are able to measure the association between previous scheme participation and different occupational statuses on the labour market, which gives us a more varied and complete understanding of the outcomes of scheme participation. Comparing non-participants with participants leaves us still with the fundamental problems about selection into participation in labour market schemes. However, we have controlled for the observed selection in the regression analyses. The main measures used in the analyses are reported in the footnote[1].

Characteristics of scheme participants

In all, 38% of the nearly 8,200 young people participating in this study had participated in a labour market scheme. There were considerable differences between the countries, however. Of the countries covered in this chapter, 43% of Finnish, 60% of Swedish, 10% of French and 35% of German youth had participated in a labour market scheme. When we compared those study participants who had been in a labour market scheme with those who had no previous scheme experiences, the results showed that young persons with scheme experiences differed from those young persons who had not participated in labour market schemes. The picture is not coherent, but overall, young persons with scheme experiences were somewhat more vulnerable. They were older, did not have previous work experience and had longer duration of unemployment. They were less likely to live with their parents, less likely to be migrants and more likely to have followed a vocational education path.

However, the cross-country comparison showed a somewhat diversified picture. In Finland, the profile of the scheme participants was more vulnerable as there were substantial differences with regard to age, gender, residence with parents, lack of work experience and duration of unemployment. In Sweden, too, scheme participants differed from non-participants with regard all the variables, except for the percentage of young people without previous work experience. In Germany, there were differences between the two groups with regard to all the variables, except for gender and residence with parents, whereas only work experience differentiated the two groups in France. Generally, one can conclude that there seems to be a stronger selection into scheme participation in Finland, Germany and Sweden than in France.

To evaluate labour market policy programmes, it is important also to study the recurrence of scheme participation as well as the outcomes of positive subjective experiences of the schemes. In general, 20% of those young persons with previous scheme experiences had been in a scheme more than once. However, the frequency of recurrent participation varied, being substantially higher in the Nordic countries than in France and Germany. Overall, 22% of Finnish, 38% of Swedish, 4% of French and 15% of German scheme participants had been in a scheme more than once. When one looked at the subjective experiences, the differences between the countries disappeared. In all four countries, the unemployed young people had positive experiences of scheme participation; for instance 88% of Finnish, 79% of Swedish, 84% of French and 78% of German scheme participants agreed with the statement 'I learned something new'. The mean value on the scale measuring positive subjective scheme experience that is used in the further analyses of this study was 3.1 in Finland, 2.6 in Sweden, 3.2 in France and 1.9 in Germany. The most positive experiences were found in Finland and France, followed by Sweden, whereas the least positive scheme experiences were found in Germany.

Outcomes of participation in labour market schemes: do scheme participants benefit from activation?

At the time of the interview 30% of the young people were still unemployed, whereas others had found employment (33%), were in education (14%), or on a labour market scheme (14%); 9% were on sick leave, maternity leave or in the army. Generally, unemployed youth who had been in a scheme were more often unemployed or had returned to labour market schemes compared with those young persons who had never been in a scheme (Figure 11.4). Young persons without previous scheme experiences were also more often in employment. Nevertheless, it is important to note that there were no differences between the two groups according to the level of educational attainment at the time of the interview.

By using logistic regression we have analysed the outcomes of labour market policies in four different countries with different unemployment levels and different labour market policies (Table 11.1). However, our analyses cannot distinguish between the different labour market programmes as each country runs a variety of programmes. Still, in a broad sense one can distinguish between the Nordic universalistic regime and the employment-centred regimes in France and Germany; and between the extensive activation policies in Sweden, the less extensive in Finland and France, and the mixed model of Germany.

Figure 11.4: Occupational status at the time of the interview by scheme participation

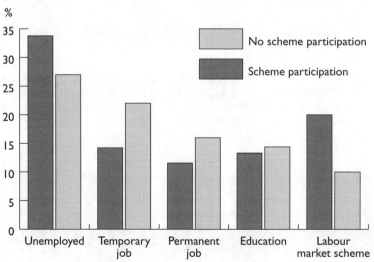

Table 11.1: Positive and negative outcomes of scheme participation in various European countries (standardised beta coefficients)

FINLAND / SWEDEN

	FINLAND					SWEDEN				
	Unemployment	Temporary employment	Permanent employment	Education	Labour market scheme	Unemployment	Temporary employment	Permanent employment	Education	Labour market scheme
Overall outcomes:										
Scheme participation	0.73**	-0.83*	-0.27	0.18	-1.15*	-0.18	-0.27	0.34	0.44*	-1.00**
Recurrent participation	-0.68***	0.13	-0.09	-0.54*	2.38***	-0.21	-0.30	-0.37*	-0.48**	2.3***
Positive scheme experiences	-0.13*	0.19	0.18	-0.01	0.04	0.06	0.04	0.00	0.00	-0.05
Subgroup outcomes:										
Immigrants	-0.91	-0.91	0.76	0.85	0.22	-0.22	0.15	-0.20	-0.07	-0.06
Longer–term unemployed	-0.01	0.01	-0.03	0.01	-0.02	0.00	0.01	0.04	-0.01	-0.02
Youth without work experience	-0.32	0.44	-0.21	0.13	-0.05	-0.08	0.12	-0.18	0.32	-0.17
-2 Log likelihood	1,835.08	1,129.4	801.4	1,304.5	924.2	2,354.5	1,685.4	1,321.3	1,677.2	1,504.4

FRANCE / GERMANY

	FRANCE					GERMANY				
	Unemployment	Temporary employment	Permanent employment	Education	Labour market scheme	Unemployment	Temporary employment	Permanent employment	Education	Labour market scheme
Overall outcomes:										
Scheme participation	1.01*	-0.36	0.36	-0.33	-1.8*	1.33***	-0.74***	-0.14	-0.52	1.13***
Recurrent participation	-0.43	-0.45	-1.45**	0.71	3.36***	-0.16	-0.96***	0.24	-0.22	0.76**
Positive scheme experiences	-0.22	0.05	0.01	-0.04	0.08	-0.39***	0.22*	-0.03	-0.17	-0.02
Subgroup outcomes:										
Immigrants	0.07	-0.09	-0.38	-0.29	0.38	-0.38	-0.63	0.82	0.15	0.30
Longer–term unemployed	0.01	0.00	0.01	-0.01	-0.02	-0.02	0.00	0.02	-0.01	-0.01
Youth without work experience	-0.42	0.30	0.70	-0.40	0.87	-0.33	1.28	1.47	-0.29	0.41
-2 Log likelihood	1,908.7	2,250.4	2,087.9	1,316.6	1,220.2	1,707.8	1,347.8	995.3	993.4	1,445.6

Note: *$p<0.05$, **$p<0.01$, ***$p<0.001$; $n = 1,506$ in Finland and 1,964 in Sweden, $n = 1,986$ in France and 1,612 in Germany; in the analyses gender, age, immigrant status, living with parents, no vocational education, months of unemployment and work experience were also controlled for.

In the Nordic countries, particularly in Finland, previous scheme participation is associated with higher unemployment risks, lower employment in a temporary job as well as lower levels of participation in a labour market scheme. However, recurrent scheme participation increased highly the chances of being in a scheme again when interviewed. As a consequence, the risk of being unemployed was somewhat lower than for the group of unemployed without recurrent scheme experiences. Sweden differed from Finland in that previous scheme participation was associated with increased enrolment in education and no increased unemployment risks. In Finland, on the other hand, positive scheme experiences were associated with lower levels of unemployment.

In the employment-centred regimes, France and Germany, former scheme participation was associated with higher risks of unemployment. As in the other countries, it was those who had repeatedly participated in schemes that were in a scheme again when interviewed. In France this group was also to a lesser degree in permanent employment and in Germany they were to a lesser extent in temporary employment than those who had not been repeatedly in schemes. It is also important to note that in Germany positive scheme experiences were substantially associated with lower risks of unemployment as well as higher levels of employment in a temporary job.

In the study, special emphasis was laid on analysing the outcomes of scheme participation for specific groups of young people as previous research has demonstrated that immigrants, longer-term unemployed youth and unemployed youth without work experience are in a more vulnerable position on the labour market. Since the main aim of labour market schemes is to prevent labour market marginalisation, it is important to study whether the schemes seem to have this effect among the more vulnerable groups of young people. The results demonstrated no substantial interactions between the subgroups and scheme participation. However, there were some *trends* that are important to mention. Particularly in Finland, and to some lesser extent in Germany, immigrants who had participated in a scheme were more often permanently employed and in education compared with immigrants who had not been in a scheme. Immigrants who had been in a scheme were to a less extent unemployed and in a temporary job compared with immigrants who had not been in a labour market scheme. A positive trend was also found for scheme participants without previous work experience. Especially in France and Germany but also to some extent in Finland, unemployed young people without work experience who had participated in a scheme were more often in employment compared with their counterparts in the group who had no scheme experiences. This indicates that labour market schemes do in fact have some effect for more vulnerable groups. However, the question whether these programmes provide sustained employability remains unanswered.

Conclusion

When analysing the role of labour market policies, employment is seen as a necessary precondition for social integration. On the other hand, Beck (2000) has argued that the requirement of full employment is a chimera. In respect of young people, this argument is very important. It poses the question of how youth is seen in modern society. Is it perhaps a time for education? If so, youth unemployment takes on a quite new meaning, as Mørch (1997) argues. Employment, unemployment and jobs are therefore not the main part of the lives of young people. High youth unemployment rates can be understood as a signal to stay in education, as Reiter and Craig claim in Chapter One, but they point out that this also means that the period of dependency is extended. Thus, it should not be forgotten that unemployment in society is a problem that affects many individuals, and it continues to be a problem also for young people who want to enter the labour market and become independent adults.

What conclusions can we then draw from our findings? Generally, we found a trend that there was some positive impact of participation in labour market programmes among more vulnerable groups. We found the most positive outcomes of scheme participation in Sweden, where scheme participation substantially increased enrolment in education. In Sweden, there was also no increase in unemployment risks among scheme participants, whereas scheme participation increased unemployment risks in the other studied countries.

However, in all countries recurrent scheme participation was associated with increased probability of being in a scheme again when interviewed. This result indicates that there is a group of unemployed young persons who circulate from scheme to scheme. This is similar to previous research (Edin and Holmlund, 1994; Furlong, 1993; Hammer, 1996; Spies, 1996) that has demonstrated that some of those who participate in labour market schemes constantly circulate between initiatives and unemployment. Furthermore, the study by Korpi (1994) demonstrated that the probability of finding employment diminishes the more the person has participated in different programmes. In addition, our study found that recurrent scheme participation is associated with reduced employment chances in Sweden, France and

Germany. Furthermore, in Finland and in Sweden recurrent scheme participation is associated with reduced enrolment in education.

Motivational factors did play a role in preventing marginalisation, but not in all countries. We found that especially in Finland and Germany positive subjective scheme experiences were associated with lower risks of unemployment. In Germany positive experiences from schemes were also associated with higher levels of employment in a temporary job. Motivational factors, however, should not be misinterpreted as behavioural factors. On the contrary, it says something about the quality of the schemes. If young people are motivated and find schemes useful, they do seem to have an effect. This puts focus on how programmes are implemented and how young people's wishes are taken into account.

From a policy perspective, it is important to acknowledge the results of our study. Outcomes of scheme participation can be positive, but they seem to be most effective in a country with a long history of active labour market policies and where schemes are more integrated into employment policies, as is the case of Sweden. On the other hand, labour market policies seem not be effective in countries with a high general unemployment level, such as Finland. One of our most important findings is the outcomes of recurrent scheme participation, which were negative in all countries. Circulating from scheme to scheme seems to decrease young persons' future chances in education as well as on the labour market. Therefore, we find it very important that, when young people participate in labour market schemes, these schemes should be a part of their own future plans as bridges to future education or employment. This indicates that schemes should be strongly integrated into labour market and educational institutions and not merely seen as projects in their own right. Furthermore, the quality of the schemes is crucial, as positive subjective scheme experience increases the likelihood of positive outcomes.

Note

[1] Outcome variables were *unemployment, employment in a temporary job, employment in a permanent job, education,* and *participating in a labour market scheme. Scheme participation* was measured by asking respondents whether they had previously participated in a labour market scheme or not. *Recurrent scheme participation* was assessed by a dummy variable measuring whether respondents had participated in labour market schemes more than once. *Positive scheme experiences* were assessed by asking respondents whether they agreed with the following statements: 'I learned something new', 'It was

good to be active', 'It was interesting', 'I gained self-confidence' and 'It was a nice atmosphere'. Those participants who had never participated in a labour market scheme were coded '0' on the variables.

Fractured transitions: the changing context of young people's labour market situations in Europe

Harriet Bradley and Jacques van Hoof

This volume has sought to shed light on the changing fortunes of young people in Europe's labour markets and has highlighted a number of key policy dilemmas. The evidence we have amassed has shown how young people are at the sharp end of global economic change: it is they, rather than their elders, who experience the flexibility and precariousness described by Richard Sennett (1998). They are more likely to be unemployed, more likely to be in dead-end jobs and non-standard work, are less well paid and have more difficulty settling into long-term careers. Bianchi's chapter on Italy (Chapter Ten) offers an extreme example of this, where the employment rights gained by organised labour in the past mean that older workers cannot be removed from their protected jobs, thus restricting entry opportunities for the young. Along with Greece, Italy has currently the highest youth unemployment rate in Europe.

On the positive side, younger people are experiencing higher levels of education and training than previous generations, which may in the long term stand them in good stead. However, as many chapters have indicated, even degree-level education is no guarantor of a job. Fóti et al's chapter (Chapter Six) has highlighted the plight of well-educated youth in Hungary and Slovenia. In these countries there is a risk of 'over-education' because the level of employment seems to be lagging behind the rise of the educational level. Similarly, in the UK and the Netherlands (among other countries) many students on completing undergraduate degrees will take temporary low-skilled employment in bars, restaurants and call-centres, sometimes as a way to make money for travel or further study, sometimes as a way to find out a little more about the world of employment and their own capacities before launching themselves into a more 'serious' career trajectory. The involvement of students, both during their degrees and subsequently, in low-skilled work of course further restricts openings for youngsters without qualifications. While unqualified unemployed young people are offered a wealth of schemes and training opportunities in all European countries, research reveals that here, too, the education strategy has its limits. Malmberg-Heimonen and Julkunen's chapter (Chapter Eleven) shows that, while participating in schemes may aid young people to find employment, a significant number may get trapped in a scenario of recurrent scheme membership.

All this points to a number of key dilemmas for EU states. What types of education and training are most effective in helping young people find employment? Is a move from general to vocational education the best solution? Who should offer support in the lengthened period of dependency brought about by unemployment and longer participation in education? Should it be the state or the family? How can the victims of unemployment and social exclusion be integrated into the labour market? Is activation the right solution? How important is motivation in getting young people into education, employment and training? What kind of welfare provision is best for young people?

The chapters in this book have offered various insights and answers to such questions. In this final section, we start by offering a sociological overview on changing youth transitions, unemployment and citizenship, and end up with some observations about policy trends and suggestions for the future.

Changing transitions

It is instructive to return to one influential model of youth transitions developed in the UK by Ashton and Field (1976). They outlined three routes of transition: the 'extended careers' of those with higher education entering the professional and managerial arena, 'short-term' careers such as banking or craft apprenticeships available to lower middle- and upper-working-class youths, and 'careerless' routes involving entry to unskilled jobs.

This book has confirmed how radically this pattern of transition has altered. It is clear that Ashton and Field's account no longer captures the complexity of labour market trajectories, where people are much more likely to shift between categories and activities as described in Chapters Three and Five. Two major changes are evident. First, transitions have been greatly *lengthened*, as highlighted by many previous commentators (for example, Hollands, 1990; Furlong and Cartmel, 1997). This is in part caused by the expansion of both higher and further education, but it is also due to the longer time it takes young people from all backgrounds to settle down into a steady 'career path'.

Second, transitions have become *more precarious and more complex*. Young people's individual trajectories often take the form of Plug and du Bois-Reymond's 'yo-yo' movements in and out of various activities and work statuses: study, temporary employment, unemployment, training, self-employment, part-time or full-time employment, 'fiddly jobs' in the black economy (MacDonald, 1994), domestic and household work. They may undertake several of these at once. Thus, there is no longer any sense of a simple linear pathway from youth to adult employment and economic independence. Young people are increasingly unlikely to have established themselves in their mid- or late twenties in a traditional career path or a 'job for life'. For this reason, researchers have started to move beyond the 15-24 age group in order to fully understand the nature of transitions, and to utilise more longitudinal methodologies. Both these trends are reflected in the research reported in this volume.

Moreover, the complexity of transitions has been heightened by the major upheaval in gender roles that has taken place since the 1980s (Bradley et al, 2000). In many European societies young women are now out-performing young men in school, entering higher education in greater numbers and competing more successfully with young men for jobs, while the decline in manufacturing and traditional apprenticeships has closed down many opportunities formerly available to young men from manual backgrounds. Migration, increasingly common across Europe, has also had a key impact. Young migrants or young people from minority ethnic groups are likely to face special problems of transition – for example, a recent study of young Turks and Kurds in Britain revealed rates of school exclusion, truancy and low qualifications that led to the young people running the risk of being trapped within the 'ethnic enclave' of employment in kebab shops, sandwich bars and other small community businesses (Modood et al, 2004). The special disadvantages facing young people from minority groups or who are counted as 'foreigners' were explored by Craig et al in Chapter Seven. Young refugees, again a growing group across Europe, are particularly vulnerable to social exclusion, unemployment and racism, along with the illegal migrants, often from North Africa, who can be seen selling 'Prada' handbags in the streets of cities such as Venice and Madrid.

Researchers consequently have turned their attention to the plurality of 'transitions'. Moreover, it is now recognised that there is a need to study transitions more holistically, often focusing on three interrelated aspects of young people's lives: their labour market careers, their housing careers, and the establishment of their own families and households. These are seen as interrelated because it is clear, for example, that the family circumstances of young people (both in terms of the support offered by their families of origin and the responsibilities incurred when they set up their own families) have a crucial impact on labour market opportunities and choices.

As our chapters have shown, many complex factors have contributed to this change to fractured, precarious and lengthened transitions. These include:

1. changes in the structure of labour market opportunities consequent upon broader processes of economic change, such as the rise of post-industrial, service-based economies and decline of traditional manufacturing in the more developed societies, the spread of computer technology and the 'E' economy;
2. the development of management policies designed to promote 'flexibility' at work and among the labour force;
3. the rise of mass long-term unemployment in most European societies during the 1980s and 1990s;
4. the increased proportion of young people staying on after post-compulsory education and taking up places in further and higher education, partly in response to government responses to unemployment;
5. the proliferation of state and private sector training schemes and programmes, again a typical government response to youth unemployment;
6. the rapidly rising cost of housing in many societies;
7. the feminisation of the labour force, which means increased competition for young men;
8. new patterns of migration within Europe, especially since the reintegration of former Soviet-bloc nations into Europe, and from outside Europe, including refugees and asylum seekers.

Against these factors, it may be worth pointing out that a major demographic trend, the ageing of the population and the reduction in proportion of the younger cohorts, may in the longer term have some positive effects for young people and improve their labour market position. However, we should not be surprised if the less well-educated young people profit least from it.

Behind these socioeconomic changes lie even larger-scale issues of globalisation, increased market competition, the changing international division of labour, and the collapse of the former Soviet Union. These structural forces have impinged significantly on the lives of young people in Europe. As a result of these forces, we have seen that many more young people are likely to find themselves being dependent on either their families or the state for longer.

Many young people are likely to stay dependent on their parents for longer than in the past, especially young men who, in Britain for example, are three times more likely than young women to stay at home after finishing schooling and twice as likely to return home after initially leaving. It was already the case that in Mediterranean countries such as Spain and Italy it was the norm for young people to stay in the parental home until they married or started their own households. As Jones reports in Chapter Two, 53% of young Spanish people aged 25-29 live at home with their parents. While this pattern is less common in northern societies, we have suggested that they are clearly moving in this direction. It is only in some of the Scandinavian countries, with their relatively generous levels of social security, that young people are able to maintain a higher degree of independence in their housing transitions. However, this will only persist as long as the level of social security in these countries remains high. Should this decline, they might become quite vulnerable because parental support is not such a tradition. These processes are already having a negative impact on young people in Finland.

Losing out: youth, unemployment and exclusion

As we argued in the Introduction, the major policy concern consequent upon the changes described earlier has been the rise of mass youth unemployment across Europe. While the exact proportions are variable and dependent on the general economic performance of each country, its policies on youth and its sectoral composition, there is little doubt that there is a common trend. In 1998 40% of the unemployed in Europe were under 25 years old (Carle and Hammer, Chapter Eight).

At the heart of this problem is the decrease in the number of job opportunities in what was traditionally the 'youth employment' market. Primarily these jobs are in manufacturing; there has been a loss both of unskilled factory work and of skilled apprenticeships, although the latter has been experienced less in the countries of northern Europe (for example, Denmark, Germany and the Netherlands). Where new service jobs have been created, for example in retail or catering and leisure, young entrants to the labour force who might expect to get such unskilled low-paid jobs have increasingly found themselves in competition with other sources of labour, such as married women, migrant workers, students and even newly qualified graduates. Certainly in Britain and the Netherlands, employers show a preference for these categories of worker over low-skilled young people, and are increasingly reluctant to employ unqualified school leavers, whom they see as lacking in work experience and work discipline.

Whether this loss of employment opportunities has resulted in the growth of an unemployed or under-employed 'underclass' is not a debate that will be entered into here. This trend does, however, raise questions about the growth of the alternative or unofficial economy. In Britain many officially 'out of work' young people may find a source of income in 'fiddly jobs', criminal activity and, particularly, in the thriving drugs subculture. Low-level self-employment is another option: there has been a rise in street selling (especially common in Europe among young legal or illegal immigrants) in craft markets: young people may work the popular music festival scene, selling refreshments and New Age artefacts. While economic improvement in many countries has led to some recent decline in youth unemployment, this remains a major problem with considerable social implications (for example, a rise in crime and vandalism, ethnic tensions and racism, and a burgeoning drugs culture among young people).

We have offered in this section a structural account of the rise of youth unemployment. Governments across Europe have attempted to find structural solutions to the problem: encouraging young people to stay on at school and to enter further or higher education (although, as we have seen in the chapters of Fóti et al (Six) and Bianchi (Ten), this may be only deferring the problem); strengthening or initiating programmes of vocational education (Chapters Nine and Ten); and devising wide varieties of programmes to assist and train unemployed, unqualified youngsters (Chapter Eleven). As time has gone by, such programmes have increasingly taken the form of 'workfare' schemes, and tended to focus on the particular needs of individual young people. As Reiter and Craig so powerfully argue in Chapter One, the thrust of much contemporary youth policy is to individualise the problem, ascribing unemployment to lack of motivation and low employability. The target is to change young people's attitudes, demeanour and behaviour. The results of the cross-European survey reported in Hammer (2003), and in Chapters Four, Eight and Eleven, are particularly crucial here. For example, this research demonstrates that, along with material deprivation, young unemployed people are more likely to experience a decline in psychological well-being. Mental health problems may contribute to young people being trapped in a cycle of structural disadvantage. However, most importantly, in their exploration of job-seeking behaviour and attitudes, Álvaro and Garrido (Chapter Four) find that there is no lack of motivation or desire to find work among the young employed and that they actively pursue job-seeking strategies. This challenges the assumptions of many youth unemployment schemes.

Winners and losers: the consolidation of a low-wage economy

Given the rise of youth unemployment and deprivation, it is not surprising that government policy on youth has concentrated on support and training for the young unemployed, and that much research on youth has focused on this group (for example, the work of Hammer and colleagues (2003) or Chatrik et al (2000) on the 'disappeared'). However, it is important to note that these are not the only young people who are being affected by neo-liberal economic development, the rise of flexible capitalism and the service economy.

It is possible to speak of a polarisation between the young excluded and a minority of highly qualified young people who are able to take advantage of the new parameters to attain highly paid professional and managerial careers: in a report on the youth programme in Britain funded by the Joseph Rowntree Foundation, Gill Jones termed this the 'Youth Divide' (2002). Such a divide is evident in most European countries. However, a number of chapters in this book indicate that the picture is more complex.

First, in most European countries there is a sizeable 'intermediate' category between the young excluded and the minority of highly qualified young people. We refer here to those young people in skilled industrial occupations and (increasingly) those in relatively stable jobs in the financial, commercial, social/cultural and personal services. In fact, many countries are trying to bolster up this category by improving vocational education. This group is probably more significant in those countries where a developed system of vocational education exists, such as Germany, Netherlands and Denmark. Jobs in these areas are increasingly being feminised, and it may be seen as a vulnerable category because young people in these intermediate jobs are more likely to have a 'traditional' outlook and be less adaptable to flexible conditions (see Chapter Three by Plug and du Bois-Reymond). The prospects for this category will be decisive for the future of the youth labour market.

Second, as shown in Chapters Five and Six, many young people who are in jobs still face disadvantageous conditions: low pay, casual or temporary work, insecure employment and uncertain futures. They are more likely than their parents to experience spells out of the labour market, either forced (unemployment) or voluntary (travel, study). With the end of 'jobs for life' many young people face a future with the prospect of no pension or very limited pension provisions. Those who are in high-status jobs may find themselves caught up in a 'long hours culture' that is inimical to family life and a healthy 'work–life balance'.

The research of Bradley and colleagues and du Bois-Reymond and colleagues suggests that work–life balance is a key issue for young people. These studies showed that young people had neither abandoned the work ethic to become leisure-centred, nor become fixated on work to the exclusion of all else. Rather, they were committed to developing and planning a rewarding working life, but also continued to place high priority on family and relationships, while hoping to enjoy a rich leisure life with travel being particularly a desideratum. In some ways these young people seem to be saner than their more workaholic elders (see Pahl, 1995), but it may also be that such a search for balance is an illusion. It also points to the continuation of sex differentiation in labour market histories. Both in Bristol and the Netherlands young women tended to favour the more 'traditional' options of stopping employment or working part-time when children came along, rather than seeking to maintain their careers and share both wage and domestic labour equally (a 'modern' option). As we saw, Plug and du Bois-Reymond (Chapter Three) found that less-qualified working-class people were more likely to be traditional in their choices, but the Bristol study indicated that a majority from all class backgrounds took this view, although there was a small group of highly qualified work-oriented women who were determined not to compromise their careers. However, the majority of women who opt for traditional ways to balance home and work are likely to continue to lose out against men in terms of career development, levels of pay and pensions.

In such an environment, of insecurity, fractured trajectories, yo-yo movements and lengthened dependence, it is clear that the various kinds of capital provided by families (economic, social and cultural) are becoming ever more important. We can talk of a privatisation or familiarisation (see Jones' Chapter Two) of welfare with families forced to bear the brunt of support for young adults well into their twenties.

Moreover, broader networks of support (community, extended kin, friendship groups and so on) are likely also to be crucial to young people as they make their way in the world. In this sense, the possession of positive or 'bridging' social capital is increasingly at play in the polarisation of young people's life chances. Families help young people in a variety of ways, including providing them with shelter and subsistence, helping them buy homes, cars and material goods, providing work and business contacts, helping them find jobs or even employing them, and looking after young children. Friends are also important in helping find jobs. By contrast, what might be seen as 'negative' social capital, which pulls young people into destructive or criminal networks, may be an important contributor to processes of social exclusion. A limited and localised network may trap young people in lower-paid labour markets and limit their horizons.

While the focus of youth employment policy is, reasonably enough, on current problems, all this suggests that a wealth of future social problems may be accruing. Young people move from job to job, inhibiting the likelihood of occupational pensions. Lengthened stays in education and redundancies/early retirement are curtailing the period of 'working life' at both ends, with a likely impact on savings and pension entitlements. Low wages contribute to this effect. In sum, we can see a major crisis about support in old age occurring. This will place a further burden on families and it also raises the issue of how the next generation will be able to cushion their own children against unemployment and precarious employment.

Young people and citizenship: a politically marginalised generation?

The above discussion has focused on economic aspects of youth disadvantage. It is important to recognise that social exclusion extends beyond material deprivation and involves social marginalisation and exclusion from full participation in other aspects of social activity. Two themes have particularly occupied our attention.

First, we are concerned with the way young people from minority ethnic groups are excluded from citizen rights in many countries, as discussed by Craig et al in Chapter Seven. Research has suggested that contemporary citizenship is defined by active labour market involvement (Walby, 1997). Thus the unemployed and marginalised are in effect second-class citizens. Again this especially affects minority ethnic young people because they are much more likely to be unemployed. Young women, who as we have seen are still more likely to withdraw from the labour market, also continue to be debarred from full citizen rights.

Second is the way current circumstances, especially unemployment, serve to isolate young people from political participation. In Chapter Eight Carle and Hammer reveal a complex picture. Unemployed young people are somewhat less likely to be politically active than employed youth. They are not in trade unions, which are an important site of political socialisation. This may account for the slight tendency to informal modes of political action noted by Carle and Hammer. Such young people are more likely to be left-leaning, although a minority may be drawn to extreme-right nationalist parties as an outlet for their resentment and frustration. They are more likely to show distrust for the formal political system, although Carle and Hammer found this less the case in Scandinavia, perhaps reflecting better state welfare support provision. All this is not because they are against political activism, but they have fewer channels of access and fewer resources. Thus the young unemployed show diminished levels of citizenship. Carle and Hammer suggest that this has not yet led to either increased militancy or very high degrees of alienation, but rather to apathy in the face of powerlessness. However, the sporadic outbursts of rioting and youth violence in places with high unemployment alert us to the potential for social disruption. We still need to know a lot more about young people's political behaviour and attitudes, which are likely, anyway, to be variably affected by the specific political cultures and power configurations of different nations.

Welfare, activation and dualism

Specificity is also an issue when considering welfare responses, since an initial conclusion from the work of our COST group was that welfare provision was highly differentiated, with countries developing their unique policies to deal with specific problems and reflecting the countries' precise positions in terms of economic development and sectoral composition. However, in this volume we have used various adaptations of Esping-Andersen's well-known typology of social democratic, liberal and conservative welfare regimes to describe clusters of countries that we have found to have broadly similar youth policies. Jones' modified version of this typology was set out in Chapter Two and includes two extra categories. Latin Rim countries are characterised by a less developed welfare state and a high degree of familialism. Finally, a new cluster of post-Soviet societies face their own problems as a result of the abrupt transition to neo-liberal economics and capitalism. In particular, as Fóti et al's Chapter Six shows, the new spectre of widespread youth unemployment poses problems for youth in those countries with their newly awakened consumption aspirations.

However, beyond that we can see some common trends across Europe that reflect the growth of flexible capitalism and global interchange, so we end this discussion by highlighting a few policy responses that seem to be emerging across Europe: the *individualising* tendencies within *activation* policies; more *targeted* provision of training; a stress on *vocational* learning; the development of *dualised* systems and of *lifelong learning* to facilitate access to the labour market and employability; and the need to offset gender inequities with *family-friendly policies*.

In Chapter One Reiter and Craig argue that the tendency within state policy reflects the culture and ideology of individualism that has been promoted by neo-liberalism and presents success and failure as the responsibility of the individual. The Dutch and British studies suggest that in many countries young people are buying into this ideology, which stresses ideas of merit, achievement, planning and hard work. Accordingly, as we have shown, many schemes now focus on engagement and motivation of young people as a way to reintegrate them into the workforce. A key trend, therefore, is the switch from *passive* to *active* approaches with a workfare element. The aim of these new schemes is to increase employability. Typical of such an approach is the new Connexions programme in Britain, which aims to provide a universal and 'joined-up' advice service for all young people aged 13-18. This scheme is based on consistent monitoring, the provision of a 'personal adviser' to act as mentor and counsellor, and the development of individualised targets and work plans.

Targeting is also crucial. As youth unemployment rises and resources are stretched, programmes are increasingly focused on a 'hard core' of 'at risk' young people who are multiply disadvantaged and often have failed to prosper under previous training and education attempts. Moreover, a 'one size fits all' model is rejected, as trainers and providers seek to tailor courses to the needs of particular groups – for example, drug users or teenage parents, those with special educational needs or minority ethnic youth. This again is a key feature of Connexions. This attempt to define differing needs could be seen as an extension and development of the 'dual system' (academic and vocational pathways), which up to now has proved very successful in countries such as Germany and the Netherlands. Such an approach recognises the importance of diversity and 'multiple positioning' (Bradley, 1999) in social support systems.

A very important trend to be witnessed both in the Western European countries and the countries of the 'New Europe', such as Slovenia and Hungary, is *vocationalism*, the policy of improving and upgrading vocational education and training. Inspired by the example of Germany's 'dual system' (a systematic combination of on-the-job training and school-based vocational education leading to recognised qualifications), many countries are experimenting with new ways of combining education and work experience training as a way to improve the transition from school to work. Increasingly, a basic level of vocational skills is seen as the best guarantee against youth unemployment. In this volume two cases were discussed in detail: Italy, where the move towards vocational training is a recent development, and the Netherlands, where public vocational education has a long tradition, but government and industry together are now trying to strengthen the dual element by integrating apprenticeship training into the public system. In the latter case, according to van Hoof, some of the limitations of the vocational strategy become apparent. First, most of the time there is a tension between the short-term perspective of training young people for direct employability (which is favoured by many employers) and a long-term view of skill development emphasising trainability and employability in a broader sense. Vocational education tends to follow the immediate skill demands of industry too closely, which may jeopardise the labour market integration of qualified young people in the long run. Second, the upgrading of vocational education may create a threshold at the lower level of the system of vocational education for those young people who only have a minimum of general education, and in this way contribute indirectly to the process of losing out described earlier. Third, systems of vocational education are often beset by high drop-out rates, which have to do with a lack of previous schooling by some of the participants but also with the attraction of paid work. Although there are indications that vocational education and training facilitate the transition from school to work (see Chapter Nine), it is no easy road towards the solution of youth unemployment.

Another key strand is the shift to *lifelong learning*, which follows from the end of a job for life. States increasingly recognise that people are likely to change occupations in the course of a lifetime. Bianchi (Chapter Ten) points to the mismatch in Italy between young school leavers' attributes and employers' demands. There is therefore a need for people to have easy access to skills training as their jobs and the attributes of jobs in general change. Evidence from Britain and the Netherlands suggests that young people have bought into the culture of training and retraining. Rather than being overwhelmed and dismayed by flexibility and insecurity, young people respond to it pragmatically and even in some cases with enthusiasm. Thus access to educational provision (further and higher education) and training must be made more easily accessible to groups other than initial school leavers. However, this is easier said than done. The main reason is that in most countries lifelong learning is mainly provided by the market (Crouch et al, 1999) and opportunities for lifelong learning are highly contingent upon having a job. By having a job young people get access to organisational (sponsored) training, but even then they remain dependent on decisions of their employer to focus training on particular groups of workers. It is well known that firms' training is not evenly distributed among employees and that some categories (women, minority ethnic employees, low-skilled workers) get less than their share. Therefore, these categories depend on outside interventions for access to lifelong learning. In some countries the government plays an active role — for example in France, where employers are legally obliged to spend a part of total wages on training. Subsidising training costs of some target groups is another option being used in some countries, as is the creation of facilities for educational leave. In other countries (including the Netherlands and the UK), employers and trade unions have taken an initiative by introducing training rights for employees in collective agreements, and establishing jointly administered training funds to cover part of the training costs (van Hoof, 2000). However, in spite of these initiatives, there is still a long way to go in many countries before young people have easy access to and financial support for the full range of training and educational opportunities.

Additionally, there remains a gender skew in pay and opportunities. While young women across Europe are equalling or surpassing their brothers in educational achievement, troubles still develop when children come along. While only a percentage of the studied age group is as yet affected by this, it is important that young women's initial achievements are not negated by family arrangements. The Scandinavian models of childcare provision and parental rights (such as the Norwegian 'Daddy weeks', which require fathers to spend some time alone with their infants) are justly renowned and should be extended across Europe and the conservative, liberal and familial regimes as part of the development of a *family-friendly working environment*.

Along with gender, other forms of social division must not be forgotten. Issues of ethnicity and racism are of particular concern. Study in this area is made harder by the lack of official statistics or ethnic monitoring systems in many countries. In the context of continued youth disadvantage along with increased diversity, a major task for future labour market research is the collection of data, both quantitative and qualitative, to illuminate the special dilemmas and difficulties faced by different categories of youth.

Finally, we have discerned a major weakness in contemporary youth employment policies. All the trends we have discussed centre on the young people themselves. It is their supposed lack of 'will' and 'skill' that is seen as the cause of problems and that therefore has to be corrected by activation, training and so on. On the contrary, policy options directed to the demand side of the youth labour market, and measures to stimulate youth employment by creating jobs, are often completely lacking. A similar conclusion was reached in the recent study of the EGRIS group of European youth researchers (Walther et al, 2002). There is a need for job schemes in addition to activation and training schemes. As we have seen, much traditional youth employment has disappeared, while many new low-skilled and semi-skilled jobs are now turned into part-time jobs for students and women. It appears as if job creation schemes (both schemes for subsidised jobs in general and schemes targeted at unemployed young people such as those utilised in Denmark and the Netherlands) have been replaced by activation and training schemes, under the inspiration of neo-liberal policy thinking.

Conclusion

Reiter and Craig in Chapter One have highlighted the contradictions and tensions in these new policies on youth unemployment. In focusing on individual motivation and employability, they may help some individual young people, but they fail to address the structural causes of social exclusion, marginalisation, unemployment and poverty and, above all, the lack of suitable jobs. Indeed active labour market policies may only serve to deepen social divisions, of gender, ethnicity, class and region. Normative elements, which enter into the definition of 'employability', mean that schemes attempt to remodel young people into displaying 'acceptable' forms of behaviour that are at odds with certain class, ethnic and gender cultures. There are requirements for mobility, long working hours and particular habits of speech and dress that disadvantage the already disadvantaged. As Reiter and Craig state, such normative prescriptions are based upon a misperception of youth as 'lazy and unwilling'.

There is pressure on young people to get into the labour market at all costs, and employers and employment agencies collude in offering low-paid jobs to young people. Policies designed to prevent state dependency are only succeeding at a macro level in contributing to lengthened transitions and dependency, where young people are unable to achieve independent living and establish households. The prolonging of education and greater opportunities for training, while they may be welcomed in theory as an aid to self-development and self-sufficiency, have failed as yet to solve the problems of youth unemployment and poverty. Neo-liberal economic systems create structural unemployment: individualising youth policies do little to relieve it.

References

Abrahamson, P. (1999a) 'The Scandinavian model of welfare', in *Comparing social welfare systems in Nordic Europe and France*, Nantes: Mire Drees Collection, pp 31-60.

Abrahamson, P. (1999b) 'Activation and social policies: comparing France and Scandinavia', in B. Palier and D. Boguet (eds) *Comparing social welfare systems in Nordic Europe and France*, Nantes: Mire Drees Collection, pp 403-17.

Accornero, A. and Carmignani, F. (1986) *I paradossi della disoccupazione*, Bologna: Il Mulino.

Alacevich, F. (1998) *Annual Report on negotiation and consultation in Italy*, First Report issued for the European-wide research coordinated by the Institut des Sciences du Travail (IST), University of Louvain La Neuve (UCL): European Commission.

Allatt, P. and Yeandle, S. (1992) *Youth unemployment and the family*, London: Routledge.

Álvaro, J.L. (1992) *Desempleo y bienestar psicológico*, Madrid: Siglo XXI.

Álvaro, J.L. and Garrido, A. (2000) 'Youth and the social protection system in Spain', Paper presented at the meeting of the COST A13 Working Group 4, December, Madrid.

Ambrosini, A. (ed) (2000) *Un futuro da formare*, Brescia: La Scuola.

Anastasia, B. and Corò, G. (1999) 'Lavori e non lavoro: la strada obliqua', in I. Diamanti (ed) *La generazione invisibile*, Milano: Il Sole 24 ore.

Andersen, J.G. and Jensen, P.H. (eds) (2002) *Changing labour markets, welfare policies and citizenship*, Bristol: The Policy Press.

Aramburu-Zabala, L. (1998) 'Determinantes psicosociales de la búsqueda de empleo', *Revista de Psicología del Trabajo y de las Organizaciones*, vol 14, pp 315-31.

Armstrong, D. (ed) (1997) *'Status 0': A socio-economic study of young people on the margin*, Belfast: Northern Ireland Economic Research Centre, Queens University Belfast.

Arts, W. and Gelissen, J. (2002) 'Three worlds of welfare capitalism and more? A state-of-the-art report', *Journal of European Social Policy*, vol 12, no 2, pp 137-58.

Ashton, D. and Field, D. (1976) *Young workers*, London: Hutchison.

Attias-Donfut, C. and Wolff, F.C. (2000a) 'Complementarity between public and private transfers', in S. Arber and C. Attias-Donfut (eds) *The myth of generational conflict: family and state in ageing societies*, London: Routledge, pp 47-68.

Attias-Donfut, C. and Wolff, F.C. (2000b) 'The redistributive effects of generational transfers', in S. Arber and C. Attias-Donfut (eds) *The myth of generational conflict: Family and state in ageing societies*, London: Routledge, pp 22-46.

Bagguley, P. and Mann, K. (1992) 'Idle thieving bastards? Scholarly representations of the "underclass"', *Work, Employment and Society*, vol 6, no 1, pp 113-26.

Ball, S. (2003) *Class strategies and the education market: The middle classes and social advantage*, London: Routledge.

Banks, M. and Ullah, P. (1987) 'Political attitudes and voting among unemployed youth', *Journal of Adolescence*, vol 10, no 2, pp 210-16.

Barbagli, M. (1974) *Disoccupazione intellettuale e sistema scolastico in Italia*, Bologna: Il Mulino.

Barbagli, M. and Saraceno, C. (eds) (1997) *Lo stato delle famiglie in Italia*, Bologna: Il Mulino.

Bates, I. and Riseborough, G. (1993) *Youth and inequality*, Milton Keynes: Open University Press.

Bauman, Z. (1998) *Work, consumerism and the new poor*, Buckingham: Open University Press.

Bauman, Z. (2002) *The individualized society*, Cambridge: Polity Press.

Bay, A.H. and Blekesaune, M. (2002) 'Youth, unemployment and political marginalization', *International Journal of Social Welfare*, vol 11, no 2, pp 132-9.

Beaud, S. (2002) *80 per cent d'une classe d'âge au Bac ... et après?*, Paris: La Découverte.

Beauftragte der Bundesregierung fur Auslanderfragen (2002) *Daten und fakten zur Auslandersituation*, Auflage: Bonn.

Beck, U. (1992) *Risk society: Towards a new modernity*, London: Sage Publications.

Beck, U. (2000) *The brave new world of work*, Cambridge: Polity Press.

Beck, U. and Beck-Gernsheim, E. (2002) *Individualization*, London: Sage Publications.

Beck, U., Giddens, A. and Lash, S. (1994) *Reflexive modernization: Politics, tradition and aesthetics in the modern social order*, Cambridge: Polity Press.

Behrens, M. and Evans, K (2002) 'Taking control of their lives? A comparison of the experience of unemployed young adults (18-25) in England and new Germany', *Comparative Education*, vol 38, no 1, pp 17-37.

Bergmark, Å. and Palme, J. (2003) 'Welfare and unemployment crisis: Sweden in the 1990s', *International Journal of Social Welfare*, vol 12, pp 108-22.

Berthoud, R. (1999) *Young Caribbean men and the labour market*, York: YPS.

Bertrand, O. (2002) 'Jeune, musulman et français, une identité difficile à faire accepter', *Libération*, vol 15, pp 6-8.

Besozzi, E. (ed) (1998) *Navigare tra formazione e lavoro*, Roma: Carocci.

Bevc, M. (2002) *Uèinkovitost dodiplomskega študija v Sloveniji, druga longitudinalna analiza (Effectiveness of undergraduate studies in Slovenia, second longitudinal analysis)*, Ljubljana: Institute of Economic Research.

Bianchi, F. and Giovannini, P. (eds) (2000) *Il lavoro nei paesi d'Europa*, Milano: Angeli.

Bison, I. and Esping-Andersen, G. (2000) 'Unemployment, welfare regime, and income packaging', in D. Gallie and S. Paugam (eds) *Welfare regimes and the experience of unemployment in Europe*, Oxford: Oxford University Press, pp 69-86.

Björgö, T. (1997) *Racist and right-wing violence in Scandinavia*, Oslo: Tano Ashehoug.

Blanchflower, D.G. and Freeman, R.B. (2000) 'The declining economic status of young workers in OECD countries', in D.G. Blanchflower and R.B. Freeman (eds) *Youth employment and joblessness in advanced countries*, Chicago, IL: The University of Chicago Press, pp 19-55.

Bleich, E. (2003) *Race politics in Britain and France*, Cambridge: Cambridge University Press.

Bloch, A. and Schuster, L. (2002) 'Asylum and welfare: contemporary debates', *Critical Social Policy*, vol 22, no 3, pp 393-415.

Boltanski, L. and Chiapello, E. (2002) 'The new spirit of capitalism', Paper presented at the Conference of Europeanists, 14-16 March, Chicago (mimeo).

Bouget, D. (2002) 'Movements by the unemployed in France and social protection: the fonds d'urgence sociale experience', in J. Goul Andersen and P. Jensen (eds) *Changing labour markets, welfare policies and citizenship*, Bristol: The Policy Press.

Bouget, D. and Brovelli, G. (2002) 'Citizenship, social welfare system and social policies in France', *European Societies*, vol 4, no 2, pp 161-84.

Bourdieu, P. (1998) *Acts of resistance. Against the new myths of our time*, Cambridge: Polity Press.

Bradley, H. (1999) 'Inequalities: coming to terms with complexity', in G. Browning, A. Halcli and F. Webster (eds) *Theory and society: Understanding the present*, London: Sage Publications.

Bradley, H. (1996) *Fractured identities*, Cambridge: Polity Press.

Bradley, H., Erickson, M., Stephenson, C. and Williams, S. (2000) *Myths at work*, Cambridge: Polity Press.

Breedveld, K. (2001) *Van arbeids – naar combinatie-ethos*, Werkdocument, Den Haag: SCP.

Britton, L., Chatrik, B., Coles, B., Craig, G., Hylton, C. and Mumtaz, S. with Bivand, P., Burrows, R. and Convery, P. (2002) *Missing Connexions? The career dynamics and welfare needs of 16-17 year-olds*, Bristol/York: The Policy Press/Joseph Rowntree Foundation.

Bynner, J. and Ashford, S. (1994) 'Politics and participation – some antecedents of young people's attitudes to the political system and political activity', *European Journal of Social Psychology*, vol 24, no 2, pp 223-36.

Bynner, J., Londra, M. and Jones, G. (2004) *The impact of government policy on social exclusion among young people: A review of the literature*, Breaking the Cycle Series, Social Exclusion Unit, London: Office of the Deputy Prime Minister.

Bynner, J., Elias, P., MacKnight, A., Pan, H. and Pierre, G. (2002) *Young people's changing routes to independence*, York: Joseph Rowntree Foundation.

Byrne, D. (1999) *Social exclusion*, Buckingham: Open University Press.

Caplan, R., Vinokur, A., Price, R. and van Ryn, M. (1989) 'Job seeking, re-employment, and mental health: a randomised field experimental study', *Journal of Applied Psychology*, vol 74, pp 759-69.

Carle, J. (2000a) *Opinion och aktion. En sociologisk studie av ungdomar och miljö* (*Opinion and action – a sociological study of youth and environment*), Göteborg: University of Göteborg.

Carle, J. (2000b) 'Political activity in the context of youth unemployment – experiences from young people in six Northern European countries', *YOUNG*, vol 8, no 4, pp 16-39.

Carle, J. (2002) 'Jóvenas y relaciones familiares en Suecia', *Revista de Estudies De Juventud*, vol 58, no 2, pp 79-92.

Carle, J. (2003) 'Political participation and welfare regimes', in T. Hammer (ed) *Youth unemployment and social exclusion in Europe*, Bristol: The Policy Press, pp 193-205.

Carle, J. and Hammer, T. (2003) 'Method and research design', in T. Hammer (ed) *Youth unemployment and social exclusion in Europe*, Bristol: The Policy Press, pp 121-9.

Caroleo, F. and Pastore, F. (2003) 'Youth participation in the labour market in Germany, Spain and Sweden', in T. Hammer (ed) *Youth unemployment and social exclusion in Europe*, Bristol: The Policy Press, pp 109-35.

Castles, S. (2000) *Ethnicity and globalization*, London: Sage Publications.

Cavalli, A. and Galland, O. (eds) (1993) *L'allongement de la jeunesse*, Actes Sud.

Cazes, S. and Nesporova, A. (2003) *Labour markets in transition: Balancing flexibility and security in Central and Eastern Europe*, Geneva: ILO.

CBS (Centraal Bureau voor de Statistiek) (2001) *Jeugd 2001*, Voorburg/Heerlen: CBS (www.cbs.nl).

CENSIS (2001) *35° Rapporto sulla situazione sociale del paese*, Milano: Angeli.

CEREQ (2002) *Quand l'école est finie. Premiers pas dans la vie active de la Génération 98*, Marseille: CEREQ.

Chabbert, I. and Kerschen, N. (2001) 'Towards a European model of employability insurance? Interaction between Europe and the member states', in P. Weinert, M. Baukens, P. Bollérot, M. Pineschi-Gapènne and U. Walwei (eds) *Employability: From theory to practice*, International Social Security Series, vol 7, New Brunswick, NJ: Transaction Publishers, pp 91-112.

Chahal, K. (2000) *Ethnic diversity, neighbourhoods and housing*, York: Joseph Rowntree Foundation.

Chandola, T. (2001) 'Ethnic and class differences in health in relation to British South Asians: using new national statistics socio-economic classification', *Social Science & Medicine*, vol 52, pp 1285-96.

Chatrik, B. and Convery, P. (2000) *New Deal handbook* (3rd edn), London: Unemployment Unit and Youthaid.

Chatrik, B., Coles, R., Craig, G., Hylton, C. and Mumtaz, S. (2000) 'The disappeared: how many are there and where have they gone?', Paper for the Youth Research Conference, September 3, University of Keele, mimeo.

Coffield, F. (2000) *The necessity of informal learning*, Bristol: The Policy Press.

Coleman, J.C. (1997) 'The parenting of adolescents in Britain today', *Children and Society*, vol 11, pp 44-52.

Coles, B. (1995) *Youth and social policy: Youth citizenship and young careers*, London: UCL Press.

Coles, B. (2000a) *Joined up youth research, policy and practice*, Ilford: Barnardos.

Coles, B. (2000b) 'Slouching towards Bethlehem: youth policy and the work of the Social Exclusion Unit', *Social Policy Review 12*, Lavenham: Social Policy Association.

Coles, B. (2003) 'Connexions: an outbreak in purple and orange', *Benefits*, vol 11, no 2, pp 93-8.

Colombo, M. (2001) *Scuola e comunità locali*, Roma: Carocci.

Craig, G. (1991) *Fit for nothing?*, London: Children's Society.

Craig, G. (1999) '"Race', social security to poverty', in J. Ditch (ed) *Introduction to social security*, London: Routledge, pp 206-26.

Craig, G. (2002) 'Ethnicity, racism and the labour market: a European perspective', in J. Goul Andersen and P. Jensen (eds) *Changing labour markets, welfare policies and citizenship*, Bristol: The Policy Press, pp 149-82.

Craig, G. (2003a) 'Involving children in policy development', in C. Hallet and A. Prout (eds) *Hearing the voices of children*, Brighton: Falmer, pp 38-56.

Craig, G. (2003b) 'Globalization, migration and social development', *Journal of Social Development in Africa*, vol 2, pp 49-76.

Craig, G. (2004) 'Citizenship, exclusion and older people', *Journal of Social Policy*, vol 3, no 1, pp 95-114.

Craig, G., Elliott-White, M. and Perkins, N. (1999) *Mapping disaffected youth*, Lincoln: Lincolnshire Training and Enterprise Council.

Cretney, S.M. and Masson, J.M. (1997) *Principles of family law* (6th edn), London: Sweet and Maxwell.

Crompton, R. (1997) *Women's work in modern Britain*, Oxford: Oxford University Press.

Crompton, R. and Sanderson, K. (1990) *Gendered jobs and social change*, London: Unwin.

Crouch, C. (2000) 'Die europäische(n) gesellschaft(en) unter dem druck der globalisierung', *Jahrbuch für Europa – und Nordamerika-Studien*, vol 4, pp 77-99.

Crouch, C. (2001) *Sociologia dell'Europa occidentale*, Bologna: Il Mulino.

Crouch, C. and Streeck, W. (1997) *Political economy of modern capitalism. Mapping convergence and diversity*, London: Sage Publications.

Crouch, C., Finegold, D. and Sako, M. (1999) *Are skills the answer? The political economy of skill creation in advanced industrial countries*, Oxford: Oxford University Press.

Crouch, C., Eder, K. and Tambini, D. (2001) 'Introduction: dilemmas of citizenship', in C. Crouch, K. Eder and D. Tambini (eds) *Citizenship, markets, and the state*, Oxford: Oxford University Press, pp 1-21.

Crow, G. and Rees, T. (1999) '"Winners" and "losers" in social transformations', *Sociological Research Online*, vol 4, no 1.

Cseke, H. (2003) 'Kezdõ lépés' ('Initial step'), *Figyelõ* (Observer, Hungarian economic weekly), Budapest, 25 December 2003-7 January 2004.

CYPU (Children and Young People's Unit) (2001) *Tomorrow's future: Building a strategy for children and young people*, London: CYPU.

Cyrus, N. (nd) 'Ein anwerbestopp und seine ausnahmen. Aktuelle formen grenzüberschreitender Beschäftigung', *der Bundesrepublik Deutschland* (www.radapl.de/anwerbe.htm).

Dahrendorf, R. (1995) *Quadrare il cerchio. Benessere economico, coesione sociale e libertà politica*, Roma-Bari: Laterza.

Deacon, A. (1976) *In search of the scrounger*, LSE Occasional Papers, London: Bell.

Dean, H. (1995) 'Paying for children', in H. Dean (ed) *Parents' duties, children's debts*, Hampshire: Arena.

Dean, H. and Taylor-Gooby, P. (1992) *Dependency culture: The explosion of a myth*, London: Harvester Wheatsheaf.

Dean, H. and Melrose, M. (1999) *Poverty, riches and social citizenship*, London: Routledge.

Dearden, C. and Becker, S. (2000) *Growing up caring: Vulnerability and transition to adulthood – young carers' experiences*, Leicester: Youth Work Press and the Joseph Rowntree Foundation.

de Beer, P.T. (2001) *Over werken in de postindustriële samenleving*, Rijswijk: SCP.

de Jong, U. and Berkenbosch, J. (2001) 'Toegankelijkheid', in R. van der Velden (ed) *Toegankelijkheid, intern rendement en doorstroom*, Zoetermeer: Stuurgroep Evaluatie WEB.

de Maio, A. (2000) 'Presentazione', in S. Cortellazzi (ed) *Percorsi per l'apprendistato*, Milano: Guerini e associati.

de Swaan, A. (1982) 'Uitgaansbeperking en uitgaansangst. Over de verschuiving van bevelshuishouding naar onderhandelingshuis-houding', in A. Swaan (ed) *De mens is de mens een zorg*, Amsterdam: Meulenhoff, pp 81-115.

Denters, B. (2002) 'Size and political trust: evidence from Denmark, the Netherlands, and the United Kingdom', *Environment and Planning C-Government and Policy*, vol 20, no 6, pp 793-812.

Devadason, R., Bradley, H., Fenton, S., Guy, W. and West, J. (2001) 'Which way is up? Changing discourses of inequality and young adults' labour market trajectories', Paper presented at Work, Employment and Society Conference, University of Nottingham.

de Witte, H. (1992) 'Unemployment, political attitudes and voting behaviour', *Politics and the Individual*, vol 2, no 1, pp 29-41.

Dex, S., Robson, P. and Wilkinson, F. (1999) 'The characteristics of the low-paid: a cross-national comparison', *Work, Employment and Society*, vol 13, no 3, pp 503-4.

DfEE (Department for Education and Employment) (2000) *Connexions: The best start in life for every young person*, London: DfEE.

DHSS (Department of Health and Social Security)(1985) *Reform of social security*, Green Paper, Cmnd 9517, London: HMSO.

Diefenbach, H. (2002) 'Bildungsbeteiligung und Berufseinmündung von Kindern und Jugendlichen aus Migrantenfamilien', in *Sachverständigenkommission 11, Kinder und Jugendbericht* (ed) Band 5: Migration und die Europäische Integration, Opladen: Leske & Budrich, pp 98-70.

Dieleman, A. (2000a) 'Individualisering en ambivalentie in het bestaan van jongeren', *Pedagogiek*, vol 20, no 2, pp 91-111.

Dieleman, A. (2000b) *Als de toekomst wacht… Over individualisering, vertrouwen en de sociale integratie van jongeren in West-Europa*, Assen: van Gorcum.

Diepstraten, I., Ester, P. and Vinken, H. (1999) *Mijn generatie*, Tilburg: Syntax.

Dietrich, H. (2001a) 'Wege aus der jugendarbeitslosigkeit – von der arbeitslosigkeit in die maßnahme?', *MittAB*, vol 34, no 4, pp 419-39.

Dietrich, H. (2001b) *JUMP. Das Jugendsofortprogramm*, IAB Werkstattbericht, no 3.

Dietrich, H. (2003) 'Scheme participation and employment outcome of young unemployed people: empirical findings from nine European countries', in T. Hammer (ed) *Youth unemployment and social exclusion in Europe: A comparative study*, Bristol: The Policy Press, pp 83-108.

Doets, C., Hake, B. and Westerhuis, A. (eds) (2001) *Lifelong learning in the Netherlands. The state of the art in 2000*, s–Hertogenbosch: CINOP.

du Bois-Reymond, M. and Lopéz Blasco, A. (2003) 'Yoyo transitions and misleading trajectories: from linear to risk biographies of young adults', in A. Walther, A. Lopéz Blasco and W. McNeish (eds) *Dilemmas of inclusion: Young people and policies for transitions to work in Europe*, Bristol: The Policy Press, pp 19-42.

du Bois-Reymond, M. and Stauber, B. (2003) *Biographical turning points in young people's transitions to work across Europe*, RC 34 Publication, Aldershot: Ashgate.

du Bois-Reymond, M., te Poel, Y. and Ravesloot, J. (1998) *Jongeren en hun keuzes*, Bussum: Coutinho.

du Bois-Reymond, M., Plug, W., te Poel, Y. and Ravesloot, J. (2001) 'And then decide what to do next… Young people's educational and labor-trajectories: a longitudinal study from the Netherlands', *Nordic Journal of Youth Research*, vol 9, no 2, pp 33-52.

du Bois-Reymond, M., Plug, W., Stauber, B., Pohl, A. and Walther, A. (2002) *How to avoid cooling out? Experiences of young people in their transition to work across Europe*, Working paper no 2, Research Project YOYO, Leiden: University of Leiden.

EAPN (European Anti-Poverty Network) (1999) *Racial discrimination and poverty in Europe*, Brussels: EAPN.

ECB (European Central Bank) (2002) *Labour market mismatches in Euro area countries*, Frankfurt am Main: March.

ECRI (2000) *European Commission against racial discrimination and intolerance*, Second report on Greece, Strasbourg: Council of Europe.

Edin, P.A. and Holmlund, B. (1994) *Arbetslösheten och arbetmarknadens funktionssätt*, Bilaga 8 till Långtidsutredningen, Stockholm: Fritze.

Egerton, M. (2002) 'Higher education and civic engagement', *British Journal of Sociology*, vol 53, no 4, pp 603-20.

EGRIS (European Group for Integrated Social Research) (2001) 'Misleading trajectories: transition dilemmas of young adults in Europe', *Journal of Youth Studies*, vol 4, no 1, pp 101-18.

Esping-Andersen, G. (1990) *The three worlds of welfare capitalism*, Cambridge: Polity Press.

Esping-Andersen, G. (1995) *Welfare states in transition*, London: Sage Publications.

Esping-Andersen, G. (1999a) *Social foundations of post-industrial economies*, Oxford: Oxford University Press.

Esping-Andersen, G. (1999b) 'Serve la deregolazione del mercato del lavoro? Occupazione e disoccupazione in America e in Europa', *Stato e Mercato*, no 56.

Esping-Andersen, G. (2001) 'A welfare state for the 21st century', Paper presented at the Nordic Alternative seminar, 12 March, Stockholm.

ESS (Employment Service of Slovenia) *Annual Reports 1993, 1994, 1995, 1996, 1997, 1998, 1999, 2000, 2004*, Ljubljana.

Ester, P. and Vinken, H. (2001) *Een dubbel vooruitzicht. Doembeelden en droombeelden van arbeid, zorg en vrije tijd in de 21e eeuw*, Bussum: Coutinho.

European Commission (1995) *White paper on education and training. Teaching and learning – Towards the learning society*, Luxembourg: Office for Official Publications of the European Communities.

European Commission (2000) 'A memorandum on lifelong learning', European Commission Staff Working Paper.

European Commission (2001) *A new impetus for European youth*, European Commission White Paper Com(2001)681, Brussels: Luxembourg: Commission of the European Communities.

Fallon, P. and Verry, D. (1988) *The economics of labour market*, Oxford: Philip Allan.

Feather, N.T. (1992) *The psychological impact of unemployment*, New York, NY: Springer-Verlag.

Feather, N.T. and O'Brien, G.E. (1987) 'Looking for employment: an expectancy-valence analysis of job seeking behaviour among young people', *British Journal of Psychology*, vol 78, pp 251-72.

Fenton, S., Devadason, R., Bradley, H., Guy, W. and West, J. (2001) 'In and out of work: job changing, life changing and young adult identities', Paper presented at the European Sociological Association Conference, Helsinki.

Finch, J. and Mason, J. (1993) *Negotiating family responsibilities*, London: Routledge.

Forlani, L. (1999) *Patto sociale e formazione: Nuovi impegni, impegni da rinnovare*, February, mimeo.

Forsyth, A. and Furlong, A. (2000) *Socioeconomic disadvantage and access to higher education*, Bristol/York: The Policy Press/Joseph Rowntree Foundation.

Fóti, K. (1997) 'Youth unemployment in Hungary', personal communication.

Fóti, K. (2000) 'Social protection of youth in Hungary', Paper presented at the meeting of the COST A13 Working Group 4, December, Madrid.

Fóti, K. (ed) (2003) *Alleviating poverty: Analysis and recommendations*, Human Development Report for Hungary 2000-2002, Budapest, Institute for World Economics of the Hungarian Academy of Sciences, and Bratislava: UNDP RBEC.

France, A. and Wiles, P. (1997) 'Dangerous futures: social exclusion and youth work in late modernity', *Social Policy & Administration*, vol 31, no 5, pp 59-78.

Frickey, A. and Primon, J.-L. (2002) 'Jeunes issus de l'immigration: les diplômes de l'ensignement supérieur ne garantissent pas un gal accus au marché du travail', *Formation Emploi*, vol 79, pp 31-50.

Furlong, A. (ed) (1999) *Integration through training. Comparing the effectiveness of strategies to promote the integration of young people in the aftermath of the 1997 Luxembourg Summit, Final report*, University of Glasgow: Department of Sociology.

Furlong, A. (1993) 'The youth transition, unemployment and labour market disadvantage. Gambling on YTS', *Youth and Policy*, vol 41, pp 24-35.

Furlong, A. and Cartmel, F. (1997) *Young people and social change. Individualization and risk in late modernity*, Buckingham/Philadelphia: Open University Press

Furlong, A. and Cartmel, F. (2003) 'Unemployment, integration and marginalisation: a comparative perspective on 18- to 24-year-olds in Finland, Sweden, Scotland and Spain', in T. Hammer (ed) *Youth unemployment and social exclusion in Europe: A comparative study*, Bristol: The Policy Press, pp 29-43.

Furlong, A. and Forsyth, A. (2003) *Losing out? Socioeconomic disadvantage and experience in further and higher education*, Bristol/York: The Policy Press/Joseph Rowntree Foundation.

Furlong, A. and Cartmel, F. (2004) *Vulnerable young men in fragile labour markets: Employment, unemployment and the search for long-term security*, York: Joseph Rowntree Foundation.

Gábor, K. (2002) 'A magyar fiatalok és az iskolai ifjúsági korszak. Túl renden és osztályon?' ('Hungarian youth and the school youth period. Beyond grades and classes?'), in A. Szabó, B. Bauer and L. Laki (eds) *Ifjúság 2000 (Youth 2000 – collection of studies)*, Budapest: National Youth Research Institute, pp 230-58.

Gallie, D. (2002) 'The quality of working life in welfare strategy', in G. Esping-Andersen et al (eds) *Why we need a new welfare state*, Oxford: Oxford University Press, pp 96-130.

Gallie, D. and Alm, S. (2000) 'Unemployment, gender, and attitudes to work', in D. Gallie and S. Paugam (eds) *Welfare regimes and the experience of unemployment in Europe*, Oxford: Oxford University Press, pp 109-34.

Gallie, D. and Paugam, S. (2000) 'The experience of unemployment in Europe: the debate', in D. Gallie and S. Paugam (eds) *Welfare regimes and the experience of unemployment in Europe*, Oxford: Oxford University Press, pp 1-25.

Gallie, D. White, M., Cheng, Y. and Tomlinson, M. (1998) *Restructuring the employment relationship*, Oxford: Oxford University Press.

Gallino, L. (1998) *Se tre milioni vi sembran pochi*, Torino: Einaudi.

Gangl, M. (2002) 'Changing labour markets and early career outcomes: labour market entry in Europe over the past decade', *Work, Employment and Society*, vol 16, no 1, pp 67-90.

Garrido Luque, A. (1992) *Consecuencias psicosociales de las transiciones de los jóvenes a la vida activa*, Madrid: Universidad Complutense.

Gazier, B. (2001) 'Employability – the complexity of a policy notion', in P. Weinert, M. Baukens, P. Bollérot, M. Pineschi-Gapènne and U. Walwei (eds) *Employability: from theory to practice*, International Social Security Series, vol 7, New Brunswick, NJ: Transaction Publishers, pp 3-23.

Giddens, A. (1973) *The class structure of the advanced societies*, London: Hutchinson University Library.

Giddens, A. (1991) *Modernity and self-identity*, Cambridge: Polity Press.

Giesek, A., Heilemann, U. and von Loeffeholz, H. (1994) 'Economic implications of migration into the Federal Republic of Germany 1988-1992', in S. Spencer (ed) *Immigration as an economic asset: The German experience*, Stoke on Trent: Trentham Books.

Gilbert, N. and van Voorhis, R.A. (eds) (2001) *Activating the unemployed. A comparative appraisal of work-oriented policies*, International Social Security Series, vol 3, New Brunswick, NJ: Transaction Publishers.

Gillis, J.R. (1974) *Youth and history. Tradition and change in European age relations 1770 – present*, New York, NY: Academic Press.

Giovine, M. (1994) 'Miti e problemi. Sistema duale e sequenze formative in alternanza', in *Italia e Germania: sistemi a confronto*, dossier di 'Scuola democratica', no 3-4.

Glastra, F. and Meijers, F. (eds) (2000) *Een leven lang leren? Competentieontwikkeling in de informatiesamenleving*, Den Haag: Elsevier Bedrijfsinformatie.

Glover, S., Gott, C., Lizillon, A., Portes, J., Price, R., Spencer, S., Srinvasan, V. and Willis, C. (2001) *Migration: An economic and social analysis*, RDS Occasional Paper no 67, London: Home Office.

Godfrey, C., Hutton, S., Coles, R., Bradshaw, J., Craig, G. and Johnson, J. (2002) *The costs of social exclusion of 16-18 year-olds*, Research Report 347, Nottinghamshire: DfES.

Goul Andersen, J (1999) 'Changing labour markets, new social divisions and welfare state support: Denmark in the 1990s', in S. Svallfors and P. Taylor-Gooby (eds) *The end of the welfare state?*, London/New York: Routledge/ESA Studies in European Society, pp 13-33.

Goul Andersen, J. (2002) 'Work and citizenship: unemployment and unemployment policies in Denmark, 1980-2000' in J. Goul Andersen and P. Jensen (eds) *Changing labour markets, welfare policies and citizenship*, Bristol: The Policy Press, pp 59-85.

Gowricharn, R. (2002) 'Integration and social cohesion: the case of the Netherlands', *Journal of Ethnic and Migration Studies*, vol 2, pp 259-73.

Granato, N. and Kalter, F. (2001) 'Die Persistenz ethnischer Ungleichheit auf dem deutschen Arbeitsmarkt', *KZfSS*, vol 53, pp 497-530.

Green, A., Maguire, M. and Canny, A. (2000) *Keeping track: Mapping and tracking vulnerable young people*, Bristol/York: The Policy Press/Joseph Rowntree Foundation.

Green, S. (2002) *Immigration, asylum and citizenship: Britain and Germany compared*, London: Anglo-German Foundation.

Griffin, C. (1993) *Representations of youth: The study of youth and adolescence in Britain and America*, Cambridge: Polity Press.

Gualmini, E. (1998) *La politica del lavoro*, Bologna: Il Mulino.

Guillemard, A.-M. (2001) 'The advent of a flexible life course and the reconfiguration of welfare', Keynote speech, COST A 13 Conference, *Social policy, marginalization and citizenship*, November, Aalborg University, Denmark.

Hall, P.A. and Soskice, D. (2001) 'An introduction to varieties of capitalism', in P.A. Hall and D. Soskice (eds) *Varieties of capitalism: The institutional foundations of comparative advantage*, Oxford: Oxford University Press, pp 1-68.

Hall, T., Coffey, A. and Williamson, H. (1999) 'Self, space and place: youth identities and citizenship', *British Journal of Sociology of Education*, vol 20, no 4, pp 501-13.

Halman, L. (2001) *The European values study: a third wave* (Source book of the 1999/2000 European Values Study Surveys), Tilburg: EVS/WORC/Tilburg University.

Hammer, T. (1996) 'History dependence in youth unemployment', *European Sociological Review*, vol 13, pp 17-33.

Hammer, T. (1998) 'Living on the "dole": income, coping and the probability of re-employment', in I. Julkunen and J. Carle (eds) *Young and unemployed in Scandinavia – a Nordic comparative study*, Copenhagen: Nord, pp 79-93.

Hammer, T. (2001) 'Arbeidsløse sosialklienter i de nordiske land', *Tidsskrift for velferdsforskning*, vol 4, no 2, pp 120-34.

Hammer, T. (2002) 'Youth unemployment, welfare and political participation. A comparative study of six countries in Northern Europe', in J. Goul Andersen and P. Jensen (eds) *Changing labour markets, welfare policies and citizenship*, Bristol: The Policy Press, pp 129-48.

Hammer, T. (2003a) 'The probability for unemployed young people to re-enter education or employment: a comparative study in six Northern European countries', *British Journal of Sociology of Education*, vol 2, pp 209-23.

Hammer, T. (ed) (2003b) *Youth unemployment and social exclusion in Europe: A comparative study*, Bristol: The Policy Press.

Hammer, T. and Julkunen, I. (2003) 'Surviving unemployment, a question of money or families? A comparative study of youth unemployment in Europe', in T. Hammer (ed) *Youth unemployment and social exclusion in Europe*, Bristol: The Policy Press, pp 135-55.

Hammer, T. and Carle, J. (2005: forthcoming) *Welfare and citizenship among unemployed youth in Europe*.

Hammerstedt, M. (2001) 'Disposable income differences between immigrants and natives in Sweden', *International Journal of Social Welfare*, vol 10, pp 117-126.

Hanesh, W., Steltzer-Orthofer, C. and Baltzer, N. (2001) 'Activation policies in minimum income schemes', in M. Heikkilä and E. Keskitalo (eds) *Social assistance in Europe. A comparative study on minimum income in seven European countries*, Helsinki: Stakes.

Hantrais, L. (2000) *Social policy in the European Union* (2nd edn), London: Macmillan.

Harris, N.S. (1989) *Social security for young people*, Aldershot: Avebury.

Harsløf, I. (2003) 'Processes of marginalisation at work: integration of young people in the labour market through temporary employment', in T. Hammer (ed) *Youth unemployment and social exclusion in Europe: A comparative study*, Bristol: The Policy Press, pp 45-67.

Heath, S. and Kenyon, L. (2001) 'Young single professionals and shared household living', *Journal of Youth Studies*, vol 4, no 1, pp 83-100.

Heckmann, F. (1999) 'Integration policies in Europe: national differences or convergence?', Paper given at European Research Conference, Obernai, France (mimeo).

Heijke, H., Borghans, L. and Smits, W. (2001) *De WEB tussen vraag en aanbod*, Zoetermeer: Stuurgroep Evaluatie WEB.

Heikkilä, M. (ed) (1999) *Linking welfare and work*, Dublin: European Foundation for the Improvement of Living and Working Conditions.

Helve, H. and Wallace, C. (eds) (2001) *Youth, citizenship and empowerment*, Aldershot: Ashgate.

Hills, J. (1996) *New inequalities*, Cambridge: Cambridge University Press.

Hirsch, D. (1997) *Social protection and inclusion*, York: York Publishing Services.

Hofstede, G. (1998) *Masculinity and femininity. The taboo dimension of national cultures*, London: Sage Publications.

Hogewind, S.N. and Dijkstra, S. (2001) *Slachtoffers van de informatiesamenleving. Opgroeien, werken en integreren in een nieuwe tijd*, Den Haag: Stichting Maatschappij en Onderneming.

Holdsworth, C. (2003) 'The transition out of the parental home in Britain, Spain, and Norway', End of Award Report to the ESRC (www.regard.ac.uk).

Holdsworth, C. and Dale, A. (1997) 'Ethnic differences in women's employment', *Work Employment and Society*, vol 11, no 3, pp 435-57.

Holdsworth, C. and Morgan, D. (2002) 'Family support during the transition out of the parental home in Britain, Spain and Norway', Paper presented at the Social Values, Social Policies Conference, 29-31 August, Tilburg.

Hollands, R. (1990) *The long transition: Class, culture and youth training*, London: Macmillan.

Honneth, A. (ed) (1993) *Kommunitarismus. Eine debatte über die moralischen grundlagen moderner gesellschaften*, Frankfurt am Main: Campus.

Horgan, G. and Rodgers, P. (2000) 'Young people's participation in a new Northern Ireland society', *Youth & Society*, vol 32, no 19, pp 107-37.

Hövels, B. (1994) *Beroepsonderwijs en arbeidsbestel: kiezen voor perspectief*, Nijmegen: KUN.

Hövels, B. (2004) *Country report: the Netherlands*, Nijmegen: Knowledge centre for Vocational Training and Labour Market (mimeo).

Hult, C. and Svallfors, S. (2002) 'Production regimes and work orientations: a comparison of six western countries', *European Sociological Review*, vol 18, no 3, pp 315-31.

Hutson, S. and Jenkins, R. (1989) *Taking the strain*, Milton Keynes: Open University Press.

Hvinden, B. and Halvorsen, R. (2001) 'Emerging notions of active citizenship in Europe', Paper presented at the 5th Conference of the European Sociological Association, Helsinki, Finland, 28 August-1 September.

Hyyppä, H. (1999) *Varanto varastossa: koulutus sivistää, jalostaa ja varastoi joutoväkeä*, University of Turku: Research Unit of the Sociology of Education (RUSE) reports no 3.

Iacovou, M. and Berthoud, R. (2001) *Young people's lives: A map of Europe*, Colchester: University of Essex, Institute for Social and Economic Research.

Iannelli, C. (1999) 'Individual educational decisions: a study of the low levels of educational attainment in Italy', Thesis for the Degree of Doctor of the E.U.I. (S. Domenico – Fiesole), Florence.

IARD (2001) *Study on the state of young people and youth policy in Europe*, Report for the European Commission D.G. for Education and Culture, Contract n. 1999 – 1734/001-001, IARD: Milan.

Ichino, P. (1996) *Il lavoro e il mercato*, Milan: Mondatori.

Iglesias, E., Robertson, E., Johansson, S.-E., Engfeldt, P. and Sundqvist, J. (2003) 'Women, international migration and self-reported health. A population based study of women of reproductive age', *Social Science & Medicine*, vol 56, pp 111-24.

Ignjatović, M. (2000) 'The social security of children and young people in Slovenia', Paper presented at the meeting of the COST A13 Working Group 4, December, Madrid.

IRP (Istituto di Ricerche sulla Popolazione) (1998) *Gli ideali degli italiani sulla popolazione*, Working Paper No 1, Rome: IRP.

IRR (Institute of Race Relations) (2000) *The dispersal of xenophobia*, London: IRR.

ISFOL (2001) *Federalismo e politiche del lavoro, Rapporto 2001*, Milan: Angeli.

Istance, D. and Williamson, H. (1996) *16- and 17-year olds in Mid-Glamorgan not in education, training or employment (Status 0)*, Bridgend: Mid-Glamorgan Training and Enterprise Council.

Istance, D., Rees, D. and Williamson, H. (1994) *Young people not in education, training or employment in South Glamorgan*, Cardiff: South Glamorgan Training and Enterprise Council.

ISTAT (1996) 'Inserimento professionale dei laureati', *Informazioni*, no 10.

ISTAT (2001) *Dinamica e caratteristiche del mercato del lavoro, Rapporto 2001*.

Jahoda, M. (1982) *Employment and unemployment. A social-psychological analysis*, Cambridge: Cambridge University Press.

Jahoda, M., Lazarsfeld, P. and Zeisel, H. (1933) *Marienthal: The sociography of an unemployed community*, New York, NY: Aldine-Atherton.

Jenkins, R. (1983) *Lads, citizens and ordinary kids*, London: Routledge

Jessop, B. (2002) 'Liberalism, neoliberalism and urban governance: a state-theoretical perspective', *Antipode*, vol 3, pp 473-494.

Johansson, H. (2001) 'Activation policies in the Nordic countries: social democratic universalism under pressure', *Journal of European Area Studies*, vol 1, pp 63-78.

Jones, G. (1991) 'The cost of living in the parental home', *Youth and Policy*, vol 32, pp 19-29.

Jones, G. (1992) 'Short-term reciprocity in parent–child economic exchanges', in C. Marsh and S. Arber (eds) *Household and family: Divisions and change*, Basingstoke: Macmillan, pp 26-44.

Jones, G. (1995) *Leaving home*, Buckingham: Open University Press.

Jones, G. (2001) 'Fitting homes? Young people's housing and household strategies in rural Scotland', *Journal of Youth Studies*, vol 4, no 1, pp 41-62.

Jones, G. (2002) *The youth divide: diverging paths to adulthood*, York: Joseph Rowntree Foundation (pdf available at www.jrf.org.uk).

Jones, G. and Wallace, C. (1992) *Youth, family and citizenship*, Milton Keynes: Open University Press.

Jones, G. and Martin, C.D. (1999) 'The "Young consumer" at home: dependence, resistance and autonomy', in J. Hearn and S. Roseneil (eds) *Consuming cultures: Power and resistance*, Basingstoke: Macmillan, pp 17-41.

Jones, G. and Bell, R. (2000) *Balancing acts? Youth, parenting and public policy*, York: York Publishing.

Jones, G., O'Sullivan, A. and Rouse, J. (2004) 'Because it's worth it? Education beliefs among young people and their parents in the UK', *Youth and Society* special issue (eds L. McDowell and C. Jeffrey) *Global change, local lives: Youth in a comparative perspective*, Sage Publications.

Julkunen, I. (2000) 'A leap forward or a ride on a carousel?', *YOUNG*, vol 1, pp 3-21.

Julkunen, I. (2002) *Being young and unemployed: Reactions and actions in Northern Europe*, Helsinki: SSKH Skrifter 14.

Kalter, F. and Granato, N. (2002) 'Demographic change, educational expansion, and structural assimilation of immigrants. The case of Germany', *European Sociological Review*, vol 18, pp 199-216.

Kanjuo-Mrčela, A. and Ignjatović, M. (2004) 'Neprijazna fleksibilizacija dela in zaposlovanja – potreba po oblikovanju varne fleksibilnosti' ('Unfriendly flexibilization of work and employment – the need for flexicurity'), in I. Svetlik and B. Ilić (eds) *Razpoke v zgodbi o uspehu. Primerjalna analiza upravljanja človeških virov v Sloveniji*, Ljubljana: Založba Sophia, pp 230-58.

Karsters, C., du Bois-Reymond, M. and Plug, W. (2004) *FATE: Family and transition in Europe (NL)*, Final report for the Netherlands, Leiden: University of Leiden.

Keune, C. and van Horssen, C. (2002) *Trendstudie allochtone jeugd: Vooruitgang of stilstand. Maatschappelijke positie, beleid en onderwijs in de periode 1989-1998*, Utrecht: Verwey-Jonker Instituut.

Keuzenkamp, S. and Hooghiemstra, E. (eds) (2000) *De kunst van het combineren. Taakverdeling onder partners*, Den Haag: SCO.

Kieselbach, T. (ed) (2001) *Living on the edge. An empirical analysis on long-term youth unemployment and social exclusion in Europe*, Opladen: Leske & Budrich.

Klemm, K. (2000) 'Bildungsexpansion, erfolg und mißerfolg sowie bildungsbeteiligung', in W. Böttcher, K. Klemm and T. Rauschenbach (eds) *Bildung und soziales in Zahlen*, Weinheim and München: Juventa.

Kohli, M. (1986) 'Social organization and subjective construction of the life course', in A. Sørensen, F. Weinert and L. Sherrod (eds) *Human development and the life course: Multidisciplinary perspectives*, Hillsdale, NY: Lawrence Erlbaum Associates.

Kohli, M. (1999) 'Private and public transfers between generations: linking the family and the state', *European Societies*, vol 1, no 1, pp 81-104.

Korenman, S. and Neumark, D. (2000) 'Cohort crowding and youth labour markets: a cross-national analysis', in D.G. Blanchflower and R.B. Freeman (eds) *Youth employment and joblessness in advanced countries*, Chicago, IL: University of Chicago Press, pp 57-105.

Korpi, T. (1994) *Escaping unemployment*, Institutet for Social Forskning, Stockholm: Stockholm University

Korte, A.W. de and Bolweg, F. (1994) *De nieuwe werknemer?!: een verkenning naar vernaderingen in werknemerswensen en de managementconsequenties daarvan*, Assen: Van Gorcum.

Kovatcheva, S. (2001) 'Youth research in Central and Eastern Europe: changes and challenges on the way to European youth research co-operation', in *Youth research in Europe: The next generation; perspectives on transitions, identities and citizenship*, Strasbourg: Council of Europe Publishing, pp 47-56.

Kovatcheva, S. (2000) *Sinking or swimming in the waves of transformation? Young people and social protection in Central and Eastern Europe* (www.youthforum.org/en/our_work/youth_work/linkper cent205.pdf).

Kymlicka, W. and Norman, W. (1994) 'Return of the citizen: a survey of recent work on citizenship theory', *Ethics*, vol 104, pp 352-81.

La Rosa, M., Dall'Agata, C., Giullari, B., Grazioli, P. (1996) 'Nuova cittadinanza, nuovo welfare, disoccupazione e politiche attive del lavoro', in E. Bartocci (ed) *Le incerte prospettive dello stato sociale*, Rome: Donzelli.

Lazaridis, G. and Koumandraki, M. (2001) 'Youth citizenship and unemployment: the case of passive and active labour market policies towards the young unemployed in Greece', *Sociological Research Online*, vol 5, no 4, U24-U46.

Leisering, L. and Walker, R. (1998) 'New realities: the dynamics of modernity', in L. Leisering and R. Walker (eds) *The dynamics of modern society*, Bristol: The Policy Press, pp 3-16.

Lenhardt, G. (1984) *Schule und demokratische Rationalität*, Frankfurt and Main: Suhrkamp.

Levi, M. and Stoker, L. (2000) 'Political trust and trusworthiness', *Annual Review of Political Science*, vol 3, pp 475-507.

Levitas, R. (1996) 'The concept of social exclusion and the new Durkheimian hegemony', *Critical Social Policy*, vol 46, no 16, pp 5-20.

Lipset, S. (1960) *Political man*, New York, NY: Doubleday.

Lister, R. (1990) 'Women, economic dependency and citizenship', *Journal of Social Policy*, vol 19, no 4, pp 445-67.

Lister, R. (2000) 'Citizenship: theoretical perspectives and developments in European welfare states', Paper presented at the 12th International Conference of Europeanists on Gender, Citizenship and Subjectivities, March, Chicago.

Lister, R. (2001) 'New Labour: a study in ambiguity', *Critical Social Policy*, vol 21, no 4, pp 425-48.

Lister, R. (2002) 'Citizenship and changing welfare states', in J.G. Andersen and P.H. Jensen (eds) *Changing labour markets, welfare policies and citizenship*, Bristol: The Policy Press, pp 39-58.

Livi Bacci, M. (1999) 'Quanto "contano" i giovani?', in I. Diamanti (ed.) *La generazione invisibile*, Milan: Il Sole 24 ore.

Lødemel, I. and Trickey, H. (eds) (2000) *An offer you can't refuse: Workfare in international perspective*, Bristol: The Policy Press.

Lodovici, M.S. (2000) 'The dynamics of labour market reform in European countries', in G. Esping-Andersen and M. Regini (eds) *Why deregulate labour markets?*, Oxford: Oxford University Press, pp 30-65.

Lozzi, M. (2000) 'Il quadro normativo della formazione professionale', in M. Ambrosini (ed) *Un futuro da formare*, Brescia: La Scuola, pp 47-64.

Lukes, S. (1976) *Power. A radical view*, London and Basingstoke: Macmillan Press.

MacDonald, R. (1994) 'Fiddly jobs, undeclared working and the "something for nothing" society', *Work, Employment and Society*, vol 8, pp 507-30.

MacDonald, R. (ed) (1997) *Youth, the 'underclass' and social exclusion*, London: Routledge.

MacDonald, R. and Marsh, J. (2001) 'Disconnected youth?', *Journal of Youth Studies*, vol 4, pp 373-91.

Mackert, J. and Müller, H.-P. (2000) 'Der soziologische gehalt moderner Staatsbürgerschaft. Probleme und Perspektiven eines umkämpften Konzepts', in J. Mackert and H.-P. Müller (eds) *Citizenship, Soziologie der Staatsbürgerschaft*, Wiesbaden: Westdeutscher Verlag, pp 9-42.

MacPherson, W. (1999) *Official report on the inquiry into the death of Steven Lawrence*, London: The Stationery Office.

Manawar, J.-K. (2003) 'The right to riot', *Community Development Journal*, vol 38, no 1, pp 32-42.

Marshall, T.H. (1950) 'Citizenship and social class', in T.H. Marshall and T. Bottomore (1992) *Citizenship and social class*, London: Pluto Press, pp 2-51.

Marshall, T.H. (1973) *Class, citizenship and social development*, Westport: Greenwood Press.

Marshall, T.H. and Bottomore, T. (1992) *Citizenship and social class*, London: Pluto Press.

Marsland, D. (1986) 'Young people, the family and the state', in D. Anderson, and G. Dawson (eds) *Family portraits*, London: Social Affairs Unit, pp 87-94.

McLeod, J.M. (2000) 'Media and civic socialization of youth', *Journal of Adolescent Health*, vol 27, no 2, pp 45-51.

Mihevc, B. (2003) *Skrb za kakovost, uèinkovitost študija in prenova študijskih programov na Univerzi v Ljubljani, Poroèilo o kakovosti UL 2003 (Considering quality, effectiveness of studies and renewal of study programmes at University of Ljubljana, Report on quality at University of Ljubljana 2003)*, Ljubljana: University of Ljubljana.

Millar, J. and Warman, A. (1996) *Family obligations in Europe*, London: Joseph Rowntree Foundation and Family Policy Studies Centre.

Ministero del Lavoro e delle Politiche Sociali (2001a) Libro Bianco sul mercato del lavoro in Italia. Proposte per una società attiva e per un lavoro di qualità, Rome.

Ministero del Lavoro e delle Politiche Sociali (2001b) Rapporto di monitoraggio, no 2, Rome.

Ministero del Lavoro e delle Politiche Sociali (2002) Monitoraggio delle politiche occupazionali e del lavoro. Nota di aggiornamento, no 1, Rome.

Ministry of Health, Welfare and Sport (1998) *Review of national youth policy*, Den Haag: Haeghepoorte.

MLFSA (Ministry of Labour, Family and Social Affairs) (2003) *Joint assessment of the employment policy priorities of Slovenia*, Ljubljana: MLFSA.

Modood, T., Berthoud, R., Lakey, J., Nazroo, J., Smith, P., Vivdee, S. and Beishon, S. (1997) *Ethnic minorities in Britain*, London: Policy Studies Institute.

Modood, T., Bradley, H. and Enneli, P. (2005) *Young Turks and Kurds*, York: Joseph Rowntree Foundation.

Mørch, S. (1997) 'Youth and activity theory', in J. Bynner, L. Chisholm and A. Furlong, *Youth, citizenship and social change in a European context*, Aldershot: Ashgate, pp 245-61.

Moscati, R. and Rostan, M. (2000) 'Higher education and graduate employment in Italy', *European Journal of Education*, no 2, pp 201-9.

Negri, N. and Saraceno, C. (1996) *Le politiche contro la povertà in Italia*, Bologna: Il Mulino.

Newbold, B. and Danforth, J. (2003) 'Health status and Canada's immigrant population', *Social Science & Medicine*, vol 57, pp 1981-95.

NIBUD (2002) *Nationaal Scholieren Onderzoek 2001/2002* (www.nibud.nl).

Ni Cheallaigh, M. (1995) *Apprenticeship in EU member states*, Berlin: Cedefop.

Noiriel, G. (1988) *Le creuset français. Histoire de l'immigration XIXème-XXème siècles*, Paris: Le Seuil.

OECD (1996) *Employment outlook*, Paris: OECD.

OECD (2000a) *Education at a glance: OECD indicators*, Paris: OECD.

OECD (2000b) *From initial education to working life: Making transitions work*, Paris: OECD.

OECD (2001a) *Education at a glance 2001: OECD Indicators*, Paris: OECD.

OECD (2001b) *Employment outlook*, Paris: OECD.

OECD (2004) *Employment outlook*, Paris: OECD.

O'Higgins, N. (2001) *Youth unemployment and employment policy. A global perspective*, Geneva: International Labour Office.

Onderwijsraad (2003a) *Leren in een kennissamenleving*, Den Haag: Onderwijsraad.

Onderwijsraad (2003b) *Tel uit je zorgen. Onderwijszorgen van leerlingen, ouders, leraren en het bredere publiek gepeild*, Den Haag: Onderwijsraad.

Osler, A. (1997) *The contribution of community action programmes in the fields of education, training and youth to the development of citizenship with a European dimension*, Final Synthesis Report, Brussels: European Commission.

Pahl, R. (1995) *After success*, Cambridge: Polity Press.

Parekh, B. (Chair) (2000) *The future of multi-ethnic Britain*, London: Runnymede Trust.

PIU (Performance and Innovation Unit) (2002) *Ethnic minorities and the labour market*, London: PIU, Cabinet Office.

Pitcher, J. (2002) 'Policies and programmes to address disadvantage among young people: issues for evaluation', *Evaluation*, vol 8, no 4, pp 474-95.

Platt, L. (2002) *Parallel lives?*, London: Child Poverty Action Group.

Platt, L. and Noble, M. (1999) *Race, place and low income distribution*, York: York Publishing Services.

Plougmann, P. (2002) 'Internalisation and the labour market of the European Union', in J. G. Andersen and P. Jensen (eds) *Changing labour markets, welfare policies and citizenship*, Bristol: The Policy Press, pp 15-38.

Plug,W. and du Bois-Reymond, M. (2003) *YOYO Dutch final interview report*, Leiden: University of Leiden.

Plug,W., Zeijl, E. and du Bois-Reymond, M. (2003) 'Young people's perceptions on youth and adulthood. A longitudinal study from the Netherlands', *Journal of Youth Studies*, vol 6, 2, pp 127-44.

Poel,Y. te (ed) (2002) *Arbeid en zorg in de levensloop van jonge volwassenen. Een onderzoek naar het realiseren van arbeid- en zorgscenario's door jonge ouders en jongvolwassenen zonder kinderen*, Onderzoeksrapport SOZA.

Powel,J. and Wagner, S. (2002) 'Zur Entwicklung der Überrepräsentanz von Migrantenjugendlichen an Sonderschulen in der Bundesrepublik Deutschland seit 1991', *Gemeinsam Leben*, vol 10, no 2, pp 65-70.

Preuss, U.K. and Everson, M. (1996) 'Konzeptionen von Bürgerschaft in Europa', *Prokla*, vol 26, no 4, pp 543-64.

Raffo, C. and Reeves, M. (2000) 'Youth transitions and social exclusion: developments in social capital theory', *Journal of Youth Studies*, vol 2, pp 147-66.

Rahn W.M. and Transue, J.E. (1998) 'Social trust and value change: the decline of social capital among American youth, 1976-1995', *Political Psychology*, vol 19, no 3, pp 545-56.

Rantakeisu, U., Starrin, B. and Hagqvist, C. (1996) *Ungdomsarbetslöshet. Vardagsliv och samhälle*, Lund: Studentlittertaur.

Reiter, H. (2003) 'Past, present, future: biographical time structuring of disadvantaged young people', *YOUNG*, vol 11, no 3, pp 253–80.

Reyneri, E. (1997) *Occupati e disoccupati in Italia*, Bologna: Il Mulino.

Richter, I. and Sardei-Biermann, S. (eds) (2000) *Jugendarbeitslosigkeit. Ausbildungs und Beschäftigungsprogramme in Europa*, Opladen: Leske & Budrich.

Riphahn, R. (1999) *Immigrant participation in social assistance programmes*, University of Munich (mimeo).

Riphahn,T.R. and Serfling, O. (2002) 'Neue Evidenz zum Schulerfolg von Zuwanderern der Zweiten Generation in Deutschland', in *Vierteljahreshefte zur Wirtschaftsforschung*, vol 71, no 2, pp 230-48.

Ripoll, P., Salanova, M., Rodríguez, I., Bravo, M.J., Hontangas, P. and Prieto, F. (1994) 'La conducta de búsqueda de empleo: aplicación de un modelo de expectativa-valencia', *Revista de Psicología Social Aplicada*, vol 4, no 1, pp 43-51.

ROA (2002) *Schoolverlaters tussen onderwijs en arbeidsmarkt*, Maastricht: Researchcentrum voor Onderwijs en Arbeidsmarkt (Research Centre for Education and the Labour Market).

ROA (2003) *De arbeidsmarkt naar opleiding en beroep tot 2008*, Maastricht: Researchcentrum voor Onderwijs en Arbeidsmarkt (Research Centre for Education and the Labour Market).

Róbert, P. (2002) 'Átmenet az iskolából a munkaerõpiacra' ('Transition from school to labour market'), in I.Tóth, T. Kolosi and G.Vukovich (eds) *Társadalmi Riport* (Social Report), Budapest: TÁRKI.

Roberts, K. (1995) *Youth and employment in modern Britain*, Oxford: Oxford University Press.

Roberts, K. (2001) *Class in modern Britain*, London: Palgrave.

Roberts, K. (2003) 'Problems and priorities for the sociology of youth', in A. Bennett, M. Cieslik and S. Miles (eds) *Researching youth*, Houndmills: Palgrave, pp 13-28.

Roberts, K., Fagan, C., Fóti, K., Jung, B., Kovatcheva, S. and Machacek, L. (1999) 'Tackling youth unemployment in East-Central Europe', *Journal of East-European Management Studies*, vol 3, pp 238-51.

Roche, M. (1992) *Rethinking citizenship. Welfare, ideology and change in modern society*, Cambridge: Polity Press.

Rodgers, G., Gore, C. and Figueiredo, J. (eds) (1995) *Social exclusion: Rethoric, reality, responses*, Geneva: ILO.

Rosdahl, A. and Weise, H. (2001) 'When all must be active: workfare in Denmark', in I. Lødemel and H. Trickey (eds) *An offer you can't refuse: Workfare in international perspective*, Bristol: The Policy Press, pp 159-80.

Rubery, J., Smith, M. and Fagan, C. (1999) *Women's employment in Europe. Trends and prospects*, London: Routledge.

Rubery, J., Smith, M., Fagan, C. and Grimshaw, D. (1998) *Women and European employment*, London: Routledge.

Rudd, P. (1997) 'From socialization to postmodernity: a review of theoretical perspectives on the school-to-work transition', *Journal of Education and Work*, vol 10, no 3, pp 257-78.

Ryan, P. (2000) *The school to work transition: A cross national perspective*, Working Paper no 14, Cambridge: University of Cambridge.

Ryan, W. (1976) *Blaming the victim*, New York, NY: Vintage Books.

Salverda, W. (2000) 'Youth unemployment: a Dutch solution?', in A. Serrano Pascual (ed) *Tackling youth unemployment in Europe: Monitoring the European employment strategy*, Brussels: European Trade Union Institute.

Saraceno, C. (1998) *Mutamenti della famiglia e politiche sociali in Italia*, Bologna: Il Mulino.

Sassen, S. (1994) *Cities in a world economy*, Thousand Oaks, CA: London: Pine Forge Press.

Scheepers, P., te Grotenhuis, M. and Gelisson, J. (2002) 'Welfare states and dimensions of social capital: cross-national comparisons of social contacts in European countries', *European Societies*, vol 4, no 2, pp 185-207.

Schröder, L. (1991) *Springpojkar och språngbrädor,* Uppsala: Institutet för social forskning 18.

Schweer, M.K.W. and Erlemeyer, A. (2001) 'Youth, politics and trust: significance of trust for the political activity of youth', *Gruppendynamik-Zeitshrift für Angewandte Sociolpsychologie,* vol 32, no 1, pp 61-70.

Schwinn, T. (2001) 'Staatliche Ordnung und moderne Sozialintegration',*Kölner Zeitschrift für Soziologie und Sozialpsychologie,* vol 53, no 2, pp 211-32.

SCP (Sociaal en Cultureel Planbureau) (1998) *Sociaal Cultureel Rapport 1998. 25 jaar sociale verandering,* Rijswijk: SCP.

SCP (2000) *Sociale en Culturele Verkenningen 2000: Nederland in Europa,* Rijswijk: SCP.

SCP (2003) *Rapportage jeugd 2002,* Den Haag: SCP.

Sen, A. (1986) *Scelta, benessere, equità,* Bologna: Il Mulino.

Sen, A. (1994) *La diseguaglianza,* Bologna: Il Mulino.

Sennett, R. (1998) *The corrosion of character: The personal consequences of work in the new capitalism,* New York, NY: W.W. Norton and Company.

SER (Sociaal Economische Raad) (2002) *Het nieuwe leren: Advies over een leven lang leren in de kenniseconomie,* Den Haag: SER.

Serrano Pascual, A. (ed) (2000) *Tackling youth unemployment in Europe,* Brussels: European Trade Union Institute.

SEU (Social Exclusion Unit) (1998) *Truancy and school exclusion,* Cm 3957, London: SEU/The Stationery Office.

SEU (1999) *Bridging the gap,* Cm 4405, London: SEU/The Stationery Office.

Shavit, Y. and Müller, W. (2000) 'Vocational secondary education. Where diversion and where safety net?', *European Societies,* vol 2, no 1, pp 29-50.

Sik, E. and Nagy, I. (2002) 'Rugalmas munka, rugalmas család?' ('Flexible work, flexible household?'), in T. Kolosi, O. Vukovich and G. Tóth (eds) *Társadalmi Riport* (Social Report), Budapest: TÁRKI, pp 256-70.

Silberman, R. and Fournier, I. (1999) 'Les enfants d'immigrés sur le marché du travail', *Formation Emploi,* vol 65, pp 31-55.

Silver, H. (1994) 'Social exclusion and social solidarity: three paradigms', *International labour Review,* vol 133, nos 5/6, pp 531-78.

Smith, E.S. (1999) 'The effects of investments in social capital of youth on politics and civic behaviour on young adulthood: a longitudinal analysis', *Political Psychology,* vol 20, no 3, pp 553-80.

Smith, J., Gilford, S. and O'Sullivan, A. (1998) *The family background of young homeless people*, London: Joseph Rowntree Foundation and Family Policy Studies Centre.

Solga, H. (2002) 'Jugendliche ohne Schulabschluss und ihre Erwerbsbiographien', in K.U. Schnabel, J. Baumer, A. Leschinsky and K.U. Mayer (eds) *Das Bildungswesen in der Bundesrepublik Deutschland*, Strukturen und Entwicklung im Überblick, Reinbek.

SORS (Statistical Office of the Republic of Slovenia) (2003) *Slovenia in figures, 2003*, Ljubljana: SORS.

SORS (2002) *Statistical Yearbook 2002* (www.stat.si/letopis_n.htm) (26.5.2003).

SORS (1999) *Level of living*, no 4, Rapid Reports, no 215.

SORS (1993-1998) *Labour Force Survey*, 1993-1998.

SORS (1998a) *Social protection*, Rapid Reports, no 152.

SORS (1998b) *Labour market*, Rapid Reports, no 317.

Spies, H. (1996) 'Workfare – emancipation or marginalization?', in M. de Goede, P. de Klaue, J. van Ophen, C. Vevhaar and A. de Vvies (eds) *Youth unemployment, identity and policy*, Leuwaarden: Fryske Akademi, pp 191-213.

Steijn, B. and Hofman, A. (1999) 'Zijn Lager Opgeleiden de Dupe van de Toestroom van Studenten op de Arbeidsmarkt? Over verdringing aan de onderkant van de arbeidsmarkt', *Tijdschrift voor Arbeidsvraagstukken*, vol 15, no 2, pp 149-61.

Stille, F. (1999) 'Ethnic minorities and recent immigrants on the labour market: an introduction', European Employment Observatory, mimeo.

Stuurgroep Evaluatie WEB (2001) *De WEB: Naar eenvoud en evenwicht. Eindrapport*, Zoetermeer: Stuurgroep Evaluatie WEB.

Svallfors, S. and Taylor-Gooby, P. (eds) (1999) *The end of the welfare state? Response to state retrenchment*, London and New York, NY: Routledge/ESA Studies in European Society.

Taris, T., Heesink, J. and Feij, J. (1994) *Tijdschrift voor Arbeidsvraagstukken*, vol 10, no 1, pp 17-25.

Taylor-Gooby, P. (1999) 'Hollowing out versus the new interventionism', in S. Svallfors and P. Taylor-Gooby (eds) *The end of the welfare state? Response to state retrenchment*, London and New York, NY: Routledge/ESA Studies in European Society, pp 1-13.

Teichler, U. (2000) 'Graduate employment and work in selected European countries', *European Journal of Education*, vol 2, pp 141-56.

ter Bogt, T. and van Praag, C.S. (1992) *Jongeren op de drempel van de jaren negentig*, Rijswijk: Sociaal en Cultureel Planbureau.

Timera, M. (1999) 'Logiques familiales, communautaires et scolarisation des jeunes filles d'origine africaine noire en France', *Formation Emploi*, vol 65, pp 57-75.

Togeby, L. (1989) *Ens og forskellelig. Gräsrodbevegelser I Norden*, Århus: Politica.

Trbanc, M. (2000) *Overview of the disadvantaged youth problem and the contribution of a certification system*, Ljubljana: Phare MOCCA Programme.

Turner, B.S. (1990) 'Outline of a theory of citizenship', *Sociology*, vol 24, pp 189-217.

Ule, M. (2002) 'Young people in the risk society', in B. Tivadar and P. Mrvar (eds) *Flying over or falling through the cracks? Young people in the risk society*, Ljubljana: MESS, Office of the Republic of Slovenia for Youth.

Ule, M. and Rener, T. (eds) (1998) *Youth in Slovenia: New perspectives from the nineties*, Ljubljana: Ministry of Education and Sport, Youth Department.

Ullah, P. and Banks, M. (1985) 'Youth unemployment and labour market withdrawal', *Journal of Economic Psychology*, vol 6, pp 51-64.

van Asselt, R. and Visser, K. (1999) 'Doorstroomkwalificatie MBO-HBO', in *Jaarboek Kwalificatiestructuur 1999*, s-Hertogenbosch: CINOP.

van der Linden, F.J. and Dijkman, T.A. (1989) *Jong zijn en volwassen worden in Nederland*, Nijmegen: Hoogveld Instituut.

van der Velden, R.K.W. and Wolbers, M. (2001) 'De integratie van schoolverlaters op de arbeidsmarkt in de Europese Unie: de rol van institutionele factoren', in N. van der Heuvel, F. Holderbeke and R. Wielers (eds) *De transitionele arbeidsmarkt. Contouren van een actief arbeidsmarktbeleid*, Den Haag: Elsevier Bedrijfsinformatie.

van Hoof, J. (1997) 'Nieuwe institutionele kaders en de aansluiting tussen beroepsonderwijs en de arbeidsmarkt', *Tijdschrift voor Arbeidsvraagstukken*, vol 14, no 1, pp 85-96.

van Hoof, J. (2000), 'Youth unemployment, vocational education and training policy in the Netherlands', in H. Bradley (ed) *Young people in the labour market*, COST A13 Work-In-Progress Report.

van Hoof, J. (2001) *Werk, werk, werk? Over de balans tussen werken en leven in een veranderd arbeidsbestel*, Amsterdam: Boom.

van Hoof, J. (2002a) 'Work as a central life interest in post-industrial society', Paper presented at the World Congress of Sociology, July 2002, Brisbane (mimeo).

van Hoof, J. (ed) (2002b) *Werken moet wel leuk zijn*, Assen: Van Gorcum.

van Hoof, J. and Dronkers, J. (1980) *Onderwijs en arbeidsmarkt*, Deventer: Van Loghum Slaterus.

van Oorschot, W. (2002) 'Miracle or nightmare? A critical review of Dutch activation policies and their outcomes', *Journal of Social Policy*, vol 3, pp 399-421.

Veendrick, L. (1993) *Het loon van de last*, Groningen: Wolters-Noordhoff.

Vergani, A. (2000) 'I nuovi contenuti della formazione professionale', in M. Ambrosini (ed) *Un futuro da formare*, Brescia: La Scuola, pp 65-80.

Vinken, H. (1997) *Political values and youth centrism. Theoretical and empirical perspectives on the political value distinctiveness of Dutch youth centrists*, Tilburg: Tilburg University Press.

Vinken, H., Ester, P., Dekkers, H. and van Dun, L. (2002) *Aan ons de toekomst. Toekomstverwachtingen van jongeren in Nederland*, Assen: Van Gorcum.

Vinken, H., Ester, P., van Dun, L. and van Poppel, H. (2003) *Arbeidswaarden, toekomstbeelden en loopbaanoriëntaties. Een pilot-study onder jonge Nederlanders*, Tilburg: OSA.

Vinokur, A. and Caplan, R.D. (1987) 'Attitudes and social support: determinants of job-seeking behaviour and well being among the unemployed', *Journal of Applied Psychology*, vol 17, no 12, pp 1007-24.

Viprey, M. (2002) *L'insertion des jeunes d'origine étrangère*, Report for the Conseil Economique et Social, Paris.

Virtanen, T. (1998) 'Racist violence from the part of skinheads: the expression of hate in Finland', in H. Helve (ed) *Unification and marginalization of young people*, Helsinki: Finnish Youth Research Society, pp 96-109.

Vroom, V.J. (1964) *Work and motivation*, New York, NY: John Wiley & Sons.

Walby, S. (1997) *Gender transformations*, London: Routledge.

Wallace, C. (2001) 'Youth, citizenship and empowerment', in H. Helve and C. Wallace (eds) *Youth, citizenship and empowerment*, Hampshire: Aldershot, pp 11-31.

Wallace, C. and Kovacheva, S. (1998) *Youth in society: The construction and deconstruction of youth in East and West Europe*, London: Macmillan.

Wallace, C., Spannring, R. and Haerpfer, C. (2000) 'Youth, citizenship and social capital in Europe', Paper for the Youth Research Conference, 3 September, University of Keele (mimeo).

Walther, A., Stauber, B. and Biggart, A. et al (eds) (2002) *Misleading trajectories. Integration policies for young adults in Europe*, Opladen: Leske & Budrich.

Wanberg, C.R., Watt, J.D. and Rumsey, C. (1996) 'Individuals without jobs: an empirical study of job-seeking behaviour and re-employment', *Journal of Applied Psychology*, vol 81, pp 75-87.

Warr, P., Cook, J. and Wall, T. (1979) 'Scales for the measurement of some work attitudes and aspects of psychological well-being', *Journal of Occupational Psychology*, vol 52, pp 129-48.

Weil, P. (2002) *Qu'est ce qu'un français? Histoire de la nationalité française depuis la Révolution*, Paris: Bernard Grasset.

Weise, H. and Broogaard, S. (1997) *Aktivering av kontanthjaelpsmodtagere*, Köpenhamn: Socialforskningsinstituttet, 21.

Williams, F. (1999) 'Good enough principles of welfare', *Journal of Social Policy*, vol 4, 667-87.

Williamson, H. (1997) 'Status zero, youth and the "underclass"', in R. Macdonald (ed) *Youth, the 'underclass' and social exclusion*, London: Routledge.

Willis, P. (1984) 'Youth unemployment', *New Society*, 29 March, 5 April, 12 April.

Wilthagen, T. (2002) '*The flexibility-security nexus: New approaches to regulating employment and labour markets*', Tilburg: OSA/Institute for Labour Studies (OSA Working Paper WP2002-18).

Wyn, J. and White, R. (1997) *Rethinking youth*, London: Sage Publications.

York University Centre for Housing Policy (2004) Centrepoint Youth Homelessness Index.

Zeijl, E. (2001) *Young adolescents' leisure: A cross-cultural and cross-sectional study of Dutch and German 10-15-year-olds*, Opladen: Leske & Budrich.

Index

Page references for notes are followed by n